# SILENT
### AND
# UNSEEN

# SILENT

## AND

# UNSEEN

On Patrol in Three Cold War Attack Submarines

## ALFRED SCOTT McLAREN

NAVAL INSTITUTE PRESS
ANNAPOLIS, MARYLAND

This book was brought to publication with generous assistance of
Marguerite and Gerry Lenfest.

Naval Institute Press
291 Wood Road
Annapolis, MD 21402

Library of Congress Cataloging-in-Publication Data
McLaren, Alfred Scott.
  Silent and unseen : on patrol in three Cold War attack submarines / Alfred Scott
McLaren.
     pages cm
  Summary: "Silent and Unseen is a memoir of a submariner's life on a U.S. attack subma-
rine during the Cold War by Capt. Alfred S. McLaren, an experienced submarine officer
and nuclear attack submarine commander. He describes in riveting detail the significant
events that occurred early in the Cold War during his seven years, 1958-1965, on board
three attack submarines: the USS Greenfish (SS 351), USS Seadragon (SSN 584), and
USS Skipjack (SSN 585). He took part in the first submerged transit of the Northwest
Passage, a Baffin Bay expedition, and, as commander of USS Queenfish (SSN-651), a
North Pole expedition that completed the first survey of the entire Siberian Continental
Shelf"— Provided by publisher.
  Includes bibliographical references and index.
  ISBN 978-1-61251-845-9 (hardback) — ISBN 978-1-61251-846-6 (ebook) 1. McLaren,
Alfred Scott. 2. United States. Navy—Submarine forces—Biography. 3. United States.
Navy—Officers—Biography. 4. Submariners—United States—Biography. 5. Submarines
(Ships)—United States—History—20th century. 6. Seadragon (Submarine : SSN-584) 7.
Skipjack (Submarine : SSN-585) 8. Greenfish (Submarine : SS-351) 9. United States—
History, Naval—20th century. 10. Cold War—Biography. I. Title.
  V63.M2867A3 2015
  359.0092—dc23
  [B]
                                    2015003774
∞ Print editions meet the requirements of ANSI/NISO z39.48–1992 (Permanence
of Paper).
Printed in the United States of America.

23  22  21  20  19  18  17  16  15        9  8  7  6  5  4  3  2  1
First printing

The USS *Greenfish*, USS *Seadragon*, and USS *Skipjack* insignias on pages 5, 63, and 139
are from the U.S. Navy.

*To the officers and crews with whom I served on attack submarines during the Cold War and to all my brother submariners who served our great nation, silently and unseen, during this turbulent era.*

# Contents

# Photos and Illustrations

# Acknowledgments

I wish to acknowledge and thank, from the bottom of my heart, my wife of twenty-six wonderful years, Avery Battle Russell, for her loving and steadfast encouragement and support from the time I first began this book in 1996 until its completion in 2014. I also wish to thank her for her absolutely superb editorial advice and countless hours of editing during the course of preparing this book for publication.

Heartfelt thanks go to Ms. Wendy Gulley, archivist at the Submarine Force Museum and Library, Groton, Connecticut, for allowing me access to the submarine boat books, scrapbooks, and cruise books, and for her patient and invaluable assistance during a series of visits. I also thank Cdr. Don Ulmer and former *Greenfish* shipmate Jim Kyser for refreshing my memory with regard to *Greenfish*'s maneuvering room and engineering spaces.

I also thank Lt. Cdr. Thomas J. Cutler, USN (Ret.), director of professional publishing at the Naval Institute Press, for his encouragement and sage advice as I pursued publication of this book. I further thank Marlena Montagna and Gary Thompson — editorial assistant on the editorial staff of the Naval Institute Press — for helping me bring this book to fruition. Finally, my heartfelt thanks go to Ms. Alison Hope for an extremely thorough and invaluable copy edit of my original manuscript.

In conclusion, I thank my former wife, the late Mary Louise Eisenhower, and my children for their loyal and steadfast support in holding down the home front during the many, many months I spent at sea and away from home on board three Cold War attack submarines: USS *Greenfish*, USS *Seadragon*, and USS *Skipjack*.

# Introduction

**M**y first book, *Unknown Waters*, recounted just one of many exciting submarine Cold War missions that I was fortunate, as a U.S. Navy submarine officer, to be a part of.[1] Among other subjects, the book related how I came to pursue a career in submarines, how Rear Adm. Hyman G. Rickover (later vice admiral, eventually full admiral) selected me for nuclear submarines, and some detail of my pre- and postcommissioning executive officer's tour that preceded my taking command of USS *Queenfish* (SSN 651) in 1969.

In this book, *Silent and Unseen: On Patrol in Three Cold War Attack Submarines*, I describe some of the more significant events that occurred on board the first three of five attack submarines on which I served: USS *Greenfish* (SS 351), USS *Seadragon* (SSN 584), and USS *Skipjack* (SSN 585). I hope to convey even more fully than I did in *Unknown Waters* the day-to-day life of a U.S. Navy submariner during the Cold War. I hope, too, to convey how interesting and satisfying a life it is for a young man, and I assume for a young woman one day soon, who might consider pursuing a career in submarines and joining a centuries-old undersea fraternity.

An important strand runs throughout this book: that of the events, experiences, personalities, and particularly the commanding officers who helped to direct the course of my submarine career and to shape me into the commanding officer that I eventually became. The commanding officers that a young submarine officer serves with will have a profound effect on how well prepared he is—not only to do his job day to day, but also to assume his own command years later. This was particularly true in attack submarines, both diesel and nuclear, during those high-risk years of the Cold War.

Attack boats in my era bore the brunt of Cold War mission requirements. Sometimes it seems as if the officers and crewmembers were almost continually at sea. Each of these missions, which were essentially reconnaissance and intelligence collection and at times early warning, were of potentially great, even extraordinary, value to the government of the United States. Each mission involved a tremendous commitment of a very expensive national military asset and the precious lives of anywhere from 75 to 115 of the nation's finest and best-trained young men. Each one also represented a wholehearted commitment by the families who steadfastly supported them.

The success of all these missions depended heavily on accurate outside intelligence, geographical positioning of the boat and, most importantly, the readiness of the individual attack-boat team. I was to learn very early that the latter was made up of three inseparable parts: material readiness of the boat; preparatory training and deployment readiness of the entire crew; and the knowledge, experience, and physical and psychological readiness of the commanding officer. All had to be forged together into the best team possible.

Always of keen interest to me, and I am sure to each crewmember, was one question: "Will we be safe at sea with the commanding officer we have?" Along with that question were others: "Will our commanding officer be able to develop us into the best team possible?" "Will he be able to inspire us and lead us to success in all we do, including the Cold War missions assigned?" And, finally, "Will he be able to gain us the recognition and respect we deserve as a team?" No one could ever really know the answers to these questions until an individual commanding officer had proved himself through the skillful and safe handling of a life-threatening occurrence, or the conduct of an even-more demanding arduous mission.

Above all, during the course of a mission the situational awareness, courage, and professional capability and skill of the commanding officer stood out. I was to serve with at least two distinct types during my career: the indecisive and timorous and the skilled and daring. I learned a great deal from both types. From the former I learned what not to do. From the latter I learned what could be foolhardy and what was always worth doing.

Cold War missions more often than not required sufficient closing of the potential enemy to collect fully the intelligence desired, usually within weapons range—theirs and ours. But, unlike a war patrol, the U.S. attack boat strived to remain completely undetected throughout and did nothing more than count coup, so to speak, as the high-priority intelligence desired was collected. The boat would then, ideally, withdraw as silently and unseen as it had approached. It was the degree to which a submarine commanding officer executed these actions successfully that separated the men from the boys.

I served with one captain in peacetime who, no matter what opportunity might present itself, seemed to be totally incapable psychologically of closing a potential enemy to gather the intelligence that his boat and crew team were sent out to acquire. He preferred to remain at the outer limit of visibility and detectability, to the increasing impatience and disgust of his officers and crew.

Another captain I served with was, by contrast, so brave and charismatic a leader at sea that his crew would have gone to the ends of the earth for him. He was, in addition, a truly professional submariner and seaman who knew every aspect of his business. He never hesitated to close a potential adversary sufficiently and, when the opportunity presented itself, to gather all the intelligence possible. He accomplished this while ensuring that our own boat remained undetected.

My remaining commanding officers fell somewhere in between these two styles. All were dedicated professionals but leaned more toward a more cautious and deliberate manner of conducting submarine missions. I learned from them as well.

A common theme among submarine sailors was stories about their skippers, officers, and crewmembers. God help the commanding officer who was unskilled, timid, and indecisive, or who was uncomfortable with either his crew or the mission assigned. Then, as now, this would become the talk of the waterfront and reach the ears of his peers, superiors, and even the Commander Submarine Force Atlantic (ComSubLant) or Commander Submarine Force Pacific (ComSubPac) himself. One poor commanding officer during my time drew the unfortunate nickname Captain Tuna, the Chicken of the Sea. That name was to follow him, probably unbeknownst to him, throughout the remainder of his career.

Although the chief focus of this book is to describe the experiences that I had under several captains who prepared me to be a submarine commanding officer one day, I also learned a great deal from my brother officers and fellow crewmembers.

*Silent and Unseen* consists of three parts, each devoted to one of the attack submarines on which I served: USS *Greenfish* (1958–59), USS *Seadragon* (1960–62), and USS *Skipjack* (1962–65). The remaining two nuclear attack submarines on which I served, USS *Greenling* (SSN 614) and USS *Queenfish* (SSN 651), I plan to discuss in a subsequent book that will focus on the immediate preparations for and the entirety of my command of *Queenfish* during the period from 1965 to 1973.

# PART I

## USS *Greenfish* (SS 351)
### Workhorse of the Pacific

USS *Greenfish* (SS 351) at sea. *U.S. Navy*

# CHAPTER 1

# Early History and Post–World War II Modifications

I t was by pure chance that I was assigned to USS *Greenfish* (SS 351) during the final days of my training at the U.S. Naval Submarine School in Groton, Connecticut. The first of five attack submarines on which I was to serve as a young officer during the Cold War, she was one of 128 *Balao*-class, diesel-electric fleet submarines built from 1942 to 1945 to fight the war in the Pacific.[1] *Greenfish* took her name from a type of fish living in the Pacific and Southwest Asian waters.

Our entire class, number 105, of some sixty young officers was scheduled to graduate on 20 December 1957. Each of us had drawn numbers for submarine and home port selection, and, in early December I found myself standing behind a good friend, Ens. James "Doc" W. Blanchard Jr., on the day we were to make our selection. Doc's number was 9 and mine 13. Neither of us could believe our luck: low numbers essentially guaranteed us any submarine and base location we wanted—from New London, Norfolk, Charleston, or Key West on the Atlantic seaboard, to San Diego and Pearl Harbor in the Pacific.

Doc and I were Navy juniors, fellow U.S. Naval Academy graduates, and good friends. Doc's father was a famous World War II submarine commander, mine a naval aviator and, at this time, commanding officer of the U.S. Naval Gunfire Support School in Coronado, California. Both of us had traveled a great deal during our upbringing, moving every two years on average and attending countless schools. We were comfortable with change and able to adjust quickly no matter where we were ultimately assigned. Our new wives, on the other hand, would probably not be, since neither had traveled much out of her hometown, except for their years in college. My wife, Mary Eisenhower, for instance, had never been farther west than

7

Rheimersburg, Pennsylvania. As a result, in the weeks preceding submarine home port selection, the four of us had decided that Key West might be the wiser choice. We would remain on the East Coast where we thought we wanted to be, close to our families; at the same time, we would escape the damp, chilly winter of New London and Norfolk. Doc and I thus left our tiny on-base married officers' quarters on that morning in early December having reassured our wives we would be picking boats out of Key West.

As Doc and I stood patiently in line waiting to select Key West submarines as we had promised, I looked at the big selection board showing boats and their available home ports. I suddenly remembered we had the unique opportunity of choosing a submarine in the most ideal and exotic location of all, Pearl Harbor, in what was then the territory of Hawaii. The thought of the beautiful yet mysterious islands, the wonderfully clement weather, and the opportunity to surf, swim, and fish year around began to fill my thoughts.

I remarked to Doc, "You know, we're really being stupid."

"What do you mean?" asked Doc.

"We don't have to pick a Key West submarine," I said.

"What!" he exclaimed.

"Doc, why don't we choose a boat in the best home port in the world? There should be several left when it's our time to pick where we want to go."

"But we promised our wives," responded Doc, adding, "They won't be happy."

"So what?" I said. "Pearl Harbor'll be a great place to operate out of—calm seas and terrific weather. Anyway, it's really our choice, and with all those beaches and the beauty of the islands, family living out there would probably vastly exceed Key West."

"Hmmm, not a bad idea," said Doc.

"Let's do it," I said. "I know Mary will give me hell, but it'll be worth it in the long run."

"OK," he agreed.

Our mutual decision crystallized, and when Doc's turn came, he picked a relatively new Pearl Harbor submarine, USS *Tang* (SS 563), patterned on the German World War II deep-diving Type *XXI* U-boats. *Tang* was commanded by a colorful, former Naval Academy football player, Lt. Cdr. John O. "Bo" Coppedge. When my turn came, I picked the very last of the Pearl Harbor boats available, USS *Greenfish,* the World War II–era submarine specially streamlined and modified into a GUPPY (greater underwater propulsion power) IIA.

Our initial elation at choosing where we really wanted to go ended abruptly, however, when we realized we were faced with the problem of explaining our choice of submarine location to our wives. Doc was sure his wife Carol would not be too unhappy with his decision, once she was past the initial shock. I was far less certain about Mary's reaction. She was already well known in our community for her strong opinions—definitely not someone who took well to unpleasant surprises. A U.S. Naval Academy classmate and good friend, John M. "Jack" Bannon, who had picked USS *Dogfish* (SS 350) in New London, went so far as to offer to put me up at his house that night and even to trade submarines if need be.

The domestic fireworks that ensued were far from pleasant when I finally got up the nerve to tell Mary the news. An emotional telephone conversation with her mother in Pennsylvania early the next morning made matters worse, since both were convinced the Hawaiian Islands were still inhabited by savages.

I stuck with my decision, nonetheless, during the tumultuous days and weeks that followed, with my wife still fuming during the subsequent drive to California with our young son. After a brief stay at the Marine Memorial Club in San Francisco, my family of three descended by military air transport to Honolulu Airport to a resounding welcome from Lt. Cdr. John T. "Jack" Knudsen, who commanded *Greenfish* at the time, and executive officer (exec) Lt. Cdr. William W. "Mac" McKenzie Jr. It was the end of January 1958, and the weather was balmy. *Greenfish*'s officers were all in Hawaiian shirts and their wives in muumuus, and they greeted us with flower leis that they draped over our shoulders. Afterward we went to the skipper's house for a wonderful night of Mai Tais and our first taste of real Hawaiian food.

The Cold War at that time had been in progress for more than twelve years, with the most recent events of significance being the formation of the Warsaw Pact in May 1955, the brutal suppression of a rebellion in Communist Hungary, and the Soviet Union's successful launching of Sputnik into orbit in early October 1957. Accordingly, assignment to a frontline GUPPY IIA promised to be exciting duty for a new submarine officer. The continuous advances in Soviet naval technology and in the naval force levels of the Soviet Union, People's Republic of China, and North Korea required almost continuous monitoring by the United States, using all means available in both the Atlantic and the Pacific. Submarines like *Greenfish*, with their ability to surreptitiously monitor and collect intelligence, were therefore expected to be increasingly deployed on Cold

War missions. Not only did the United States need to stay abreast, but it also had to develop effective means of countering new developments, whether in equipment or complete sensor and weapons systems on their ships and submarines, in order to maintain the tactical and strategic advantage that we held over all three of these countries at the time.

The original *Greenfish* was authorized in April 1942 and her keel laid on 29 June 1944. On 21 December 1945 she would be the 101st submarine to be launched at Electric Boat Company in Groton since 1933.[2] Her commissioning on 7 June 1946 was too late for her to join her famed sisters in the Pacific during World War II, but she was to play an important role in the coming Cold War.

Following commissioning and a shakedown cruise to the Caribbean and South America, plus numerous exercises with the fleet in the Atlantic and Caribbean, *Greenfish* sank the infamous German war prize, *U-234*, with live torpedoes, during a practice exercise in late 1947. After surrendering to the Allies off Newfoundland on 15 May 1945, *U-234* was discovered to be carrying special Japanese and German personnel and a unique high-technology cargo destined for Japan that included 560 kilograms of uranium oxide.[3]

In early January 1948 *Greenfish* entered the Electric Boat Company yards for a major GUPPY IIA conversion, which included changing her basic exterior hull configuration to enhance submerged speed and hydrodynamic efficiency.[4] The most significant of her modifications were removing the deck gun and streamlining her deck and superstructure; enclosing the conning tower compartment, bridge, periscope shears, and other mast supports within a one-piece faired sail made of welded aluminum; installing snorkeling equipment, which enabled her to run her diesel engines and charge her batteries while submerged; and increasing her batteries from two to four, for a total of 504 cells, to increase both her submerged speed and the length of time she could remain submerged.[5] Finally, *Greenfish*'s four high-speed electric motors were replaced with two low-speed direct-drive electric motors, to enhance sound quieting.[6]

The most significant modification within the submarine, or below decks, was to provide the capability to shift electrical connections among the four main lead-zinc batteries from a normal parallel to connection in series. This shift, used during maximum or flank speed operations only, provided sufficient electrical current, or amperage, to the two direct-drive electrical motors such that they could drive both propeller shafts at a sufficiently high RPM to attain underwater speeds in excess of twenty knots, providing the hull was free of the marine growth that normally accretes from long periods in port. Such high speeds provided a boat, when under attack, with at least one good opportunity to break free of enemy active sonar contact and escape from an antisubmarine warfare (ASW) surface vessel.

Upon completion of the conversion in August 1948, *Greenfish* was assigned to the Pacific Fleet and departed for her new home port, the U.S. naval submarine base in Pearl Harbor. With the exception of ASW and harbor-defense exercises in the Puget Sound area in early 1950, and an overhaul in Mare Island, she spent most of her time operating out of Pearl Harbor on local exercises through 1951.

The Korean War broke out in June of 1950, and in late 1951 *Greenfish* departed for the U.S. naval base and repair facility at Yokosuka, Japan, for duty in the area. From 31 January to 1 March 1952 she was on her first and only war patrol since commissioning. Following Seventh Fleet exercises off Okinawa, she returned to Pearl Harbor where local and Cold War missions kept her busy until late 1954. Noteworthy during this period was a joint operation conducted with USS *Redfish* (SS 395) during the summer of 1952 in the sea ice–covered Beaufort Sea. It was during this operation, headed by Waldo K. Lyon, PhD, director of what was to become the famous Arctic Submarine Laboratory in San Diego, that *Redfish* proved that a suitably configured diesel electric submarine could polynya hop from the Chukchi Sea north of the Bering Strait to the Canadian Arctic Islands and return.[7]

*Greenfish* entered the Pearl Harbor shipyard for another modernization overhaul in 1955, whereupon she departed for a six-month deployment to the Western Pacific (WestPac) with the Seventh Fleet. During this time she conducted several Cold War missions and embarked on a tour of Southeast Asia, visiting ports in Hong Kong, Manila, and Singapore. She was the first U.S. submarine ever to visit Rangoon, Burma.

Returning to the submarine base in Pearl Harbor in March 1956, *Greenfish* conducted local operations—exercises along the North American coast—and a number of Cold War reconnaissance missions in the Northern Pacific, the last of which was completed a few months prior to my reporting on board in late January 1958, when my seagoing submarine career began in earnest.

## CHAPTER 2

# On Board USS *Greenfish*

**W**hen I reported as a prospective watch officer and first lieutenant, *Greenfish*'s basic characteristics as a fully operational GUPPY IIA submarine were as follows:

- Displacement: 1,870 tons surfaced, 2,440 tons submerged
- Length overall: 307 feet
- Beam: 27 feet 4 inches
- Draft: 17 feet
- Speed on surface: 18.0 knots maximum, 13.5 knots cruising
- Speed submerged: 16.0 knots for 30 minutes, 9.0 knots snorkeling, 3.5 knots cruising
- Range: 15,000 nautical miles surfaced at 11.0 knots
- Endurance submerged: 48 hours at 4 knots
- Armament: Ten 21-inch torpedo tubes, six forward and four aft
- Crew: 8 officers and 72 crew[1]

*Greenfish* was also outfitted with the latest in sonar and electronic countermeasures equipment plus state-of-the-art antishipping and antisubmarine torpedoes and weapons countermeasures.

Diesel electric submarines that had been recently modified, such as *Greenfish*, had the capability of remaining submerged throughout the entire duration of a Cold War mission or a war patrol in times of active conflict. Instead of having to follow the usual World War II patrol routine of running submerged on the battery during the day and on the surface at night to both reposition and recharge batteries, GUPPY submarines could now remain submerged both day and night and only had to come to periscope depth to ventilate, communicate, and recharge their batteries using their snorkel system. Snorkeling enabled the submarine to remain completely submerged; it involved raising a special snorkel air induction/diesel exhaust mast just above the surface, opening an air induction head valve atop the mast, and starting a diesel engine. The pressure of the engine exhaust would then blow the exhaust mast free of water through a normally shut diesel exhaust valve. A second diesel engine could then be added and dedicated to recharging the four batteries, with the original diesel engine used for propulsion or both propulsion and battery recharging. When on the surface, a maximum of three of the four engines could be used to recharge the battery even more rapidly. Surface transits were still required, however, if a submarine needed to relocate or reach a particular destination at best speed. Maximum speed while snorkeling was dependent largely on sea state and on how much of the total diesel electric output would be required for recharging batteries. *Greenfish* rarely ran in excess of five to six knots.

Crews of seventy-five to eighty men normally manned diesel electric submarines of this era. All submarines—as high-speed, deep-diving warships—are compact, and *Greenfish* was no exception. By necessity they use every inch of interior space, but without compromising their war-fighting capabilities. Approximately a tenth of crewmembers had to hot bunk: that is, they had to share their bunk with a fellow shipmate, with one man climbing into a bunk as soon as its previous occupant had vacated it. Most hot bunking took place in the forward torpedo room where the most junior members of the crew slept in side-by-side pan bunks, positioned on top of the torpedo reloads.

Although all boats of this era had heating and air-conditioning systems, the systems were notoriously ill-distributed through any given submarine's interior, in spite of the improvements that had been made since the war. Adding to crew discomfort when on the surface was the fact that GUPPY submarines now had a rounded bow, versus the previous uplifted, pointed or fleet bow, causing the submarine to ride less comfortably than previously on the surface, particularly when heading directly into rough seas. Finally, none of these older submarines was particularly clean below decks. The need to cram more and more improved equipment within each submarine created innumerable and inaccessible dirt- and moisture-collection areas throughout the boat, especially in the bilges, which became breeding grounds for cockroaches.

Despite all these discomforts, submarine crews then, as during World War II and today, were made up of the finest officers and crew in the U.S.

Navy. All were volunteers, and all had been professionally and psychologically screened. They were successful graduates of rigorous basic training, submarine school, and technical training for their particular rate specialty. Most had also served some time on surface warships prior to volunteering for submarine duty. Officers during the Cold War were required to have served at least two years at sea and to have qualified as an officer of the deck under way, preferably on a destroyer in deployed fast-carrier task forces, before becoming eligible to apply for submarine school.

Pearl Harbor could not have been a more salubrious location to begin my submarine career, and I soon found *Greenfish's* officers to be a most congenial lot. After settling my family into Navy quarters, I was put to work qualifying as an in-port duty officer under the senior watch officer, Lt. Leonard Stoehr.

Lt. (jg) Alfred S. McLaren, gunnery and torpedo officer, USS *Greenfish* (SS 351), 1958. *U.S. Navy*

One thing that was quite different from my previous two years on board the destroyer USS *Gregory* (DD 802) was the notable overall spirit of goodwill and comradeship stemming from the Submarine Force Pacific's glory days of World War II. That spirit pervaded the submarine base and boat crews and their families homeported in Pearl Harbor. We worked hard in port and under way, but we also managed to have great fun during our time on shore. We especially looked forward to Friday afternoon happy hours at the submarine base officers club following a week at sea. Afterward we would go on to dinner with wardroom mates and friends, either outdoors under romantic tiki torches at the officers club or at the nearby Hickam Air Force Base. All looked forward to the frequent parties and all-officer lunches, and to the very competitive bowling nights every Thursday at which each submarine fielded teams of wardroom officers and wives. We were proud of our boats, each with its distinctive patch or insignia. We were also a hard-drinking bunch in those days, particularly when it came to Kamehameha beers and Mai Tais. That was the culture, and I don't recall a single unpleasant incident or adverse effect on anyone's personal life or operational performance and readiness from a night out on the town.

Early 1958 started at a leisurely pace. *Greenfish* spent as much time in port as under way on local operations in and around the Hawaiian Islands. With the exception of a ten-day Submarine Force Pacific submarine-versus-submarine exercise in the waters surrounding the island of Maui in the early spring of 1958, an exercise that took place annually, our operations were generally two- and three-day local area operations. These were designed to train new personnel and hone up the boat's overall readiness for its next scheduled deployment, whether that would be a one- to two-month special operation, as we called submarine Cold War operations, or a full six-month deployment to the Western Pacific.

I was ordered to relieve another officer as gunnery and torpedo officer within a week of reporting on board and to assume duties as first lieutenant as well. *Greenfish* had long since removed its deck gun, so my main responsibilities encompassed all personnel within the department, all small arms and associated gun lockers, the forward- and after-torpedo rooms, all fire-control equipment connected with tracking, and computing a hitting solution prior to launching a torpedo or torpedoes at a practice target or actual enemy. My responsibilities also included *Greenfish*'s ten torpedo tubes (six forward and four aft) and two emergency signal ejectors; and the loading, maintenance, and readiness of all torpedoes loaded on board. As first lieutenant I was in charge of all deck operations whenever we were on the surface, including all line handling when mooring or getting under way.

Although submarine school did a superb job of preparing a young officer for all these duties, I still had much to learn from my division petty officers and more-experienced officers before I gained the necessary knowledge and confidence to carry out fully all responsibilities assigned.

Loading torpedo onto USS *Greenfish* (SS 351), 1958. *U.S. Navy*

## The All-Important Submarine Battery

One of the most important things I learned in port was to ensure that *Greenfish*'s four high-capacity batteries (504 cells) were always fully charged prior to departure for the next scheduled operations. Every new officer's first responsibility was thus to learn how to inspect and prepare *Greenfish*'s huge battery and line up her interior ventilation, diesel, snorkel, and electrical systems for the safe conduct of a battery charge both in port and at sea. In conjunction, I had to learn how to monitor and supervise all aspects of the charge while it was in progress, handle any emergencies that might develop such as ventilation interruptions that could quickly lead to a battery explosion, and, finally, how to secure from a battery charge, properly and safely.

The crucial part of recharging a submarine's batteries was lining up the ventilation system in order to maintain adequate airflow over all battery cell tops. The ventilation system lineup and fan rotation/flow had to be absolutely correct for both ventilation above the battery cells and continuous exhaust of the air from all battery compartments. Submarine battery cells emit hydrogen gas as they heat up during the course of charging. It is critical that this gas be diffused and ventilated out of the battery compartments. If that was not done it could have become a serious explosive hazard once the gas percentage exceeded 3 percent overall, which could happen very quickly if, for example, ventilation fan rotations were reversed, fan rotation was too slow, or a fan was electrically faulty and began sparking or stopped rotating. Also of importance during the precharging lineup was checking for battery grounds and evidence of electrolyte leakage and loose debris on the battery cell tops. Finally, the battery-charging officer had to post warning signs where appropriate, and to broadcast over the sub's main circuit (1MC) communications system at periodic intervals the fact that a battery charge was in progress.[2]

Although I took it very seriously then, I realize now that the battery-charge qualification was probably the single most important certification among the many that I would have to achieve in the course of earning my Gold Dolphins as a submarine officer. The safety of one's submarine and crew depended on it. Just one mistake or omission or one moment of inattention could spell disaster, as it did for a sister submarine, USS *Pomodon* (SS 486). In February 1955, while *Pomodon* recharged her batteries in the San Francisco Naval Yard, a build-up of hydrogen gas caused a series of explosions and fire that not only seriously damaged the battery and submarine, but also led to the deaths of five men.[3] The cause was, in all probability, reversed flow or no flow through one or all of the battery well ventilation fans.[4]

### The Mysterious *Boing*

Back in the mid-1950s, the Soviet Union's submarine force was frequently given credit for capabilities that it did not yet have, particularly with regard to the long-range deployment of its submarines. As a result, Submarine Force Pacific spooked easily, and frequently overreacted at times when we heard something under water that we could not readily classify. Toward the end of the ten-day exercise in 1958 mentioned above, *Greenfish* was playing the role of a submerged enemy submarine when our sonar watch thought he detected a Soviet submarine in our vicinity. He initially concluded that it was a Soviet *Zulu*-class diesel electric attack submarine based on several low-frequency active sonar pings detected close aboard that sounded like loud *boings*.[5]

Our commanding officer, Lt. Cdr. Jack Knudsen, immediately took the conn, ordering *Greenfish* to head for periscope depth and then to a fully surfaced condition as per ComSubPac's standing orders in such a situation. An Uncle Joe code word alert was immediately sent off to all other exercise participants via VHF radio and via the underwater telephone in the event there might be any other U.S. submarines operating fully submerged in our near vicinity.

Once all participating submarines were on the surface and accounted for, ASW patrol aircraft were called in to search for and localize the possible Soviet intruder. An intensive search of the area over several hours using sonobuoys turned up nothing, however, and the exercise was resumed after all participating units had been repositioned. All of us on board *Greenfish* were frustrated and disappointed, of course.

This scenario was to repeat itself innumerable times in the local operating areas surrounding Pearl Harbor for the next four decades at considerable cost of valuable military resources and operational time, never resulting in the location of the supposed active-ranging Soviet submarine intruder. Then, in early November 2002, *David Starr Jordan*, a U.S. research vessel cruising Hawaiian waters, detected the same *boing* sounds and eventually tracked them down during the course of several days to a Pacific minke whale, about twenty-three feet long.[6] Some researchers believed it might be a mating call.[7] More recently, authorities have concluded that the dwarf minke whale, discovered just fifteen years ago, was and is the source of these noises.[8]

### After You, Alphonse

I learned quickly that when we went to sea for local operations of a day or more, we remained in the same summer-dress khaki uniform throughout. It was only on the longer operations of a week or more that we might take a very short submarine shower and change clothes. We turned the shower on to wet ourselves, turning the water off to soap down, and then turning on the water just long enough to rinse off. A limited freshwater capacity precluded ever taking the long, hot showers enjoyed at home or in port. The odor of human exertion was pretty rank. The boat, moreover, smelled to high heaven of diesel oil. Little wonder that each new crewmember had to quickly develop submarine nose, or near-complete nasal insensitivity to this witch's brew of evil smells. Submarines were not termed "pig boats" in the old days for nothing.

I can never forget my first shower at sea. Ensign S and I were the newest officers on board. One day when showers were allowed, the more senior officers said, to our utter surprise, "You two go ahead and take yours first." "What a gentlemanly gesture," we thought, and I urged S to go first since he was a year junior to me. It was only when I heard his anguished screams that I recognized we'd both been had: our brother officers wanted us to drain all the cold water out of the shower piping before they took their own showers.

Survival on a submarine requires several important personal attributes if one is to adapt successfully to life within the confined and always crowded spaces. The first is to possess a keen sense of alertness and responsibility toward the execution of all duties, both assigned and implied, and to execute them correctly and completely: from the minute he steps on board, shipmates depend on each crewmember to carry out his job, particularly in life-threatening or potentially life-threatening situations. This is best termed situational awareness. Just a moment of inattention while on watch during submerged operations can result in collision, flooding, fire, and a host of other calamities that can cause the loss of the submarine and all on board. The second attribute, a sense of humor, especially the ability to laugh at oneself, is absolutely essential if a new crewmember is to successfully integrate into an existing submarine crew. Finally, the third personal attribute is an ability to retreat into and live within one's own heads or inner space when necessary. Quarters below decks are so close that true privacy is virtually impossible to achieve.

## Officer Submarine Qualification

The watch-standing qualifications that I had to complete as a junior officer during the weeks and months that followed first reporting on board included diving officer of the watch and officer of the deck both surfaced and submerged. I was required to learn every detail of *Greenfish* and her equipment, systems, and characteristics from stem to stern.

As both a guide and as written affirmation, incorporating the qualifying officer's and commanding officer's signatures, was completion of a Submarine Qualification Notebook for the particular submarine. The notebook covered each system—water, hydraulic, electric—throughout the boat with an attendant list of practical factors that the individual had to complete to a qualifying officer's satisfaction. The notebook also covered all submarine evolutions, operations, and emergency procedures, both surfaced and submerged.

Successful qualification on the submarine's hydraulic systems, for example, required us to trace out or hand-over-hand the entire system or systems and, in the process, produce a drawing that showed every line and valve and related equipment, such as pumps, filters, and accumulators, that we had sighted. Qualification also required that we demonstrate the ability to operate each system safely, or any portion thereof, in the event of an immediate need, such as an operational emergency.

To qualify in submarine evolutions and operations, an officer or senior petty officer had to demonstrate to a senior officer or the captain that he could safely operate any and all equipment, including attendant valves and electrical switches and controls during all phases of a diving and surfacing operation or emergency. In addition, he had to demonstrate that he could supervise the safe operation of the entire system by qualified crewmembers, if needed. Moreover, an officer had to demonstrate the ability to get his submarine under way from a pier or tender and to make a landing upon return to port. As diving officer of the watch and as a conning officer (more senior), he had to conduct dives, surfacings, and ascents to and descents from periscope depth, and he had to conduct emergency descents below the surface to evade attack and emergency surfacings to deal with flooding, fire, or a catastrophic Freon leak, for example.

During those years and for most of my career, officer submarine qualification also included making approaches and attacks, using actual practice or dummy torpedoes, against individual surface or submerged targets, and escorted ones as well. Finally, all officers on *Greenfish* were required to demonstrate that they could break contact from and escape from an ASW vessel or a hostile submarine that had detected us.

## Military Justice, of a Sort

My first real encounter with military justice was on *Greenfish* during the spring of 1958 before our first deployment in the Northern Pacific. A crewmember had somehow gone afoul of the military justice system, and I suddenly found myself appointed by my commanding officer to head a special court-martial to be conducted on board while in our home port of Pearl Harbor. I had received some military justice training at the U.S. Naval Academy and while serving on the destroyer *Gregory* before I entered submarine training. That being said, I had never been exposed to anything involving serious disciplinary measures, much less in any sort of court-martial.

Although I no longer remember what the young man was charged with, I do recall the exec telling me before the trial that it was expected the defendant would be awarded a bad conduct discharge from the U.S. Navy. Talk about being placed in a position of responsibility to ensure justice is done and then having pressure applied by one's seniors before the trial had even begun! I should have been suspicious from the outset, because the idea of putting the most junior officer, and a lieutenant junior grade at that, into such a position was ludicrous when the boat had at least four lieutenants and one lieutenant commander who would have been more appropriate as head of a special court-martial.

The trial over which I presided was held in *Greenfish*'s wardroom and lasted some three days. During the trial, the prosecutor argued against the defendant and the defense argued on his behalf. Once their cases had been made and final arguments concluded, it was up to me to make the final judgment as whether the defendant was guilty or not guilty, and to pronounce sentence. The exec, who was following the case closely, cornered me during a break, before I had rendered my decision and pronounced judgment, and told me in unmistakable terms what my commanding officer expected me to decide. After listening to three days of argument for and against, however, I was convinced that the prosecutor had not proven his case, and that there were no grounds for awarding the young man a bad conduct discharge.

Leaving the military service with anything less than an honorable discharge is very serious, and could have profound consequences for the rest of an individual's life, particularly with regard to future employment. I was definitely not going to be part of any sort of what I considered railroading to please even my commanding officer, at that or at any other time.

Back in the "courtroom," I rendered a verdict of not guilty and adjourned the trial. Before long I found myself on the wrong side of both *Greenfish*'s executive and commanding officers.[9] Captain Knudsen somehow managed to overrule my decision, had the young man placed in a nearby Navy brig, and initiated action to give him a bad conduct discharge.

As punishment for not complying with my skipper's desire, I was ordered to visit the young man every day until he was transferred to the mainland for final processing and discharge. That was kind of like throwing Br'er Rabbit into the briar patch, and I readily complied.

The idea here, I suppose, was not just to punish, but to teach me a lesson by humiliating me. As ordered, I visited the young man each day and, from our conversations and the young man's manner, became even more convinced that I had made the right decision. I conveyed this to the exec and ended up losing even more standing with the skipper. Despite the subsequent slight dip in my fitness report under loyalty, I never regretted rendering the verdict of not guilty.

The entire ordeal caused me to lose respect for and mistrust military justice as it was practiced during my naval service of some twenty-six years. This and other incidents that I subsequently witnessed persuaded me that the powers that be, or any senior officer with court-martial authority, could railroad a decision in any direction he wanted. That harkens back to an old saying that I heard many years ago: "Military justice is to justice as military music is to music."

I learned two lessons from this unpleasant experience. The first was, Never be too quick to judge one's shipmate and fellow human being. The second was, Never allow a situation to get so far out of control on board that anything beyond a nonjudicial Captain's Mast would ever be necessary.[10] If it did, then we would have had to look to where the problem really lay with regard to onboard leadership, beginning with the commanding officer.

# CHAPTER 3

# Our First Deployment: Western Pacific 1958

**D**iesel electric submarines were the workhorses of the submarine force during the first decades of the Cold War. These boats were, with a few exceptions like the new *Tang* and *Barbel* classes, all World War II veterans, snorkel-equipped, and modified under the GUPPY program. They were also somewhat quieter and less detectable under water as a result of myriad lessons in sound quieting learned during that war. Most of these submarines were initially commanded and manned by a high percentage of war patrol veterans, many of whom had survived serious depth charge attacks by Japanese destroyers and patrol craft. The advent of nuclear power and the launch of USS *Nautilus* (SSN 571) in 1954 spurred a steady increase in the number of nuclear attack submarines being built and sent to sea, beginning in the early 1960s. As a consequence, the diesel electric submarine was gradually phased out, with its final Cold War deployments occurring in the early 1970s.

In those days, a diesel electric-powered submarine normally transited in friendly or neutral waters on the surface, using its diesel engines for propulsion. When transiting or on patrol in unfriendly waters during the Cold War, however, she had to exert maximum effort to remain completely undetected. Otherwise, U.S. surface and air forces might mistake one of their own for a Cold War adversary.

Operational constraints thus required a submarine like *Greenfish* to operate completely submerged using battery propulsion during daylight hours. Depending on the operation order, the prescribed speed of advance, and the operational situation, submerged speeds could range from a minimum of less than a knot to a maximum that approached twenty knots. The former speed could normally be maintained in excess of thirty-six hours without the need to recharge the batteries. The latter speed, however, could not be sustained for more than half an hour. Once the batteries' capacity had been reduced significantly or approached being completely discharged, the submarine would have to come to periscope depth and snorkel or surface in order to run its diesel engines both for propulsion and for recharging the batteries.

The major drawback of snorkeling at periscope depth in a Cold War patrol area was the high noise level of the diesel engines and the constant opening and shutting of the head valve as the submarine proceeded through heavy seas. When snorkeling, the submarine became infinitely more detectable to the passive sonars of unfriendly submarines or aircraft sonobuoys than if it were proceeding at or below periscope depth on battery propulsion alone. The large snorkel head valve and the diesel exhaust spray also made the submarine more detectable by visual and radar means. Nonetheless, pulling off station and using the snorkel was better than having to surface. It was also possible to conduct quick battery topping off charges of as little as twenty to thirty minutes, in contrast to a complete battery charge that might require hours to complete.

In sum, the condition and state of charge of a diesel electric submarine's batteries were always of prime importance during the early days of the Cold War. A submarine could not operate effectively without well-maintained batteries, charged as fully as possible. This was a matter of operational life or death, whether it involved a Cold War mission or an actual war patrol.

*Greenfish* departed in late May 1958 for a six-month WestPac deployment of some six weeks' duration in the Northern Pacific—my first as a young and not-yet-fully qualified submarine officer. The months in the WestPac proved to be quite intensive and eventful. They included not only exercises with the Seventh Fleet and port visits to Subic Bay, Hong Kong; and Yokosuka, Japan; but also, and more importantly to my basic education as an attack submarine and future commanding officer, the conduct of two lengthy Cold War missions in the Northern Pacific under the leadership of a new commanding officer.

One of my first duties on *Greenfish* was to qualify as a diving officer of the watch, followed by qualifying as officer of the deck in port and under way.[1] Diving officer, followed by officer of the deck under way, were also to be my normal watches during much of the WestPac deployment that we had just departed for. Fortunately, all new submarine officers reporting to their first boat had already learned all the basic skills required of a diving officer of the watch during their six months at submarine school, since we had had repeated opportunities to practice these newly learned skills during weekly at-sea training periods on various boats based out of New London/Groton.

The usual routine when transiting to patrol assignments in the vast reaches of the Northern Pacific was to run at the greatest and most economical speed, when possible on the surface. We were under strict orders, however, to remain completely undetected by both friendly and potential adversary forces, so we transited at high speed on the surface during hours of darkness and fully submerged or at periscope depth during daylight hours. The time spent exposed on the surface meant that every closing visual or radar contact that we detected posed a threat to our ability to remain undetected. The submarine was thus frequently forced to dive as rapidly as possible in order to avoid detection. The World War II–era diesel electric submarines available for Cold War operations were all capable of submerging on the order of thirty seconds or less. That was the standard that the officers and crew constantly trained for and adhered to.

Diesel electric submarines at the time transited on the surface with all main ballast tanks (MBTs; seven in *Greenfish*'s case) dry and two small variable ballast tanks, negative and safety, fully flooded. Once the order, "Dive, dive!" was given, the bow and stern planes were placed on full dive, speed was increased to full, and all MBT vents were opened. The boat would submerge beneath the surface in an increasingly negative buoyancy condition as the MBTs fully flooded with water. Once well beneath the surface en route to ordered depth, the diving officer of the watch would order, "Blow negative tank to the mark!" with speed decreased to "All ahead two-thirds!" (approximately eight knots). The diving officer of the watch would then order further decreases in speed as he proceeded to trim the boat such that neutral buoyancy was achieved and it was possible to hover at the ordered depth at dead stop, or with no way on.[2] Trim adjustments by shifting water between tanks fore and aft were also made, as necessary, to achieve a completely horizontal or zero bubble condition.

The operational depth chosen once beneath the surface depended largely on the depth of water, nature of threat, its distance from the boat, and underwater acoustic conditions expected. Generally, it was always wise to dive well beneath the predicted acoustic layer.[3]

We followed this basic routine en route to our assigned Cold War mission area during the late spring of 1958. Our basic route took us north of the Hawaiian Island chain and Midway Island. We remained on the surface until well clear of Oahu and then submerged and remained so until several hours after sunset. We then surfaced and commenced a routine of running at best speed commensurate with recharging and keeping our batteries at full capacity. An officer of the deck and two lookouts were on watch in the bridge area at all times. Since we were now charged with remaining completely undetected until our mission had been completed, hull numbers had been painted out, and we no longer flew the American flag. As we gradually approached our assigned area, we also initiated the practice of disposing of all garbage and trash in unmarked hemp gunnysacks and blowing our sanitary tanks using a quieter blow method that stopped short of actually blowing air out of the tank and into the surrounding water.

### Crash-Diving the Boat

Probably the most nerve-wracking for each officer of the deck and watch section was having to crash-dive *Greenfish* upon sighting a surface or air contact or in response to a strong radar contact, well before it was possible for the boat to be detected. This happened all too frequently. The second a visual sighting was made or electronic countermeasures reported a strong radar contact closing or strengthening, the officer of the deck would sound the diving alarm from the bridge, order, "Clear the bridge, clear the bridge!," then follow the two lookouts as they dropped down the bridge trunk to the conning tower. These three would continue down to the control room where one lookout would man and place the bow planes on full dive, while the other would do the same with the stern planes. The officer of the deck would pull the upper bridge hatch shut and quickly dog it.[4] As he dropped down into the conning tower, the quartermaster of the watch would do the same with the lower bridge access hatch. The officer of the deck would continue down to the control room and immediately take control of the boat as the diving officer of the watch.

Hearing the alarm, the chief of the watch, in the meantime, would open all MBT vents, flood negative tank, and take charge of the dive until the diving officer of the watch arrived and relieved him. At the same time, maneuvering—where the engineering plant control watch standers, such as the senior controller man and junior controller man (both electrician's mates)—would shift propulsion from diesel engine to electrical propulsion in response to the full bell ordered.[5]

In general, and depending on sea state and water clarity, a crash dive would be to at least 150 feet. If an ASW aircraft had been sighted close aboard, the dive might be to an even greater depth, along with an abrupt course change, the better to prevent detection and ensure that the boat got well beneath the acoustic layer.

The captain would be up in the conning tower by this time, and after ascertaining just what the officer of the deck and lookouts had seen, would decide what to do next. After a thorough sonar search of the baffles and after a sufficient amount of time had passed, in his estimate, the captain would, providing sonar held no close contacts, order the diving officer of the watch to take the boat up to periscope depth where he could make a quick assessment of the situation with just a minimum of *Greenfish's* attack periscope above the water surface.[6] This search was generally made at minimum speed, or turns, in order to prevent creating any detectable periscope feather, or wake.[7] The captain also had to be very careful that there were no obstacles or debris overhead and especially mindful of just where the sun or a bright moon was so that the head window did not reflect or flash light in the direction of a threat contact.

After the captain had determined it was all clear, we would return to the surface using an airless surfacing: high-pressure air was not used to blow the MBTs clear of water in this case. Instead, the boat was driven to the surface at fifteen knots ("All ahead standard") or more with the MBT vents open. Once the boat broached and was holding on the surface, the MBT vents were shut, and the low pressure blower was used to clear the MBTs of whatever water remained in each. This saved the boat's high-pressure air for emergencies. It further saved running the two high-pressure air compressors to recharge our high-pressure air banks. The compressors were also very noisy, making *Greenfish* more detectable acoustically; in addition, running them required a significant amount of electrical power.

Once on the surface, the captain was the first to rush from the conning tower up to the bridge. When the situation was determined to be all clear of contacts and stable, he would call the lookouts and the officer of the deck to the bridge to resume their watch and *Greenfish's* surface transit.

There were some watches as we approached and passed by Midway Island where we had to crash-dive three or four times during each four-hour watch in order to avoid detection by U.S. military patrol aircraft. Invariably, also, there were occasions when a rising moon or exceptionally bright star or planet was misclassified as a threat contact by an inexperienced lookout or officer of the deck, and down we dived. These incidents provoked considerable merriment among the crew, and a lookout and officer might, as a result, pick up a new nickname such as Blind Eye or Chicken Eye.

I recall hearing about a submarine school classmate of mine who was standing officer of the deck watches on another boat headed north, when he saw an unidentified flying object. He immediately called "Captain to the bridge, captain to the bridge!" on the 1MC system. This is an emergency call, of course, and any submarine captain would rush to the bridge as fast as possible, with any nearby crewmember nearly trampled in the process. In this case, my classmate suddenly realized that what he actually saw was just a seagull and passed the word, "There's no hurry, captain, there's no hurry!" The incident made the rounds of the waterfront in Yokosuka and Pearl Harbor, and it was a long time before he lived it down.

As we approached within a hundred miles or so of our assigned area, *Greenfish* shifted to a routine of running submerged at patrol-quiet during the day and snorkeling at night to recharge her batteries.[8] Even stricter rules applied with regard to preventing detection, and each watch had to be especially alert to the possibility of encountering a submarine of another nation at almost any time. A closing air, surface, or subsurface threat contact called for the immediate lowering of all periscopes and radio/electronic countermeasures masts, and for securing snorkeling.

When we were within or near our patrol area, we would also abruptly secure snorkeling at irregular intervals running from every forty-five minutes to every sixty minutes. The officer of the deck would then change course to the right or left at least 60 degrees and order sonar to search for any submerged contacts that might be closing from deep within our stern or baffles area.

Once within our assigned mission area, *Greenfish*'s crew would quickly go to a watch routine much like that required during a World War II war patrol. Although always in international waters, we were operating in an area where we knew we would not be welcome if detected. All watch stations, particularly the conning tower, control room, and engineering spaces, had to be on high alert. Both torpedo rooms also maintained a full state of readiness, with a self-defense snapshot tube ready forward for immediate action if need be.[9]

The mission we were on, my first as a new submarine officer, concentrated on the collection of Soviet electronic emissions from fire control, air, and surface search radars. I don't recall our seeing a single warship of any kind during the entire six weeks, however, due in all probability to our long range from the Soviet coast and major bases during this mission.

## Caught in the Net

I stood watch as diving officer of the watch throughout most of the submerged portions of this mission, maintaining precise depth control at all times. The observation periscope and electronic signal collection and countermeasures mast had to be kept sufficiently clear of the water for observation and for electronic emissions collection, yet not so high out of the water as to make *Greenfish* more easily detected by shore-based and airborne radars.

The most difficult times for all diving station teams were those during which heavy sea states and storm conditions prevailed and those during which tidal conditions and accompanying changes in water density were at work. Both required adroit, timely control planes action as well as clever, anticipatory minor reballasting.

Probably the most interesting challenge I faced about midway through my first patrol was when *Greenfish* suddenly ran into the remnants of a large fishing net while at periscope depth. Fortunately for us, we were on a steady course and making almost minimum turns. As the exec silently hovered nearby and the captain watched the net through the periscope, I was given full conning authority as diving officer of the watch to back our boat gradually clear of the net.

It wasn't easy, because everyone in the ship control party had to realize immediately that two key roles would be reversed. The stern planesman became the forward or bow planesman, who was responsible for making the fine adjustments to keep us at ordered depth. The bow planesman, in turn, became the stern planesman who was responsible for maintaining whatever down or up bubble, or longitudinal aspect, that would hold *Greenfish* at ordered depth. He also assumed duties as helmsman, which meant that he needed to keep the rudder at zero and be alert to make whatever fine adjustments were necessary to ensure that we backed out of the net on the reverse of the course we had entered on. Any sudden up or down angle, abrupt change of course, or even worse, loss of depth could get us even further, if not hopelessly, entangled. As diving officer of the watch in this situation, I also had control of the boat's speed, which meant that I had to use backing bells judiciously as we worked gradually to clear the fishing net.

In this situation, the first order of business was to achieve and maintain both neutral buoyancy and a zero bubble as we hovered in place, preferably with our gyro heading roughly on the course on which we had first entered the net. The word was passed for all hands to remain in their present positions, unless in an emergency. Then, as soon as things appeared to have settled down, neutral buoyancy was established and the boat was steadied on the desired heading, I ordered, "All back one-third!" soon followed by, "All stop!" as we began to move astern and away from the net. This sequence was repeated a number of times until the captain reported that the net was falling or clearing well astern of us.

Once we determined, to everyone's great relief, that we had backed completely clear of the net, its position and extent were accurately plotted. We then repositioned ourselves such that we would remain well clear of the general area of this net, which might be one of several, during the remainder of our mission.

## The Great Cockroach Race

Like all other Cold War submarine operations, life on board could be boring. *Greenfish's* crewmembers, nonetheless, always seemed to find ways to amuse themselves during off-watch hours. We enjoyed a better-than-average selection of movies. Acey-deucey and high-stakes poker games were going on almost continuously in the wardroom and after-torpedo room.

Most diesel boats, particularly those based in tropical Pearl Harbor, were heavily infested with cockroaches of every size and shape. Bugs from the Philippines, Guam, Japan, and Hong Kong later joined cousins that had boarded in Hawaii and every other place we visited in the Pacific. They thrived and mutated throughout the dark, warmer, hard-to-reach nooks and crannies and innumerable areas of old layered, flaked, and peeling paint in the bilges of these grossly unevenly heated and cooled veterans of the war against the Japanese in the Pacific. No surprise that they bred by the thousands in the forward battery compartment where the galley, freeze and chill boxes, crews mess, officers' wardroom, pantry, and berthing areas were located.

Because of the submarine's limited interior volume, every accessible space was used—it was completely filled to capacity, in fact, with machinery and equipment, piping, ventilation ducts, valves, electrical wiring, switch boxes, lockers, and temporary stowage of spare parts and stores. Add to this her crew of some seventy-five to eighty men and, as the saying goes, "There was no room left to swing a cat." For these reasons, it was difficult to keep early submarines clean, especially when we were almost continually at sea on one operation after another in both tropical and northern waters.

Cockroaches could thus be encountered everywhere and at any time during the day and night, including in one's bunk. There were times when we would grab a snack or sandwich, sit down to enjoy it, and suddenly be joined by myriad hungry roaches drawn by the tantalizing smells. Roaches occasionally showed up in our coffee or juice if we were careless enough to leave it unattended for a few moments. A constant refrain of life on a diesel submarine was the sound of crunching and squishing as phalanxes of roaches met their demise underfoot or -hand.

From time to time while in port, *Greenfish* would have to be sealed up and thoroughly fumigated, and millions of lifeless carcasses would be scooped up and disposed of. Fumigation generally was conducted before we departed on a major deployment. After that, intense efforts were made to keep these pests from coming back during the loading of food stores and spare parts. Nevertheless, they always managed to return, often within just a day or two.

In the end, we all had to learn to live with our cockroach shipmates. They obviously enjoyed submarine duty as much as we did, and they weren't going away. Some crewmembers barely noticed them after a while. Others not only noticed them but found novel ways of putting them to use for the amusement of the crew.

One weekend afternoon midway through the first lengthy submerged patrol of our deployment in an area of high intelligence interest, I was sitting in the wardroom reading when I heard bursts of laughter coming from the adjacent control room. Curiosity overcame me, and I got up to see what was going on.

Dominating the center of every diesel submarine control room was the binnacle that housed the primary gyrocompass, the Mk-19. Its flat top also served as a convenient table and was in constant use. This afternoon it was serving a novel function: Surrounding the binnacle were several members of the control room watch and a half-dozen visitors from other compartments. The top of the binnacle had been cleared off and a green felt cloth, like that used for card games, laid over it. Each of those encircling the impromptu green table had piles of coins stacked in front of them. It looked like a typical table in a gambling casino.

"What is everyone enjoying so much?" I asked myself as I edged between two onlookers to get a closer view. Immediately noticeable was a long clipboard, ordinarily used to hold watch-stander equipment recording sheets, centered on the green cloth. On its surface there had been painted five longitudinal, evenly spaced white lines with the lanes numbered from "One" to "Six." Like a racetrack of some sort, I mused.

The next thing I knew, a crewmember on my left placed a small box near the clip end of the clipboard. He inserted his thumb and forefinger into the box and extracted a struggling cockroach. Several men on either side did the same. Then, as another crewmember raised the large metal clip at the board's end, each handler gently placed the tail of his own race entrant directly beneath the clip near the center of each lane and held it there as he simultaneously gently lowered the clip onto the roach.

After bets were made on each entrant, to the accompaniment of loud laughter and shouts, the starter hit the end of the clip with his fist, raising the blade portion, which released the cockroaches, and the race was on. Those cockroaches still alive bolted forward. Cockroaches, even submarine ones, couldn't be expected to run directly down their assigned lanes, and none did. Hence, the winner was the first one to escape to the edge of the green-covered binnacle and disappear.

All good things end, and in this case they ended abruptly. Captain Knudsen awoke from a nap and walked into the control room. His loud "What the hell?" caused the impromptu race participants to scatter almost as fast as the cockroaches. As would be expected, the watch section was in for a colossal ass chewing, as was the exec and chief of the boat.

Was such a race ever repeated? Of course it was, but certainly never as well organized or as public as this first one.

The days dragged by, as they always do on a mission of this type, probably because there was nothing much of interest to observe or record in the vast reaches of the Northwestern Pacific. The day of departure arrived at long last when it was time for us to pull well clear of our assigned patrol area and allow another boat to ease in and take our place.

We were ordered to head for the Yokosuka, a good week away to the south. The routine would be pretty much as it had been on our way to station—periscope depth during the day and transiting on the surface during the hours of darkness.

### Mine Close Aboard!

One of the more harrowing experiences of my life, and probably everyone else's at the time, occurred several days later while proceeding south, at periscope depth and minimum turns, a few miles to the east of the Kurile Islands. The morning brought dense fog; visibility in any direction could not have been more than fifty feet or so. I was on watch in the conning tower, manning the periscope and rapidly rotating it through 360 degrees about once every two to three minutes as I searched for fishing boats that might detect us as well as buoys, logs, and other obstacles that might lie in our path.

It was early summer. We had just finished our Cold War mission of some forty days in the Northwestern Pacific as part of our WestPac deployment. *Greenfish* had departed our assigned area the night before last and was en route to the U.S. naval base at Yokosuka, Japan, for what we hoped might be at least a week of rest and recreation. The mission had been quiet, without any event of significance throughout our entire time on station. The requirement to remain completely undetected still applied, however, and would continue until we surfaced just off the entrance to Sugami Wan, or Tokyo Bay. The routine was the usual one of transiting fully submerged during daylight hours and on the surface at night, as we charged batteries and made as much speed as we could toward our destination.

We eased to periscope depth from time to time during the day in order to copy our special radio broadcasts and fix our navigation position. While there, we also carefully searched our immediate surroundings for possible surface and air contacts, both visually and with our electronic emissions detection equipment. That was what we were engaged in as I manned our longer, larger-barreled number two, or observation, periscope.

The environment was spooky as the fog thickened and thinned. Trying to discern anything was tiring and stressful as I strained to pick out floating objects or sight a large fishing boat or ship that might be directly ahead or close aboard. It was easy to imagine you saw something only to realize nothing was there.

Any submarine at periscope depth under these low-visibility conditions was vulnerable, and just a few seconds of inattention or daydreaming could end up damaging the periscope and any other masts or antennas that were also raised. Even worse, it could spell disaster for the submarine and crew should we collide with a large, fast-moving merchant vessel.

The responsibility for *Greenfish*'s safety weighed heavily on my shoulders as I manned the periscope. Having served for several years on the destroyer *Gregory* before entering the submarine force, I already knew these waters to be hazardous for reasons that did not involve just safe navigation. An uncountable number of antiship mines, probably numbering in the tens of thousands, had been released or positioned on the ocean bottom throughout the Northwestern Pacific during World War II and the Korean War. As was always the case, the mines and their positions were soon forgotten upon the conclusion of these significant conflicts. It was always possible that an old mine might break loose from its moorings and float to the surface—anything from the traditional horned contact mine, extensively used since the early days of World War I, to the very sophisticated yet nondescript-looking acoustic and pressure mine. The frequent typhoons that had occurred since the two wars had, as one would expect, broken many mines loose and scattered them in every direction; this was especially true throughout the Northwestern Pacific. The slightest contact with a loose floating mine, of course, could spell doom for the unsuspecting ship or submarine.

My father, the late Capt. William F. McLaren, USN, had served during the Korean War as a destroyer captain and later as a mine squadron commander. He had warned me on several occasions—before I departed on my first WestPac deployment during the summer of 1956, as a newly commissioned ensign on board the *Gregory*—about the possibility of encountering free-floating mines.

Dad McLaren was right. The *Gregory* sighted and destroyed several floating mines with its 40-mm antiaircraft batteries during the course of that six-month deployment. The circumstances and visibility were always near ideal, however, and it was an event that all hands not on watch were called topside to observe and enjoy. These events were particularly important for me, since I was the ship's antiaircraft officer and had charge of the guns involved.

As I rotated the periscope rapidly yet cautiously in a series of circles to search for and identify anything in our immediate vicinity that might pose a threat, I was always mindful of the possibility that a floating mine might suddenly appear out of the fog. It was even more worrisome when others were on the scope: What if the quartermaster of the watch and the junior officer of the deck, with whom I, as officer of the deck or conning officer, had set up a routine of fifteen minutes on the scope and thirty minutes off, did not see or recognize a mine until it was too close? It was easy to obsess on that concern. I reflected that Captain Knudsen, who never left the conning tower during our times at periscope depth, must have had similar thoughts.

I could not have been on the periscope more than ten minutes when there she was—a horned, floating mine just emerging from the fog, 20 degrees to starboard, and not more than twenty yards away. It was only partially afloat, but its horns looked threateningly close as it gently bobbed in the calm seas that surrounded us.

"Mine ahead! Mine ahead! Twenty degrees off our starboard bow! Range close aboard!" I yelled out, immediately followed by "Captain to the periscope! Captain to the periscope!"

Captain Knudsen took the periscope, confirmed my sighting, and quickly ordered, "Left 10 degrees rudder, make turns for three knots!" As the mine drifted dangerously close to starboard, he judiciously adjusted both course and speed as necessary to prevent further closure by the mine, particularly toward *Greenfish's* stern planes and propellers. His was a careful and very well-executed maneuver. Too much rudder, coupled with speed, could easily have thrown our stern into the path of the mine, yet too little would have caused us to close the mine further. Whew! It was a tense moment, and the knees of all in the conning tower were fair to shaking as we slipped by the mine, noted its position, and slowly continued on our way.

Once clear, the captain wisely ordered, "Lower all masts and scopes, ease down to one hundred fifty feet!" He realized that his conning tower watch was burned out for the moment, and it was time to take a breather.

Steady at depth, the captain had the word passed to all compartments on what had just occurred and announced we would run deep and quiet for the next several hours. He later complimented me for my alertness and remarked, "*Greenfish* was a lucky boat!" The entire event was the stuff of nightmares and what-ifs. I loathed and even feared fog, particularly dense fog, for the rest of my submarine career, and to this day I still muse and dream about what could have happened. A number of both Axis and Allied submarines, during both world wars, were not so fortunate.

The remainder of the transit was relatively uneventful operationally, with the exception of an average of at least three or four emergency deeps per watch as we were forced to avoid detection by what seemed to be an endless procession of fishing boats off the Kurile Islands and northeastern Japan.

## Spotting an Indicator

Below decks the poker games for those off watch continued, as they had every afternoon and evening throughout our entire mission. In the wardroom, where most of us played at least four to six hours every evening, things were rapidly approaching closure for a number of us as our exec, Mac McKenzie, was in the final stages of relieving us of a significant portion of the pay that we were expecting upon arrival in Yokosuka five days hence. Mac was an old hand at the game, and at his insistence we had been playing pot limit the entire voyage. That meant that a knowledgeable and experienced player had the opportunity to protect his hand by matching whatever was in the pot each time it came his time to bet. It made no difference whether he had good cards or bad cards. Whoever wanted to find out would have to match or call his bet. This could prove expensive, particularly for the novice, as most of us were. The captain joined the game from time to time but didn't really know what was going on, or I am sure that he would have stepped in. The exec was the only winner of the six officers playing, and at least three of us were down by over $100. This was back in the days when my total pay was not much more than $400 per month, which in 2014 dollars would be about $2,500.[10] Thus far, I had lost a total of $119. If I did not recoup, my total pay upon arrival in Yokosuka would not amount to more than $138 and some change, after the allotment to my wife had been deducted—not enough to cover the tremendous amount of laundry I would have to have done in Yokosuka. I would also not have any money to pay for a few drinks and dinner at the officers club or, indeed, buy a few gifts for my family. It was a profoundly depressing thought. I consoled myself with the knowledge that one other officer in our wardroom might owe the exec as much as $400.

Poker is very addictive. Although I had originally resolved early in the patrol to quit when I had lost $50, I found I just couldn't stay away from the game and the camaraderie that went with it. About six of us were sitting around the wardroom table one evening playing the exec's favorite game of seven-card high-low. High-low always ensured a large pot because, in addition to providing the opportunity of winning at least half the pot—by betting that you had the highest or the lowest hand—it also gave you the chance to bet that you had both the highest and the lowest five cards out of the seven you were dealt and take the entire pot. The catch was that, once you declared, you had to win both. If you were beaten either high or low, you lost all claim, either high or low, to the pot. With such a large pot, of course, almost everyone stayed in longer than he should have in hopes of getting either the best or the worst hand. Hence, it was not only hard to drive anyone out early by continually betting what was in the pot, but also each bet required more money than usual.

For some reason I was paying closer-than-usual attention to the exec, Mac McKenzie, who exuded confidence with each and every hand he held and who then bet accordingly. As the game went on, and the other officers and I continued to lose to the exec, I thought I detected an involuntary tic in his left eye. I had never noticed it before. The tic seemed to manifest itself each time he bet. The thought occurred to me during the play that he might be bluffing and that my hand was good enough to call him. I was looking at three aces—enough for me to stay in for at least one more round. I therefore decided to take a chance on the tic being an indicator that he was bluffing and stick it out, no matter what it cost me. Following the deal-out of the last card of seven and the last round of bets, everyone else folded, leaving only the exec and me. Clearly, everyone else thought he had garnered yet another winning hand. It was his bet and he matched the pot, which was now well over $200. He looked at me with a confident smile. Having noticed the tic in action again just seconds before, I called his bet. He declared high-low and laid down his cards. He *had* been bluffing! He had only two pair. I declared high with my three aces, and since I beat the high of his high-low, I won the entire pot.

Looking at me somewhat strangely as I joyfully raked it in, the exec seemed anxious to deal another round as soon as possible. This time it was straight five-card draw, with the best five cards winning after betting, once, drawing up to three more cards, and betting again. I held a pair of kings plus an ace to start and two small cards. Since it was my bet, I opened by betting the pot. The other officers dropped out right away, leaving only the exec and me. He called or matched me. The dealer asked us each how many cards we wanted. I asked for two, and the exec, his tic working away, stated that he was good with the five he had. This meant that he was acting as if he held either a straight (five cards in numerical sequence), a flush (all five cards of the same suit), or a full house (three of a kind plus a pair). Figuring he was bluffing again, I bet the pot. The exec, smiling broadly, matched my bet and raised me another $75. Man! His tic indicated he was bluffing again. As I was not completely sure, however, I just called his bet and laid down my two pair: kings and tens. He threw down a pair of fours in utter disgust.

I had now won back my $119 and much more besides, so I quickly got up and excused myself because I "had some submarine qualification work to get back to." The exec begged me to stay in the game, but I was adamant. I wanted to catch my breath and savor my victory.

I rejoined the seemingly endless wardroom poker game after dinner that night and, unless I had a particularly strong hand, I folded. I bet whenever I caught the exec's tic at work and most, if not all, of the other players dropped out. I caught him three more times, winning an additional $200 or more from him that evening

When we broke up at close to midnight, the exec called me aside saying, "Fred, I have an indicator of some sort that you have picked up, haven't you?" I pretended not to have any idea what he was talking about, because I was "new to the game." He was unconvinced, but walked away. At that point I was certain that I had nailed his indicator and, exacting a promise of absolute confidentiality, I shared what I thought was going on with the officer who had lost close to $400.

We both won steadily from that point on. By the time we reached port, the other officer had won a significant portion of his money back, to his very great relief. I finished with close to $250, most of which was McKenzie's money. The exec, in the meantime, had become frantic. His favorite game was being ruined for him. He called me aside several times more, begging me and then outright ordering me to tell him what his indicator was. I acted confused by his question. Needless to say, I knew that no good could possibly come to me, particularly in any future poker games, by sharing this information with him. Besides, he had been merciless to us all and seemingly cared little whether he had hurt any of his fellow officers financially. I felt strongly that he richly deserved whatever happened to him in any future poker games.

All debts were squared upon our arrival at the Yokosuka Naval Base, thanks to a Navy paymaster coming on board and paying us each in cash. The exec's wistful expression as he saw our own money return to our hands, plus some of his own, was priceless.

Once all protocols and amenities had been completed with Commander Submarine Group Seven (ComSubGrp7) those officers not having in-port duty changed into civilian clothes and headed for the submarine sanctuary, while the crew headed for their favorite bars in Yokosuka.

# CHAPTER 4

# Coming into Yokosuka

In the years immediately following World War II, through the Korean War and up through the end of the war in Vietnam, Yokosuka was, next to Hong Kong, the favorite port of all Pacific-based submariners. The large naval base and the surrounding town provided a welcome and relaxing respite from Cold War operations and the privations of the older deployed diesel boats. Both officers and senior crewmembers, if they chose, could live on shore, returning to their submarine only when duty required.

## The Submarine Sanctuary

The submarine sanctuary, as it was called for officers, occupied the top floors of a building within the naval shipyard. Within easy walking distance of where our submarines were moored, it was the first place we retreated to once on shore following a lengthy transit across the Pacific or a long and difficult operation in unfriendly waters. There were a sufficient number of rooms and comfortable beds with clean linens to accommodate all the officers of whatever submarines were moored nearby. In addition, private rooms for commanding officers were always available. The sanctuary was particularly famous for a gigantic black marble soaking bathtub. You could sit for hours up to your neck in steaming hot water with your legs fully extended and completely relax. It was the only place for most of us where we could remove the accumulated dirt and smells of weeks of close confinement on board.

In the early days, the sanctuary was used for every conceivable social get-together. Beer, wine, and hard liquor were available twenty-four hours a day from an unusually well-stocked bar that was on the honor system. Drinks were so inexpensive they were almost free.

USS *Greenfish* (SS 351) outboard in nest of diesel submarines, Pearl Harbor, 1959.
*U.S. Navy*

In addition, breakfast and lunch were served seven days a week. We could send off our laundry and dry cleaning and have it back in an hour or so. We could place radiotelephone calls home in privacy, and most of us took advantage of this on arrival in port. We also could just sit and read or write home in uninterrupted quiet.

On the other hand, the sanctuary was also an excellent launching pad for a night of eating, drinking, and heavy carousing with fellow submariners, particularly on those nights when we planned to raise hell in the sizable local officers club or repair to the infamous Kanko Hotel. The sanctuary was quite popular with an abundance of congenial on-base women—for instance, Navy nurses and department of defense school teachers there to teach the children of the U.S. armed forces stationed in the area. From time to time romances would develop that raised tensions between the soon-to-depart and the just-arrived officers, to the amusement of everyone else. Not surprisingly, the sanctuary was also the location of frequent inter-submarine wardroom poker games in the late 1950s. The best players from each boat came there looking for fresh victims, and most games ran through the night.

The sanctuary was, in short, a true refuge, where we could completely unwind in every respect. It was also the only place available where attack boat commanders could physically and mentally prepare themselves for the next long and, more often than not, exceedingly arduous mission.

ComSubGrp7 and the officer members of his small staff had their head-quarters in the sanctuary building. The commanders I met through the early years were nearly all decorated submarine war patrol veterans of World War II, and their staffs were made up of colorful submarine veterans of repeated tours of duty in Japan, Okinawa, and the Philippines. A few had spent so much time cohabitating with a local *girlsan* that they were considered to have gone "Asiatic."

One memorable character was "Frank the Friendly Boatswain's Mate," a bachelor warrant officer in his forties with many years of submarine-related duty under his belt. He could always be found at the sanctuary's bar when he was not otherwise occupied as a ship superintendent for one or more subma-rines requiring repair work. Frank was a tour guide of slightly shady repute when it came to exploring the after-dark sights and charms of Yokosuka and its surrounding environs. As he sat at the bar every evening, Frank would often hold forth about the "huge, brightly lighted hand" that suddenly appeared every night above Yokosuka and beckoned submarine sailors to sample the city's delights. The hand was, of course, imaginary, but Frank had a way of making it seem real as he enthusiastically waved his long heav-ily tattooed arms in the air, describing it and suggesting to all within earshot that they join him and head into town "to find the switch and turn it off" as the case may be, or, "turn it on again."

Most of us in WestPac were at one time or another suckered into join-ing Frank on one of his nightly forays. The routine was always the same: We would first drop in on one of his favorite Japanese restaurants to have sukiyaki and copious amounts of Kirin beer. Those still ambulatory would then head for the infamous Kanko Hotel, where there was always a good band and, for the bachelors or those who considered themselves to be so, numerous attractive young Japanese women with whom they could dance away the night. A man was expected to keep his companion for the evening well supplied with pricey drinks—which were caramel-colored and nonal-coholic—if he wanted to retain her company. By the end of evening, the unwary would find his bar bill had reached staggering proportions.

Preferences varied on how best to conclude a night on shore in a foreign port. Far and away the wisest and safest was to go for a hot bath and massage at one of the many places just off base, get our clothing cleaned and pressed, and then return to the sanctuary for some sleep and a chance to sober up for the next day.

During the good old days of WestPac submarining—the 1950s, 1960s, and 1970s—the sanctuary remained a real oasis for us all, following stressful Cold War missions. Would such a retreat be considered necessary for much-needed rest and relaxation these days? Would our frequently exuberant behavior as we wound down from missions of that era be considered proper or tolerated now? Probably not. We certainly had fun, though, as our World War II forebears did before us. Having the sanctuary boosted our morale, helped us to bond even more as brother submariners, and definitely contributed to our performance and successes at sea.

*Greenfish* finished up a longer-than-expected upkeep in Yokosuka during which time we bade a fond farewell to our commanding officer, Jack Knudsen, and welcomed a new one—hot-running Lt. Cdr. John A. "Al" Davis Jr. on 16 July 1958. We then headed south for Subic Bay in the Philippines following the same routine that we had used to transit from Pearl Harbor to our Cold War mission.

## Toward Subic Bay

In July 1958 *Greenfish* was on her way, with a new captain, to the U.S. naval base at Subic Bay. The bay itself is a deep-water harborage on the west coast of the island of Luzon in Zambales, Philippines, about sixty-two miles north-west of Manila Bay. The United States captured the Spanish base in 1899 during the Philippine–American War and controlled the bay until 1991.[1] The naval base was a major ship-repair, supply, and rest and recreation facil-ity of the United States Navy and in 1958 could handle multiple ships of any type, up to and including aircraft carriers. After a brief period of upkeep and some liberty in the adjacent town of Olongopo, we would be heading north on another Cold War mission.

## "One Hot Coffee to the Bridge"

As described, *Greenfish*, a GUPPY IIA, had been streamlined externally to enable it to attain much greater speeds under water than its World War II predecessors had been capable of. These modifications, particularly to the bow, at the same time significantly degraded this class of submarine's ability to reach the war-era surfaced speeds or to ride as well as previously in rough or heavy seas. All bridge watches in northern waters became an ordeal that required layers of warm clothing and frequent hot beverages to sustain us during cold, windy, and rainy or sleety nights on the surface.

One officer who stood these watches, Lieutenant J, was noted for his abrasiveness toward the more junior enlisted personnel. He was especially hard on the Filipino steward's mates who maintained the officers' wardroom and berthing areas on board.[2] He was definitely a man of many moods, with the most disagreeable coming out at night while he had the watch.

When Lieutenant J insisted that his mug of coffee was to be delivered to him on the bridge hot and completely filled, heaven help the hapless fellow who delivered anything less. If he did, which happened more often than not in heavy seas, he was apt to be chewed out.

A short narrow ladder connected the control room to the conning tower above; a much longer but equally narrow ladder connected the after end of the conning tower to the open bridge above. It was, therefore, quite understandable that a mug of coffee carried from the wardroom all the way to the open bridge might lose some of its warmth, not to mention quantity, en route in rough seas. No matter: The nightly less-than-satisfactory coffee deliveries and subsequent fireworks became a regular and anticipated routine providing rich entertainment for those who were bored with the movie or just couldn't sleep. The best location to take in the latest dressing down was the conning tower area just beneath the bridge.

In September 1958 several new crewmembers reported on board. Among them was a senior first-class Filipino steward's mate with many years of service under his belt, including a number of war patrols during World War II. It was instantly apparent to *Greenfish*'s crew that the petty officer was a well-seasoned hand—not a man to mess with. To Lieutenant J, however, one steward's mate was like any other. As he put it, "They are all lazy and inefficient and need a frequent jacking up."

On the night of the new steward's mate's first coffee delivery to Lieutenant J, who had the evening watch on the bridge, a few more crewmembers than normal gathered in the control room to enjoy the fireworks. The sea was extremely choppy once we were well clear of Subic Bay, and the usual dressing down took place. When the new senior petty officer returned from the bridge, there was a perceptible difference in his expression from that of previous steward's mates, however. He did not descend into the control room crestfallen. On the contrary, he had an enigmatic grin on his face mixed with a solid look of determination.

A series of miracles occurred during our next three nights on the surface. Completely full, hot mugs of coffee were being regularly delivered to Lieutenant J on the bridge. He sang the praises of the new leading steward's mate's all over the boat, citing him to the supply and commissary officer and the other steward's mates as the example to be followed. The new senior petty officer just nodded, acknowledging the praise with a faint smile. Lieutenant J was happy, and now all the other steward's mates were making hot coffee deliveries. "Good leadership in action!" pronounced Lieutenant J, and so it seemed.

Those of the crew who had been treated to the nightly unsatisfactory coffee deliveries throughout *Greenfish*'s deployment, and their vocal aftermath, grew curious as to how such a chronic problem had been so abruptly solved. They were even more curious to know how the other two steward's mates had been retrained in such a short time, drawing loud approval from other bridge watch-standing officers as well. Certainly, all agreed that our boat had acquired a much-needed top-notch petty officer at a key time.

Several days later, during a particularly rough evening transit on the surface, I happened to be in the control room conducting a submarine hydraulic systems qualification exam of several young crewmembers. Lieutenant J was officer of the deck on the bridge. The leading steward's mate passed quickly through, with a brimming mug of hot coffee, en route to the bridge. On the spur of the moment I decided to follow him to see if I could learn something about the miracle he had effected.

The leading steward's mate climbed the short ladder to the conning tower with no difficulty and, as best as I could determine, merely held the hot mug of coffee firmly and carefully. I followed him up the ladder and watched him proceed aft to the first or bottom rungs of the very long ladder up to the bridge and the foul weather that enveloped us.

*Greenfish* was wallowing like a hog as she proceeded through the rough seas at twelve knots. The navigator, Lieutenant D, a quartermaster assistant, and the helmsman were on watch in the conning tower. All were extremely busy and took little notice of the steward's mate, even when he called out, "Permission to come to the bridge?"

"Permission granted," was Lieutenant J's prompt response. The leading steward's mate stole a quick glance at the conning tower watch standers and, not seeing me at the top of the ladder, quickly bent over and took a large draft from the coffee mug that caused his cheeks to puff out like a chipmunk's. He then scampered rapidly up the ladder. "Wow," I first thought, "Lieutenant J is really going to be ticked off to discover so much coffee missing" and then, "Why would the new leading steward's mate be risking Lieutenant J's anger after receiving so much praise during the last several weeks?"

"Well, let's see what happens next," I said to myself as I climbed into the conning tower and hurried to the foot of the ladder leading to the bridge. Peering up the ladder, I observed the leading steward's mate at the top, and then, after raising the coffee mug to his lips, discharge the contents of his pouched cheeks into the cup. "Good grief," I whispered. "So that's how the problem was solved." The steward's mate thrust the mug upward and yelled, "Hot coffee, Mr. J!" "Fine job," was Lieutenant J's response as he reached down and accepted the mug from the outstretched hand and took a big gulp. "Keep up the good work." "Thank you, sir," replied the steward's mate, who started back down the ladder. I quickly withdrew and rushed down the ladder to the control room. The leading steward's mate stopped to visit with the conning tower watch for a minute and then descended into the control room. He greeted me with his slow smile as he saw me standing there. I had to turn my head to keep from laughing.

I shared with no one what I had seen as the remaining weeks of the deployment dragged by. It goes with saying that I never ordered "coffee to the bridge" or anything else while on watch, either above or below decks, during the remainder of my twenty-four years in submarines.

## Two Blankets and a Pillow

A follow-on to "one hot coffee to the bridge" took place several nights later during a nighttime transit on the surface. The seas were chaotic and choppy, with wind in excess of thirty knots, and it was very cold. As one of the bridge lookouts passed through the control room on his way to assume the watch, he was so heavily encased in foul weather gear that we called him the Abdominal Snowman.

A submarine crew can always be counted on to give nicknames, not usually flattering, to their fellow crewmembers, both officer and enlisted. All that was needed was for the unfortunate sailor to have a noticeable physical characteristic, unusual or abnormal habits, or be involved in a memorable incident either on shore or afloat. The name Abdomen-able Snowman was certain to stick with this fellow the rest of his submarine career, since he was constantly battling weight gain. Several other memorable names on board *Greenfish* were No Ass, Horse, Dog Breath, The Unwashable, and The Animal.

About midway through the midnight to 4:00 a.m. watch, our most junior Filipino steward's mate was observed entering the control room with his arms around two thick blankets and a large pillow. This sight provoked considerable hilarity, followed by ribald questions from watch personnel and bystanders in the area. When questioned just where he was going and why, the steward's mate replied that the bridge had called for the blankets and a pillow to be sent up. Hearing that, the chief of the watch stationed on the hydraulic manifold immediately called up to the bridge on the 1MC, "Bridge, control, what is going on up there? We have a steward's mate down here with two blankets and a pillow that he says you wanted delivered to the bridge." The bridge clicked the 1MC several times as if the officer of the deck was on the verge of saying something, but there was nothing but silence. The officer of the deck finally responded with "Control, bridge, chief, what on earth are you talking about?" The chief of the watch answered by repeating his earlier message. I doubt if anyone on the bridge could have missed hearing the accompanying loud laughter, whistles, and catcalls in the background. The next 1MC transmission that came from the bridge was a very emphatic "Hell, no! We asked for two black and bitters to the bridge." The chief of the watch replied, "On the way," and the control room again erupted into guffaws. The steward's mate, who was soon to acquire the nickname Tin Ear, was directed to return to the wardroom, unload the bedding he was carrying, and return with the two black coffees for the bridge as originally ordered. Forget the bitters.

# CHAPTER 5

# Off the Soviet Far East Coast

**D**uring the summer of 1958 *Greenfish* was on a Cold War surveillance and intelligence-gathering mission to the Soviet Far East. It was my second special operation as an unseasoned young submarine officer and the first with our new commanding officer, Al Davis. Just where we were cannot be revealed even today, some fifty-seven years later. How long we would be gone and where we would return was never known for sure as we departed. It depended on such things as the state of the Cold War at the time, what (if any) specific objectives were assigned, what we might encounter while on patrol, and whether we were scheduled to be relieved by another submarine. We prepared and armed for and conducted each mission as if we were on an actual war patrol, because relations were such between the United States and its allies and the Soviet bloc that the steady tension and friction could erupt into an unexpected attack and exchange of weapons at any time.

## Riding Out a Typhoon

En route to a subsequent Cold War mission during late September 1958, we had the bad luck to run into Super Typhoon Ida, one of the strongest typhoons in history. Covering a span of several hundred miles, it had formed in the Western Pacific near Guam about 20 September. Initially it headed west and then curved to the north toward Japan.[1] The sequence that overtook us began with long swells from the southeast, under a canopy of darkening cirrus clouds and a steadily decreasing barometer. Winds increased from less than twenty knots to near forty knots and then from sixty to eighty knots, as the seas rose high over the next several days. After determining the direction of the typhoon's center, we maneuvered to remain to the left or west of its track and stayed in the less dangerous or so-called navigable semicircle.

As the sea state increased, all but the oldest hands became seasick, and wondered aloud why *Greenfish* couldn't just submerge under the storm. In the meantime the watch was brought down from the bridge and into the conning tower and control room, and the bridge trunk hatches were shut and dogged tight. The captain picked up the 1MC and explained to all hands that *Greenfish* would be riding out the typhoon on the surface, on two engines, because the boat did not have the battery capacity to remain submerged long enough to weather the duration of the typhoon's passage. In the meantime, every effort must be made to secure all loose gear and supplies, and all hands not actually on watch were ordered to take to their bunks. Were we ever a sorry lot!

*Greenfish* continued a four hours on, eight hours off watch rotation, except that bridge watches were stood in the conning tower. The larger barrel, number two, periscope was up at all times, continually searching for surface contacts. It was manned on a fifteen-minutes on, thirty-minutes off rotation schedule by two officers—the officer of the deck and the junior officer of the deck—and the quartermaster of the watch. Also in the conning tower were two of the lookouts who shared helmsman duties. Also present was either the navigator or the exec as the command watch.

We were all desperately seasick as *Greenfish* pitched, rolled, and yawed in the unbelievably high waves generated by the typhoon. Those not actually on the periscope or helm were constantly barfing into the tops of the two periscope wells or on the conning tower deck around or on which they were sprawled. We soon learned what it was to go way beyond normal seasickness. As the old saying goes, "At first we were afraid we were going to die, and then we were afraid we weren't." If we ever ate or drank, I don't remember where, when, or what. I do have a vague memory of eating a sandwich while I lay on my side, but not much more. Just what we actually did to relieve the call of nature has also faded from my memory. A trip to the nearest head would have been pretty hazardous at any time in such rough seas.

Of constant concern was the danger of capsizing if the boat rolled past 50 degrees. The officer of the deck was always quick to order a low-pressure blow on the boats downside when a roll approached the extreme. As I recall, the decision was soon made to snorkel, since we were constantly cycling between the surface and our normal periscope depth of fifty-eight to sixty-two feet. The snorkel mast and head valve through which air for the engines and ships ventilation was obtained also gained us some additional height above a heavily spray-covered sea surface gone absolutely wild.

The typhoon eventually blew past us and into northern Japan where it finally dissipated. We resumed our transit to our Cold War mission station, but the typhoon had had its effect. *Greenfish* did not observe as high a level of Soviet naval activity as originally hoped for or expected. To his credit our commanding officer, Al Davis, did aggressively pursue and take maximum advantage of what activity there was. We completed the operation with an interesting collection of sonar tapes that included broadband and transient noises from a number of submarines of interest.[2] We then headed south for Yokosuka for one final upkeep before departing for Pearl Harbor, home, and Thanksgiving with our families and friends.

As an interesting side note, during our stay in Yokosuka while we were the outboard boat in a nest of five, and thus the most vulnerable, another typhoon of lesser strength approached. In addition to putting wire ropes over to better secure each boat to the wharf, the four inner boats all called back their officers and most of their crew, who with their captains rode out the storm. On *Greenfish*, where I had the bad luck to be the duty officer, Captain Davis merely confirmed that we were well secured to the wharf itself with wire ropes and then took the rest of the officers ashore to the officers club, where they rode out the storm in comfort. The captain's parting words to me were a jesting, "You got yourself into this, now get yourself out."

## Some Sunday Brunch

The boats at Yokosuka were generally moored in nests of four or five alongside a pier or wharf when in port, and traffic across the interconnecting gangplanks was always heavy during the early morning hours. The on-coming duty section had to be all on board by 7:00 in the morning, and liberty didn't start for the off-going section until about midday. Mornings, therefore, could be somewhat chaotic with at least a third of the crew stumbling and lurching about as they tried simultaneously to sober up and functionally carry out their watch standing, repair, and routine maintenance duties. The cooks were no exception.

As a rule, submarine cooks took special pains to please their fellow crewmembers with the best available from onboard and onshore food larders. Steaks, roasts, and lobsters were always in abundance, as were fresh vegetables, fruit, and fresh-baked breads and pastries of various sorts. Depending on the day, we all viewed lunch or brunch as the last best chance to get a good, solid meal under our belts before heading off for a liberty on shore where a lot more drinking than eating would be done.

*Greenfish*'s cooks and mess handlers (food servers) were a dependable lot, and our messes—both officers and crews—often received the Ney nomination from our superiors for Best Mess Afloat. We trusted them to ensure that we would always be fed well and that all loaded foodstuffs would be of the highest quality and safe to eat. Cleanliness of the galley and mess hall spaces was generally excellent, in spite of the occasional cockroach infestation, and great care was taken to maintain a high level of cleanliness. Suffice it to say that a deployed submarine could not afford to have even one of its crewmembers take sick for any reason. Any form of food poisoning, for instance, could have disastrous consequences for the entire crew. Thus sanitation and cleaning gear, disinfectants, and detergent were always in evidence. Detergent along with containers of cooking oil enjoyed a prominent position on the shelf just above the galley grill. A walk through the galleys of each submarine in the nest at Yokosuka would have revealed almost identical side-by-side stowage of detergent and cooking oil above the grills. Somewhat similar in shape, each container was clearly labeled, and to the best of anyone's memory there had never been a problem.

One peaceful Sunday morning in Yokosuka, as *Greenfish* was moored outboard and crew and officers were quietly enjoying a savory brunch of steak and eggs, we suddenly heard a tremendous commotion topside—shrill voices normally associated with an infuriated mob, yet we were moored within the confines of a large, well-secured base. What on earth was going on?, we asked ourselves as we gazed at each other in amazement. The topside watch excitedly called over *Greenfish*'s 1MC system, "Duty officer topside! Duty officer topside!" Expecting the worst, both the wardroom and crews mess rushed aft and up through the after-battery compartment hatch to the main deck.

Milling around on the gangway and topside was a clutch of shouting and obviously angry men from USS C—, alongside which we were moored. Cowering behind our topside watch, who had a firm hand on his sidearm holster, was a somewhat older sailor dressed in a soiled white uniform. He was unshaven and slovenly looking, and from his appearance it was easy to conclude that he had just returned from a night of heavy drinking.

Confronting our duty officer was an incoherent commanding officer from our sister submarine. On seeing him, the older sailor fell to the deck, wrapped his arms around the ankles of our duty officer, and began pleading for asylum, while his commanding officer and fellow crewmembers demanded he be returned on board ship. This particular skipper had a reputation for volatility and severity when sufficiently provoked. It was not hard to imagine what the man could expect in the way of rough justice if he were returned. Four *Greenfish* officers and several of our senior chief petty officers managed to ease themselves into position between the refugee and the mob and gradually calm things down.

Hearing all the commotion, groups gathered on the decks of the other two submarines in the nest. The commanding officer of one of them rushed over to *Greenfish* and with soothing words put his arm around his brother skipper and asked him what was going on. None of us had, as yet, even the slightest clue as to the reason for this quite menacing scene.

C—'s commanding officer, at this point only slightly more coherent, began pointing at the fugitive, repeating, "The cook, the cook!" The pursued individual tried to escape below decks but ran into the arms of one of our largest torpedomen who forcibly restrained him and brought him back up. No one was going to be allowed to go below decks on our submarine until we had determined what had triggered the ugly scene.

It seemed that C—'s officers and crew had just seated themselves to enjoy a sumptuous brunch as piles of sizzling steaks were being delivered to both their wardroom and crews mess. The captain forked one onto his plate, cut off a large juicy piece, and joyfully popped it into his mouth, as did the others. All of a sudden the wardroom and crews mess erupted into a chaos of swearing, spitting, gagging, and general retching. How could a favorite food that looked so delicious taste like a mixture of soap and bilge?

The first to reach the galley confirmed that their still-inebriated cook was happily cooking the morning's steaks with detergent. The acrid smell and smoke alone should have tipped him off as it began to spread through the boat, but he was too drunk to notice. Miraculously, at the approach of angry crewmembers braced to grab him, the cook found his feet, dropped every-thing, and ran for it. Bolting out the forward battery compartment hatch, he high-tailed it across the connecting gangway to our boat. "Permission to go below! Permission to go below!," he screamed frantically to our startled top-side watch as he dashed on board with his shipmates close on his heels.

In the meantime, someone on shore hearing all the commotion called the base duty officer. He arrived with members of the shore patrol to join the teeming throng topside. It was generally agreed that the shore patrol should take the errant cook into custody and depart as soon as possible, which they did. Since he really couldn't be charged with anything more serious than cooking a vile meal, he was ultimately deposited for safe keeping in a nearby transient barracks until it was decided what to do with him. Fortunately for all, the cook was allowed to disappear, never to be seen or heard from again.

Was there a submarine force–wide directive aimed at preventing such a thing from ever happening again? No. This was probably because the powers that be did not want to admit that it had ever occurred in the first place.

# CHAPTER 6

# Homeward to Pearl Harbor

A new navigator, a lieutenant, arrived during our final week in Yokosuka in late October 1958, and our old navigator, Lieutenant D, left us to join his wife in Hong Kong before going on to his new duty station. In the meantime our new navigator, Lt. Arthur M, a confirmed bachelor, made quite a name for himself on shore. He was termed a "butterfly boy" by the women because of his fickleness in choosing his evening companions. He was also termed by these same companions a "base sailor," because of his seeming lack of money when it came time to pay for the drinks. The women were always quick to discern who was a sailor or an officer, and who was fresh from sea with money to spend or a base sailor, stationed on shore in Yokosuka. Lieutenant M's reputation became the subject of much amusement during the following weeks at sea.

*Greenfish* departed Yokosuka for a lengthy transit home that would take us north of the Hawaiian Island chain. It was well into November and the weather was rough all the way. Since there was no need to remain undetected or to run submerged, other than for daily training and crew qualification operations, we remained on the surface a good deal of the time. The weather was so bad that our new navigator was almost continually seasick. Not an auspicious start for a prospective exec. As a consequence, the three of us junior officers who were working hard to complete our submarine qualification were each assigned a portion of the voyage home to complete our required navigation practical factors. It was a priceless opportunity, because we were each in effect navigator for three full days, under the nominal supervision of the exec and the chief quartermaster. Taking morning and evening star sights in heavy rolling seas from the northwest proved to be quite a challenge, but we each mastered it in turn and were able to fix the boat's position within at least five miles. *Greenfish* reached the approach to the Pearl Harbor Channel without incident.

Once back in Hawaii, *Greenfish* went into an extended upkeep of all areas and equipment of the boat, including complete repainting both inside and out. Our liberty period was to last until well into January 1959. The boat had been run hard, and both submarine and crew showed its effects. We all needed a good long rest.

When we finally returned to sea in January 1959, it was only to render ASW services, as target submarine, for U.S. Navy ASW surface forces and aircraft. The pace was not arduous. We always got under way on Monday mornings and returned to port in time for Thursday night bowling. A considerable portion of operating time was devoted during the remainder of winter and all of spring to submarine-versus-submarine operations, both to hone our skills for the next Cold War mission and to devote the requisite amount of time to help those of her officers and crew to complete their submarine qualification.

### The Cumshaw Artist

By February 1959 I had been *Greenfish*'s first lieutenant for over a year and her gunnery and torpedo officer for close to nine months. In early February I was directed to turn over these duties to Lieutenant (jg) S and to relieve him as *Greenfish*'s supply and commissary officer. The duty of supply and

R to L: Lt. Cdr. John A. Davis, commanding officer, USS *Greenfish* (SS 351); Lt. (jg) Alfred S. McLaren; supply and commissary officer CSC (SS) Valdo J. Alderson, and Supply and Commissary Department, 1958. *Courtesy of* Patrol

commissary officer was dreaded by all young submarine officers, not only because of the former role's complexity in ensuring that one's submarine had all required spare parts and stores on board, but also because the latter played a significant part in the overall morale of the crew. As an old submarine saying goes, "Food quality is 95 percent of a boat's morale."

*Greenfish* had a superb chief commissaryman, Valdo J. Alderson. He was a World War II submarine war patrol veteran with a reputation for feeding the crew extremely well on every boat he had served on board. He was also well known for his shrewdness as a trader and cumshaw artist for the overall benefit of his particular boat.[1] He was also well liked on and off the waterfront and had a great number of friends, including many submarine war patrol veterans and skippers, senior active duty submarine officers, and a few retired admirals.

Chief Alderson saw to it that on *Greenfish* we were plentifully supplied with tenderloin steaks, lobsters, smoked fish, and even frog legs, all the while remaining within our monthly ration allowance. How he accomplished this, I was never able to determine for sure. However, I did surmise that he had access to a large quantity of surplus butter, which he was able to trade, along with tins of coffee beans, for almost any food we wanted or thought we needed, particularly for ship's parties and picnics. If the submarine base commissary suppliers were offering a new type of "Horse Cock" (processed meat like salami, baloney, etc.) or filet mignon (ordinarily for the ComSubPac admiral's mess), he was able to get it. He even obtained and cooked a beautiful Smithfield ham for us one night at sea.

During the four months I had the pleasure of working with him, Chief Alderson led us to a Ney nomination for the Best Mess Afloat. In that time he also became a kind and loyal personal friend, and made a concerted effort to introduce me to former shipmates, both officer and enlisted, with whom he had served during World War II. He even made sure I had an opportunity to meet Vice Adm. Ralph W. Christie, who commanded submarine operations out of the Australian ports of Brisbane and Fremantle during that war. These former shipmates were a colorful bunch with a crusty sense of humor. To them, Valdo was known as No Ass—not because of his physique, but because of his singular lack of success with Australian women during World War II. We could listen to these war veterans for hours and learn from their endless sea stories, many of them about difficult war patrols.

The lessons I learned from Chief Alderson and his former shipmates were to stand me in good stead when I became a commanding officer more

USS *Greenfish* (SS 351) mess compartment during a meal, 1959.
*J. Kyser*

than ten years later. One of the most important was to treat everyone with respect, no matter how junior or senior, armed forces or civilian, in all dealings on board and on shore. Through them I learned, too, that a person's demeanor and personal conduct, both on shore and afloat, during stressful situations, was critical in retaining the full confidence and support of shipmates and colleagues.

### Chasing the Missing Chapter

Three officers on *Greenfish* were in the homestretch toward gaining their Gold Dolphins: Lieutenant J, Lieutenant (jg) S, and me. We were all three U.S. Naval Academy graduates—1954, 1956, and 1955, respectively—and by coincidence had all been in the same company at the Academy.

I was the first of the three of us to complete my Submarine Qualification Notebook, which covered each system—air, ventilation, water, hydraulic, electric, and so on—throughout *Greenfish*, with an attendant list of practical factors that had to be completed to a qualifying officer's satisfaction. The notebook also covered all submarine evolutions, operations, and emergency procedures, both surfaced and submerged, in port and under way.

I had only a few operational practical factors to complete before I was technically eligible to go up for final qualification in submarines. Most of these involved making successful torpedo attacks on a variety of targets, unescorted and escorted, by one or more ASW ships, and had to be signed off by the captain. Since Lieutenant J was a year senior to me and had been on board longer, I was made to wait until he had finished all aspects of his submarine qualification, including underway examination by another submarine captain on a different boat. This was quite disheartening, because I had been working hard to finish up within a year of first reporting on board. In the meantime, I submitted my completed Submarine Qualification Notebook in January 1959 to the new exec, Lt. Cdr. Robert H. Koehler, for his review and approval, which I received; I then forwarded the notebook to the captain for his final OK.

Captain Davis took the notebook in early February and placed it in one of his stateroom lockers. There it remained without comment until mid-May, becoming for me a growing source of frustration and, at times, anger and discouragement.

The days and weeks dragged by as I waited impatiently to go up for formal qualification in submarines. Much of this time was spent in port, which made the time grind even more slowly. In addition, Captain Davis was seldom around during these periods, so there weren't many opportunities for me to discuss with him how long I was to remain in what was becoming a general morale purgatory for me.

Suddenly in early March 1959 without prior warning, Lieutenant J, the officer whose completion of submarine qualification I had to wait for, completed his qualification notebook, went out almost immediately for his underway examination by another submarine skipper, passed that, received the squadron commander's blessing, and within the space of a week was presented his Gold Dolphins in front of *Greenfish's* entire crew at morning quarters. The captain, who had always seemed partial to this individual, then threw a qualification party at his home, and all officers not on watch and their spouses were required to attend. That evening, I finally began to feel that there might just be some light at the end of the tunnel.

A week or so later, this same officer received orders to report later in the month to Washington, DC, to be interviewed by Rear Adm. Hyman G. Rickover and his staff for the newly established six-month-long Advanced Nuclear Power School, at the submarine base in Groton, Connecticut. He apparently passed with flying colors and was slated to be detached in time to attend the school's second class convening the forthcoming July.

On *Greenfish* we had heard we were scheduled to deploy in the early summer on a special operation. So although Captain Davis was sorry to lose

Lieutenant J, he felt he could live with it, and life continued as before on normal, four-day local operations for ASW services, submarine-versus-submarine training, followed by generous amounts of time in port. Lieutenant J was subsequently granted time off and lengthy leave periods, and we didn't see much of him from April on.

Then something completely unexpected happened that was to infuriate *Greenfish*'s skipper. In mid-April I received dispatch orders from the U.S. Navy Bureau of Personnel to report to Washington, DC, within four days, to be interviewed by Rickover for admission to the Advanced Nuclear Power School. This was in spite of the fact that I had not yet completed formal qualification in submarines. Thinking perhaps that some skullduggery or string-pulling was involved, Captain Davis had a fit. He made efforts to get my orders cancelled, but they stood as issued. I, of course, was in a state of shock, because everyone else who had been called back from Pacific Fleet submarines had had several weeks to prepare, as best he could, for the interview. The only thing I could think to do was to read a recently published book entitled *The Atomic Submarine and Admiral Rickover*.[2] I also picked out a textbook on nuclear physics that seemed to be more clearly written than most, and when I wasn't reading the former, I was studying the latter.

I passed the interview and returned to a less-than-happy Captain Davis, who could not bring himself to extend his congratulations.[3] *Greenfish* would now be deploying without two of her most experienced officers. Captain Davis was, among other things, indignant because he had not yet recommended me for submarine qualification. This, of course, was in no way my fault, and I reminded both the exec and the captain that I had been ready for months. Adding more fuel to the flame was the fact that Captain Davis almost immediately began receiving pressure from superior officers to "Get McLaren qualified ASAP!" At that time, it was considered a great honor to be selected for nuclear submarines, and the ratio of officers selected to those not selected averaged about one in ten, which was probably based on the actual number of nuclear submarines that required manning at the time.[4]

I was to feel Captain Davis' wrath over the next several months. A number of important at-sea practical factors that only the captain could sign off on had to be completed before I could be sent for an in-port and underway examination by another submarine commanding officer and then proposed to our squadron commander for final submarine qualification. Even though I had completed all related practical factors, such as the required number of underways and landings as officer of the deck and torpedo approaches and attacks as approach officer, the captain had to recheck these as he felt necessary before giving his final OK.

During the necessary at-sea workups or practices, followed by those for Captain Davis' final approval, I learned to grit my teeth with each taunt of, "There goes nuclear power!" whenever I made the most minor of mistakes or took actions that he didn't agree with. If that wasn't enough to contend with, when the captain at last pulled my Submarine Qualification Notebook out of his stateroom locker to review it with me, we discovered that the entire electrical systems chapter that I had so laboriously created was missing.[5] The captain's initial reaction was, "Well, you are going to have to do that chapter all over." Needless to say, it was my turn to have near apoplexy, but I managed to keep my cool and temper. There was too much at stake now. I asked that the exec be immediately called in, to verify that he had seen, reviewed, and approved the notebook, including the missing chapter, before I had delivered it to the commanding officer. The exec did so.

Where had the missing chapter gone? I was sure Captain Davis knew, and I was sure that he knew whom I suspected. May it forever weigh on the conscience of the officer who, for whatever reason—possibly to complete his own Submarine Qualification Notebook—lifted that chapter.

I completed my final at-sea examination for submarine qualification in the tense weeks that followed. Under my captain's close observation, I managed to make several undetected approaches and attacks, with two practice torpedo hits, on an auxiliary vessel escorted by two echo-ranging ASW destroyers. I further demonstrated that I was able to evade and escape both ASW vessels following my attacks.[6] Captain Davis grudgingly gave his final approval and sent me on for the required in-port and underway oral and practical-factors examination by a gentleman of the first-order, Lt. Cdr. Haydn Owens, commanding officer of USS *Sterlet* (SS 392).

The examination proved to be long and difficult. I was required to complete all ballasting computations relating to the first dive of the day, to personally line up the ventilation and start the diesel engines, to get the boat under way as acting commanding officer, and to navigate *Sterlet* out of Pearl Harbor Channel to our assigned dive area. I had to execute a crash dive from the surface, act as the boat's diving officer on the first dive of the day, and successfully trim the boat to a neutral buoyancy condition. Once submerged, I turned over the dive to the regular watch officer and accompanied the captain throughout his boat while he questioned me about various ship's systems, such as hydraulic, air, water, and electrical. He frequently asked me to demonstrate my ability to operate all these, as appropriate, including responding to a flank speed order, which was called the bell, as the senior controller (an electrician's mate) in the maneuvering room. Boy, was that exciting, because of the complexity of shifting the electrical propulsion plant from parallel to series battery operation.

A near-perfect approach and attack with an exercise torpedo on an escorted yard oiler vessel, recovery of the torpedo, navigation of the Pearl Harbor Channel home, and, finally, a smooth twilight landing alongside the original pier from which we departed, finished the day. Captain Owens gave me a complete up-check on my performance, shook my hand, and wholeheartedly congratulated me, as did *Sterlet*'s officers. They took me to the nearby submarine officers club for a toast with a much-needed Mai Tai before sending me home. All in all, it was a wonderful and unforgettable experience. My wife Mary was vastly relieved to hear the good news on my return home, and we celebrated with yet more Mai Tais with neighbors and close friends.

Lt. (jg) Alfred S. McLaren receiving gold "Submarine Dolphins" from Lt. Cdr. John A. Davis, commanding officer, USS *Greenfish* (SS 351), 15 June 1959. *U.S. Navy*

I was considered formally qualified in submarines on 15 June 1959, when, in front of the entire crew, Captain Davis personally pinned my Gold Dolphins qualification badge on the left breast of my uniform shirt. There was no qualification party, however, and I was to serve on board *Greenfish* another week, at which time, on 22 June 1959, I was detached with orders to report, as a newly minted full lieutenant, to the Advanced Nuclear Power School at the U.S. naval submarine base in Groton in early July. My family and I boarded a plane two days later, flew to San Francisco, bought a new car, and drove across country to Groton.

I was to have no further contact with USS *Greenfish* or my former commanding officer for the rest of my submarine career, with the exception of receiving a letter several months later that *Greenfish* had received a Battle Efficiency "E" for the past year. The letter also acknowledged my contributions as both gunnery and torpedo officer and supply and commissary officer toward achieving this honor.

I realize in hindsight that I learned a great deal from my experiences and the two commanding officers with whom I served during the time I was on *Greenfish*. From Captain Knudsen I learned the importance of establishing a pleasant wardroom atmosphere both in port and at sea. He was friendly, available, and approachable at all times. I disagreed in one instance, however, with his method of shipboard discipline. From Captain Davis I definitely learned submarine tactics and how to handle a submarine aggressively during Cold War operations. These and many other lessons alluded to were of immeasurable benefit to me as I went on to other attack submarines and in due time became the submarine captain I wanted to be.

USS *Greenfish* was to deploy three more times while in the Pacific. The first, during the period 23 September 1959 to 11 January 1960, was to earn her a much-coveted Navy Unit Commendation for an extraordinarily successful Cold War mission under the command of my previous skipper, Al Davis. The remaining two deployments were to WestPac, where she operated with the U.S. Seventh Fleet and conducted both Cold War operations and Vietnam patrols. Following a shipyard overhaul in 1970, she was reassigned to the Submarine Force Atlantic, and then during the years that followed she made deployments to the Caribbean, the Mediterranean, and the North Atlantic for a northern European cruise.[7]

*Greenfish* was decommissioned and struck from the U.S. Naval Register on 29 October 1973. She was transferred (sold) to Brazil under the terms of the Security Assistance Program at the submarine base in Groton on

19 December 1973. She was subsequently commissioned the *Submarino Amazonas* (S-16), the eighth Brazilian Navy ship to be named for the Amazon River. She was struck from service on 15 October 1992, served for several years as a museum boat at the Centro Historico da Marinha in Rio de Janeiro, and then judged to be in too bad a condition to be fully restored. She was subsequently sold on 30 January 2004 to a scrapper at the Niteroi shipyard and immediately dismantled.[8]

# PART II

## USS *Seadragon* (SSN 584)
### Arctic Pioneer

Launch of USS *Seadragon* (SSN 584), August 1958. *U.S. Navy*

# CHAPTER 7

# My First Nuclear Submarine

In early June 1960 I received unexpected orders to report to USS *Seadragon* (SSN 584) at the Portsmouth Naval Shipyard, Kittery, Maine. I was about to complete six months of nuclear power plant prototype training and qualification as a chief operator on the land-based General Electric S-3-G Reactor Plant at West Milton, New York, which followed completion of my six months at Advanced Nuclear Power School in December 1959.[1] Prior to receiving orders to report to *Seadragon*, I had received orders to report to the *Snook* (SSN 592), a nuclear attack submarine then under construction at the Ingalls Shipbuilding Company, Pascagoula, Mississippi, and scheduled to be launched later in the year. But then one of *Seadragon*'s officers, Lt. Cdr. William G. Lalor Jr., the engineer, decided to leave the U.S. Navy. I suddenly had the good luck, although I didn't know it at the time, to be ordered on board as his numerical relief.

USS *Seadragon* was named after her illustrious World War II predecessor, the SS 194, and the eponymous seadragon, a beautiful small fish also called the dragonet, that lives in Australian waters. She was the U.S. Navy's sixth nuclear-powered submarine and the fourth and final member of the *Skate* submarine class. She had earlier been launched and commissioned at the Portsmouth Naval Shipyard, and was now in the final stages of being outfitted and loaded out for a forthcoming historic voyage to our new home port in Pearl Harbor via Baffin Bay, the Northwest Passage, and the North Pole. I would be reporting on board just in time to participate.

*Seadragon*'s sisters, *Skate* (SSN 578) and *Sargo* (SSN 583), had already made their mark as Arctic submarine pioneers.[2] *Skate*, commanded by Cdr. James F. Calvert, had been to the North Pole twice, in 1958 and 1959, and was the first submarine to surface through the sea ice at the Pole. She was also the first to operate in the Arctic Ocean during the winter. *Sargo*, commanded by Lt. Cdr. John H. Nicholson, whose highly significant accomplishments remain barely known to this day, was the first nuclear attack submarine to enter and exit the Arctic Basin through the very shallow, ice-covered Bering Strait and operate all through the Arctic Basin in the dead of winter in 1960. She was additionally the first submarine to surface routinely through thick ice, culminating in a successful surfacing through almost four feet of ice at the North Pole.

*Seadragon* was set to follow in their illustrious wake with a number of firsts of her own: the first submarine to change home ports via the Arctic Ocean, the first to examine the underside of icebergs in Baffin Bay, and the first to conduct a hydrographic survey of the Northwest Passage, from Baffin Bay via the Parry Channel and the Barrow and McClure Straits, to the Beaufort Sea.

The Cold War was at this time almost fifteen years old, and relations between the United States and the Soviet bloc had recently become even more tense as a result of the Soviets' having shot down an American U-2 spy plane, piloted by Gary Powers, in their airspace just two months previous.[3] Now, in late June 1960, this was yet one more U.S. nuclear submarine about to traverse the Arctic Ocean and achieve the North Pole fewer than six hundred nautical miles from the Soviet Union's northernmost island group, Franz Josef Land, and then skirt its territorial limits in the Chukchi and Bering Seas as she proceeded south through the Bering Strait. Would they try to intercept or hinder our transpolar voyage in any way?

*Seadragon's* keel was laid at the Portsmouth Naval Shipyard on 29 September 1956 and constructed in forty-five months—a total of 375,000 man-days—at a cost of more than $21 million. As many as a thousand men had worked on her in a single day.[4] Her overall characteristics were as follows:

- Displacement: 2,580 tons surfaced, 2,861 tons submerged
- Length overall: 267.4 feet
- Beam: 25 feet
- Draft: 22 feet 5 inches
- Propulsion system: One Westinghouse S-4-W nuclear reactor plant
- Propellers: Two five-bladed
- Speed on surface: Approximately 18 knots
- Speed submerged: Approximately 20+ knots
- Range: Unlimited

- Endurance submerged: Unlimited
- Armament: Eight 21-inch torpedo tubes, six forward and two aft
- Crew: 8 officers and 75 enlisted[5]

Cdr. George P. Steele was *Seadragon's* commanding officer during final construction, her commissioning on 5 December 1959, a shakedown cruise in the Caribbean, and for the upcoming voyage. Steele was a graduate of the U.S. Naval Academy and a seasoned veteran, having made two war patrols during World War II and then having served five years on the diesel boat USS *Becuna* (SS 319), from early 1945, during which he made two war patrols before World War II ended, to 1950. He also served as exec of a new fast attack submarine, USS *Harder* (SS 568), from 1953 through 1954, and commanded USS *Hardhead* (SS 365) for two years, from 1955 to 1957. *Seadragon's* crew could not have been under better or more experienced leadership for the arduous and potentially dangerous voyage ahead.

To say I was excited to be serving on *Seadragon* is an understatement. I was not only reporting to a brand-new, frontline nuclear boat that would be the fourth in history to explore the almost completely unknown Arctic Ocean and achieve the North Pole, but my family and I would be returning to Pearl Harbor and the idyllic environment and lifestyle we had grown to love.

By now I was a submarine-qualified officer with three Cold War operations under my belt. I could assume duties as an in-port duty officer almost immediately and requalify as an officer of the deck and diving officer of the watch in a relatively short time. I was not yet qualified as an engineering officer of the watch on *Seadragon's* Westinghouse S-4-W nuclear power plant, however. A second officer or senior chief petty officer, so qualified, would have to stand duty with me. Nevertheless, I expected to be pulling my own weight.

I reported for duty on board *Seadragon* one evening in late June 1960. It was a particularly quiet time for shipyard work. The duty officer was Lt. Joseph A. Farrell III, *Seadragon's* acting engineer officer and a fellow Naval Academy graduate, who gave me a warm welcome, as did the crewmembers I encountered. They were friendly, yet entirely professional, and clearly very proud of their submarine.

After a round of coffee, Joe took me through the boat, beginning with the forward torpedo room. As we proceeded slowly from compartment to compartment, I couldn't help but be impressed by the newness and cleanliness of everything I saw. The bilges were immaculate. Even the individual valve

stems, of several hundred hydraulic and lubricating oil and salt- and freshwater system valves, were clean and free of verdigris. I was also quite taken
by the amazing sight of a carpeted steel grand staircase that connected the
upper-level operations compartment with the living and messing quarters
level directly below. Amazing to me was the fact that, although *Seadragon*
was almost fifty feet shorter than my previous submarine, *Greenfish*, she
appeared to be much roomier. As we walked farther and farther aft, I became
increasingly aware that my new boat was vastly more complex than the one
I had just left. I had a few brief moments of despair when it dawned on me I
would have to work much harder than expected to requalify as a diving officer of the watch and officer of the deck on this very sophisticated boat.

Simultaneously elated and sobered, I joined Joe Farrell for another cup
of coffee in the wardroom, and we briefly discussed what was planned for
*Seadragon* during the remaining weeks before she departed for the Arctic
Ocean and her new home port in the Pacific. We would be going to sea for
a week or more to thoroughly shake the boat down and, in particular, to test
out the under-ice navigation and sonar systems that we would depend on
so heavily to get us through the ice-covered Northwest Passage and Arctic
Ocean safely. As I prepared to rejoin my wife and young son at the house in
Portsmouth we had rented for the month, Joe informed me I should be back
on board by 7:00 a.m. the next morning, and to remain overnight to begin
intensive training for qualification as an in-port duty officer—*forward*, as he
termed it, since I was not yet qualified as an engineering officer of the watch.
The next day I would be introduced to the captain; the exec, Lt. Cdr. James
T. "Jim" Strong; and the navigator and senior watch officer, Lt. Edward A.
"Al" Burkhalter Jr.

Worn out and beset with mixed emotions, I returned home shortly
before midnight. Mary and Fred Jr. had already retired for the night. With
two coffees under my belt and completely overwhelmed by the complexity
of my new boat, I can't say I slept very well.

I returned on board *Seadragon* well before 7:00 a.m. the following morning, arriving at the same time as the exec. Jim Strong greeted me warmly and
ushered me into the wardroom for breakfast. Already there were Joe Farrell
and two other officers: Lt. Thomas L. "Logan" Malone Jr., the operations and
diving officer; and Lt. Richard L. "Dick" Thompson, the communications
officer. Lt. (jg) Vincent J. Leahy, the supply and commissary officer; and
Al Burkhalter, the navigator and senior watch officer, soon joined us. They
were a lively bunch who obviously liked each other as they conversed and

endlessly kibitzed. Now and then a polite question would be directed my way. I quickly answered, and then the general conversation would resume. The main topic of interest seemed to be that a Commodore O. C. S. Robertson of the Canadian navy, who had transited the Northwest Passage some six years earlier as commanding officer of the Canadian icebreaker *Labrador*, would join *Seadragon* on the voyage. Rumor had it he was at least six feet six inches tall, which would be almost too tall for a small submarine and its even smaller bunks and general living space. (I was six feet four.)

I further learned we would be joined by several more special riders: Waldo K. Lyon, director of San Diego's Arctic Submarine Laboratory and a veteran of *Nautilus'*, *Skate's*, and *Sargo's* historic voyages to the North Pole. He would be the expedition's chief scientist, joined by Arthur H. "Art" Roshon, also from the Arctic Submarine Laboratory. Art was the designer of both the iceberg detector and the polynya delineator that *Seadragon* would use under the ice. Other riders included Walter I. "Walt" Wittmann and Arthur E. "Art" Molloy of the U.S. Navy Hydrographic Office, Washington, DC; Jonathan L. Schere of EDO Corporation, who would operate the upward-beamed fathometer used for measuring ice draft overhead; and Donald C. Alexander and Charles S. Stadtlander of Sperry Corporation, manufacturer of the ships inertial navigation system, which would be used in the Arctic for the first time. A final rider would be Lt. Glenn M. Brewer, an experienced U.S. Navy scuba diver and underwater photographer from the U.S. Navy Photographic Center, Washington, DC.

As breakfast was concluding, we suddenly heard "*Seadragon, Seadragon* arriving!" over the 1MC system. We all stood up, and in walked George Steele, our commanding officer. He was a tall, dignified, impressive-looking man. It was obvious that his officers very much liked and respected him.

I was introduced to the captain, and after a round of coffee he looked in my direction and asked if I would be free to join him in his stateroom for a few minutes. I replied, "Yes, sir!" and followed him when he got up from the table.

In his stateroom the captain sat on his bunk, motioning me in to take the one chair available. There he formally welcomed me on board, asked about my family and our trip to Portsmouth, and inquired as to whether we were adequately housed in the local area. I thanked him and told him we were all settled in, all was well, and that I had reported on board the previous night, ready in all respects to go to work. He stated that if there was anything my family and I needed, now or during the few short weeks remaining before we departed for the Arctic and the Pacific, I was to let him or the exec know immediately. He told me to meet with the exec later in the morning to ensure that all necessary arrangements were made for my family, household goods, and automobile to reach Pearl Harbor just before we on *Seadragon* were scheduled to arrive.

Commander Steele in a few short words conveyed that he was very happy to have "another much-needed professional," on board in time for the Arctic expedition. He did so in a way that truly made me feel professional. He further stated that, although he was certain from my background, training, and experience that I could immediately stand watch as both an officer of the deck, surfaced or submerged, or as an engineering officer of the watch back aft on the nuclear power plant, he wanted me to feel free to take whatever time I needed to fully acquaint myself and feel comfortable with my knowledge of *Seadragon's* characteristics, equipment, systems, and operating procedures before I did so.

I left the captain's stateroom completely free of the previous night's anxieties about my new boat's complexity and highly motivated to really dig in and confirm to my new commanding officer that I was in every way the professional he thought I was. How to sum up what had just occurred? The captain treated me with genuine respect as a fellow professional, even though I was still a relatively inexperienced junior submarine officer. I appreciated and responded to this and felt certain there was no way I was going to disappoint him. It was an important life lesson then and for the remainder of my life: treat those who work for you, and with whom you work, with respect from the beginning, and they will always do their utmost never to let you down.

I was only in my late twenties. During the arduous academic portion of Advanced Nuclear Power School, I discovered, out of absolute necessity, that I could, if needed, function well for months on end with no more than four to five hours of sleep per night. In the weeks to follow, I really poured on the coal to learn my new boat. It took me less than a week to qualify as an in-port duty officer, and I was subsequently able to qualify as a diving officer of the watch during *Seadragon's* final at-sea shakedown prior to departing for the Arctic on 1 August 1960.

It was during our at-sea week prior to our departure that I heard about *Seadragon's* collision with a whale or possibly a whale shark during sea trials in the fall of 1959, when she was proceeding on the surface on a very dark night. This unfortunate occurrence damaged *Seadragon's* port propeller and shaft and her bow sonar dome and made superficial dents in her superstructure, where blubber was found. The whale or shark was never seen, so no one learned what species it was or if it had survived. *Seadragon*, as a result, had to return to Portsmouth Naval Shipyard to be dry-docked and repaired. Rear Admiral Rickover, who was on board at the time, was heard to remark later, "*Seadragon* was a whale of a ship."

It turned out, to my surprise, that *Seadragon*, in addition to being built to track down and kill other submarines, was fully equipped to steer or guide a Regulus cruise missile to its target, following its launch by another submarine, and I was to be the missile guidance officer. That was interesting, but then I was less than delighted to learn that, as the newest officer, I would be expected to relieve Vince Leahy as supply and commissary officer during the course of our voyage across the Arctic Ocean. As I had previously held this onerous position (onerous to a line officer) on *Greenfish*, I felt confident I could assume these duties once again. A more agreeable assignment was as an assistant photographic officer to Lt. Glenn Brewer.

## The Transpolar Voyage

During final preparations for sea and just days before our departure, I heard by chance that we would need our dress-blue uniform for a short liberty stop in Nome, Alaska, following our exit from the Arctic Ocean. As bad luck would have it, I had already sent all such uniforms off with our household goods to Pearl Harbor, keeping only my khaki uniforms and one dress-white uniform for the summer ahead. If I didn't have my blues, I would have no liberty on shore in Nome, and I wasn't going to let that happen. A frantic search among fellow submariners who might be my size in the Portsmouth area turned up a good friend, Lt. John S. Lyman (later lieutenant commander), who had completed Nuclear Power School with me and who had just reported to USS *Thresher* (SSN 593). *Thresher* was in the shipyard for a lengthy overhaul. Not expecting to need his blues until the fall, John graciously lent me his best dress-blue uniform, white shirt, and black tie, and a pair of black shoes that fit just right.[6]

During our final days in Portsmouth we were joined for lunch by the world-famous Arctic explorer and former president of the famed Explorers Club, Vilhjalmur Stefansson, PhD, and his wife Evelyn.[7] Stefansson at that time had established the Stefansson Collection on Polar Exploration at Dartmouth College and was teaching a series of courses on the Arctic regions. He was best known for his discovery of several new islands in the Canadian Arctic Archipelago, and for his unsuccessful attempt to establish a colony on

Wrangel Island, located on the Siberian continental shelf between the East Siberian and Chukchi Seas, and to take possession of it for the United States.

It was fascinating to listen to Stefansson as he regaled us with stories of his explorations in the Canadian High Arctic. I remember in particular the faraway look in his eyes as he vividly described the environment, the colors, and the obvious love he had for the Far North. Stefansson was kind enough to loan us two extremely valuable volumes from the Stefansson Collection — the expedition journals of British explorers Sir William Edward Parry and Robert John Le Mesurier McClure.[8] He thought they might prove of value as we conducted a submerged hydrographic survey of the Northwest Passage for the first time in history. The journals were, in fact, to prove invaluable. We were later to study and read aloud from them as we navigated through the Barrow Strait, Viscount Melville Sound, and the McClure Strait.

The loading of final stores and spare parts was soon completed, and on 1 August 1960 we departed for Baffin Bay and the Northwest Passage. Many a tear was shed on this beautiful day, and as we waved goodbye to family, friends, and Portsmouth Naval Shipyard personnel, *Seadragon* backed away from the dock. We cleared the channel and headed out into the North Atlantic, submerged, and were on our way to what would prove to be a historic transpolar expedition.

The days flew by as we proceeded north up the coast of North America. We practiced emergency drills on a watch-to-watch basis and carried out a

USS *Seadragon* (SSN 584) under way, 1960. *U.S. Navy*

host of special operational procedures, such as safely surfacing into and diving from open-water leads and polynyas in preparation for operating beneath the Arctic ice pack. *Seadragon* would be under thick sea ice for what might well be several months. She would, therefore, not be able to come readily to the surface in the event of a major emergency such as flooding or fire.

I stood watch as diving officer of the watch on a regular four hours on, eight hours off basis, spending every free moment in the control room in order to qualify as officer of the deck (conning officer submerged) as rapidly as possible. There were more opportunities for me to spend in the control room than I would ever have imagined, because I rarely had a bunk to retreat to, much less to call my own, and thus had more time to qualify. *Seadragon*, like almost all U.S. submarines at that time, had more crewmen than bunks. As many as two rows of six pan bunks were placed side-by-side across the torpedo reloads forward. The most junior enlisted men on board were usually assigned these bunks, with two men sharing in hot-bunking.

To the crew's everlasting gratitude, Captain Steele decreed that no crew-member would have to give up his regularly assigned bunk to the extra officers and civilian riders, and the officers would do the hot bunking. As one would expect, none of *Seadragon*'s more senior officers was going to give up his bunk to anyone else. So, as it turned out, I found myself one of three officers assigned to a single bed in officers' quarters. The other two, Ens. William T. "Bill" Bloodworth and Dr. Lewis H. "Lew" Seaton (also lieutenant commander, and later surgeon general of the U.S. Navy), *Seadragon*'s medical doctor, having served much longer on board than I, quickly rigged it so that when one of them got out, the other was always ready to jump right in, no matter the hour. Hence, I was more frequently than not left with no place to sleep. As the days passed I got smarter and improvised, starting with sleeping upright in a quiet control room corner and then lining up three armless wardroom chairs and lying across them. I later began finding innumerable devious ways of interfering with the Bloodworth-Seaton turnover, such as getting them called to the control room so I could beat one or the other to our smelly but vacant bunk.

## Weirdburgers for Dinner

The successful final load-out of crew, spare parts, weapons, food, movies, and special mission-related equipment on any submarine is truly an art. Since serving good food on a day-to-day basis is essential for the maintenance of good morale, everyone pays close attention to what is loaded on board: meat, milk and eggs, fresh vegetables and fruit, ice cream, and dry goods such as canned vegetables and fruits, spices and sauces, and coffee, to name just a few. The general feeling is that we can handle or endure any task and operation if we know we will be sitting down to a good meal afterward.

Crews mess, USS *Seadragon* (SSN 584), Arctic Ocean, 1960. *D. Cornell*

Not known to the crew of *Seadragon*, however, the powers that be in Washington had asked that a new type of food be tested on the crew for palatability during the coming transpolar voyage. Specifically, we were encouraged to carry as much ration-dense food as possible—that is, frozen or otherwise dried products that could be reconstituted with water when needed. Powdered milk and eggs, while never popular, had been carried for years by Navy ships and submarines. Suitably packaged for storage and loaded on our particular voyage was a huge amount of dried apples, peaches, pears, apricots, onions, potatoes, carrots, beans, peas, and even cabbage. Unexpectedly, one normally popular food item, hamburger, was also loaded in large quantity in a completely unfamiliar state—canned. The crew's shock and dismay on discovering this shortly after going to sea was soon to manifest itself.

Few of *Seadragon's* officers and crew had any inkling of the substitution made prior to departure for sea, much less the reason for it. Only the captain, exec, and the supply and commissary officer (not me at that time) and a few of his people knew. On the plus side, most crewmembers noted with satisfaction the enormous quantity of steak being loaded into the freeze box. Steak was far and away the most popular food item with any submarine crew, with good hamburger, real bacon, and fresh eggs close behind.

We had been transiting north for almost four days and were now approaching the Davis Strait between Greenland and Newfoundland. A shipboard routine of watch duties, routine maintenance, and under-ice practice operations and emergency drills had been pretty well established by now. We were enjoying a never-ending parade of superb meals as *Seadragon's* cooks seemed to be outdoing themselves, whether for breakfast, lunch, dinner, or midnight rations (mid rats). All eagerly looked forward to the next meal. On one particular evening, hamburgers with all the trimmings were on the menu. "Oh, boy," was the general reaction as we impatiently waited for dinner.

The hamburgers on our plates resembled nothing anyone had ever seen before. Each looked as if a cookie cutter had precisely shaped it, rather than the classic, hand-shaped patty familiar to us. In addition, the burgers were an unappetizing bile color with a strange, rubbery consistency. Worse, they didn't taste like hamburger. Some wits among both officers and crew wondered aloud if the cooks had mistakenly loaded and cooked dog food. Old hands drew loose comparisons with dubious meats they had eaten during World War II. One thing for sure: there was almost unanimous consensus that it was repulsive. Almost all of it served that evening ended up in the garbage amid grumbles and complaints.

Submarine cooks are a sensitive, prideful lot, and ours, led by Commissaryman 1st Class Orizio Parisi, were no exception. They were extremely upset at the negative reception to their hamburgers, which included a wide variety of gagging noises and catcalls. During the course of dinner they were subjected to pointed questions as to whether any of them had actually tasted the "crap" being served that night. An impromptu competition on what to name the stuff got under way. Terms such as Buffalo Barf, Whale Shit, and Grilled Lungers were among the many ventured before the exec made a sudden appearance, joining the crew for dinner, and calming things down. *Seadragon's* head cook pleaded with Vince Leahy, the chief of the boat, Torpedoman CPO Philip Le Clair, the exec, and me to allow him to discontinue the canned hamburger portion of the ration-dense food experiment. No dice. The basic purpose of the project was explained to the officers and crew: to wit, that one day nuclear submarines such as *Seadragon* might be required to remain at sea for many months at a time. Since the freeze box and the chill box (converted to a freeze box) could not hold much more than sixty-days' worth of meat at a time, canned meat might of necessity become an important component of a maximum-capacity food stores load-out. Exec Jim Strong directed the cooks, Leahy, and me, as our part of this important experiment, to come up with not just one, but a number of "mouth-watering ways" in which our store of canned hamburger could be served.

I didn't know a thing about food except how to eat it, but as the newest officer and as prospective supply and commissary officer I was pressed into service so that the new ideas I might contribute could be worked into solving the problem. My heart sank as I realized I was about to become the most unpopular man on board.

In the days that followed, the cooks, Vince Leahy, and I pored over every available cookbook to come up with a variety of recipes for what might just as well have been canned possum as far as any of the crew knew. Hamburgers with tomato sauce, hamburgers with mustard and horseradish sauce, curried hamburgers, hamburgers scrambled with eggs, and hamburgers as a stew base were all eventually to appear on the menu. Each was greeted with the usual groans, gagging sounds, and other graphic outbursts.

One change in the crew's general eating behavior had already been noted: whenever hamburger was on the menu, attendance at that meal dropped significantly, and the demand for midnight rations increased dramatically, as did the amount of in-between meal snacking by the crew. The commissary department resorted to subterfuge and no longer identified hamburger as such. Instead, tempting meal descriptions such as Savory Brunswick Stew, Texas Chili Ragout, and Arkansas Chili (whoever heard of that?) became standard menu entries. I contributed my own share of novel names for the main course of the day, such as Arctic Ocean Scramble.

No matter how it was disguised, though, the basic taste, smell, and consistency of canned hamburger were robust, for lack of a better term. At first bite the crew could always tell what was once again being foisted off on them. "Oh yuck, weirdburgers again," protested one of the crew. The name stuck.

Near the end of our transpolar voyage, permission was finally granted to discontinue serving weirdburgers, leaving us with several hundred pounds of canned hamburgers to create space-filling ballast throughout the boat. Our supply and commissary officer managed to trade a few cases of this "exotic, under-ice submarine food" with the Coast Guard for more palatable items during our brief stop in Nome. Even more cases were off-loaded and traded in a similar fashion to the unwary and gullible shortly after our arrival at home port in Pearl Harbor. I have often thought of the fun we could have had if eBay had existed back in those days.

The ration-dense food experiment was never repeated to the best of my knowledge, although I did hear years later that the U.S. government had several million pounds of canned hamburger stored away for military emergencies.

# CHAPTER 8

# Into Davis Strait and Baffin Bay

As we approached Davis Strait, our imaginations, thoughts, discussions, and even our dreams turned more and more to those who had preceded us, the Proto-Eskimos who first sighted these waters over five thousand years ago and the Dorset and Thule Inuit who followed, and first navigated, these waters en route to the western Greenland coast. We thought also of the early Vikings: Erik the Red, in the course of his historic exploration of the Greenlandic coast from 982 to 985 AD, may have been the first to reach Disko Island, the largest island in Baffin Bay. Soon following him were an untold number of Viking explorers and hunters, who during the next three centuries pushed farther and farther north along the western coast of Greenland. We now know they reached Melville Bay in the northeastern corner of Baffin Bay, Ellesmere, Skraeling, and Rune Islands to the north, and Devon and Baffin Islands to the northwest.[1]

More relevant were our studies and discussions about the British Northwest Passage expeditions commanded by John Davis who, in 1585 and 1587, charted Davis Strait. He was followed by Robert Bylot, with William Baffin as pilot, who in 1616 charted all the coasts of Baffin Bay and discovered the three major outlets from Baffin Bay: Smith, Jones, and Lancaster Sounds. Renowned British explorers William Edward Parry, commander of HMS *Hecla*, during a British Northwest Passage expedition from May 1819 through November 1820, and Sir John Franklin and Francis Crozier, commanders of HMS *Erebus* and HMS *Terror*, respectively, during the period 1845 to 1848, determined Lancaster Sound to be the main entrance to the Northwest Passage.[2] Once we had finished our work in Baffin Bay we would begin our survey of the Northwest Passage at the mouth of Lancaster Sound and follow the routes of those who had gone before.

## Icebergs Galore!

As we proceeded through the Davis Strait between Baffin Island and Greenland shortly after midnight on 10 August, excitement gripped the crew on sighting the first ice on *Seadragon's* upward-beamed fathometer, and mounted with each passing minute as more and more ice and what appeared to be icebergs were detected northward toward Baffin Bay.

At approximately 4:20 a.m. Captain Steele decided to bring us to periscope depth and then to the surface. There we found ourselves in the vicinity of a cottage-size piece of glacial ice, termed a bergy bit, that sonar had held for the better part of an hour. Beyond lay the southern edge of the Baffin Bay ice pack, glistening in the sun, as it stretched across the horizon from east to west just a mile ahead of us. Also in view some fifteen miles to the north and across the Arctic Circle was our first huge iceberg.

Every member of the crew was given an opportunity to come up on deck and briefly view the vast and mysterious white world that we had entered and under whose depths we would be operating for the next month. Their serious expressions and atypical quietness attested to its sobering effect.

Once all had taken a good look and were safely below, the deck hatches were shut, and the officer of the deck and two lookouts cleared the bridge, slamming the two sail trunk hatches shut as they quickly dropped down into the control room. The diving officer, Lt. Logan Malone, took charge of the dive, and *Seadragon* submerged and set course toward the nearby bergy bit in order to calibrate both the iceberg detector and the upward-beamed fathometer. After several passes beneath from a depth of six hundred feet, we determined that the berg extended eighty-two feet beneath the surface and was two hundred feet wide. We also found that the AN/SQS-4 sonar could detect and display bergy bits as a back-up to the iceberg detector.[3]

*Seadragon* returned to the surface to close and visually inspect the much larger iceberg to the north, projecting some seventy-four feet above the surface, with its longest axis about 313 feet. We then descended to become the first submarine in any navy to pass directly beneath a full-sized iceberg.

At a depth of six hundred feet we made a series of sonar runs at various speeds in the near vicinity of the iceberg. Even at a flank speed of 20.5 knots, both the iceberg detector and the SQS-4 tactical sonar were able to make initial contact at three thousand yards, which appeared to confirm that *Seadragon* would have more than ample time to avoid any icebergs we might suddenly encounter. We now felt ready to undertake the more difficult and history-making task of navigating directly beneath a typical large, deep-draft iceberg.

*Seadragon* eased down to a depth of 650 feet and headed directly toward the iceberg at a moderate speed of less than ten knots. As we made several passes beneath, the upward-beamed fathometer registered a draft of 108 feet—not as deep as we expected. It also revealed the longest underwater axis of the iceberg to be 822 feet. Our hydrographer and sea ice expert Walt Wittmann calculated that this baby had a staggering total mass of 600,000 tons. The day's work bolstered our confidence in the under-ice sonar equipment and in our ability to maneuver in and around icebergs inside or outside the Baffin Bay ice pack.[4] We were now ready for even bigger game.

Course was taken at sixteen knots toward the northwest and the Baffin Bay middle pack, later perfectly described by Capt. Gerald E. Synhorst as "a huge raft of pack ice that remains even in the summer. Icebergs travel in a counterclockwise fashion around this middle pack. Baffin Bay's middle pack is distinctly different from the ice pack of the Arctic Basin. Frozen into it are large icebergs that sometimes penetrate more than a thousand feet into its depths."[5]

We had reached the middle pack and been transiting under it for several hours when, early on 11 August, Captain Steele decided it was time to come to the surface and send a position report to the ComSubLant in Norfolk, Virginia. Our under-ice suite was working perfectly, with the upward-beamed fathometer showing a continuously varied and jagged under-ice topography directly above us. The underwater TV camera mounted on *Seadragon's* bow recorded a never-ending stream of sea ice passing like clouds overhead.

Shortly thereafter we reached a large area of open water. *Seadragon's* conning officer executed a Williamson Turn and returned to the center of the open-water area.[6] The special under-ice diving and surfacing team then conducted *Seadragon's* first real surfacing, using the standard procedures we had developed for making vertical ascents in ice-covered waters. We emerged within a very large polynya that contained a vast gleaming field of broken, rotting ice floes and pressure ridges. A few small icebergs were in evidence, although nothing of the scale that we wanted to examine.[7]

### Rogovin's Missing Salami

Toward the end of our last Portsmouth upkeep, Torpedoman 2nd Class Ira Rogovin was put in charge of *Seadragon's* after-torpedo room. This compartment contained two 21-inch torpedo tubes, four Mk-37 acoustic torpedoes, and an emergency signal ejector. The compartment provided bunking for as many as eight of the crew, including at least one or two other torpedomen.

Rogovin was a self-described gourmet of the smelliest sausages, the more potent the garlic-loaded salamis the better. His mother sent them to him, and he generally had two or three of the sausages hanging from the compartment overhead. The after-torpedo room was both Rogovin's regular watch station and his berthing area. He had pretty much made himself at home in this compartment following *Seadragon's* commissioning. From time to time during the course of each day Rogovin would slice off pieces of one sausage or the other as he felt the need for a snack, and heaven help the lower-rated crewmembers occupying this compartment who complained of the smells. Even the off-going conning officers who inspected this compartment, along with all others following the completion of their watches, found its general odor, combined with human sweat, hard to stomach.

One day as we approached Baffin Bay the unthinkable occurred. Rogovin had been out of his compartment—some called it his cave—for a few hours during a series of training lectures in the crews mess. On his return to the after-torpedo room, he discovered that one of his most precious salamis was missing and all hell broke loose. Everyone who happened to be in the after-torpedo room, even those asleep in their bunks, were put to work searching for the errant sausage. This one, we were told, was a mottled dark brown on the order of a foot and a half long. Rogovin was beside himself.

The search party looked everywhere, and scoured the bilges almost inch by inch because the stomach-turning bilges were a receptacle for everything dropped accidentally or intentionally.[8] No luck. Rogovin's search gradually moved forward from compartment to compartment as *Seadragon* proceeded across the Arctic Ocean. He suspected all who shared the after-torpedo room with him, plus anyone who had ever emitted a rude remark or two about the smell or appearance of the sausages.

Rogovin continued his search through the entire transit of the Arctic Basin, the voyage south from the Bering Strait to Pearl Harbor, and during our first repair upkeep in Pearl Harbor. Then, one morning halfway through our third week in port, Rogovin happened to open the after signal ejector, and out slid a long, green, mold-covered, dripping, reeking cylindrical shape: his long-missing sausage.

Rather than rejoice and share his good fortune with the rest of the crew, Rogovin swore the two witnesses to his find to absolute secrecy. He further kept it from the commanding officer and exec and the chief of the boat, to whom he had complained about the theft of his sausage. Why was this? Because Rogovin was supposed to inspect, clean, and test for proper operation at least once a week *Seadragon's* two signal ejectors and torpedo tubes that penetrated the hull and through which emergency flares and torpedo evasion devices might be fired should there be dire operational need, and he wasn't doing it.

It is useless to try to keep a secret on board any submarine, and Rogovin's discovery came to the attention of the chief of the boat and the exec. They in turn informed the commanding officer. Although I knew that Captain Steele was secretly amused, a Captain's Mast was scheduled. At the Mast he gave Rogovin a stern chewing out for his neglect of the after signal ejector and dismissed him with the warning that it must never happen again.

Rogovin took the long-lost sausage to the nearest water spigot on the pier and spent well over an hour cleaning it up with soap and brush. After rinsing it off, he restored it to its usual place, swinging from the overhead of the after-torpedo room. I never observed him cutting off and eating a piece from this particular sausage, but those who had the misfortune to do so reported that the smell was overpowering.

Who put the sausage in the signal gun? We never found out, but our guess was that it was a fellow torpedoman.

### Baffin Bay's Iceberg Alley

We were now well within Baffin Bay. Navigator Al Burkhalter and Leading Quartermaster 1st Class Frances Wines fixed our position navigationally and sent off the required position report. The ice pack was in constant motion, requiring the officer of the deck to continually maneuver *Seadragon* to keep our twin bronze screws well clear of an endless procession of wicked-looking floes. The screws were vulnerable since they extended several feet beyond the widest part of the boat's hull.

Scientific personnel came topside to take water samples, measure wind velocity, and collect environmental data. I went up to the bridge, as deputy plankton-catching officer, to empty the plankton sampler. The latter was a truly Rube Goldberg device that caught these miniscule sea organisms in twenty-four fine net bags. Either Dick Thompson, the project officer; Sonarman 1st Class George Harlow; or I did this every time we came to the surface. We unloaded each bag into a special container and replaced it with a fresh bag. We then carried the bags below decks and loaded them into a special box located within *Seadragon's* freeze box, the same freeze box that stored our meat. (It didn't take long for some wag to suggest maybe it was plankton making the canned hamburger taste so foul.) Crewmen constantly asked me how many I had caught, were they zoo- or phytoplankton (I had no idea), and could they see one of each? Very funny, when all we could see was goop in the bottom of each bag.

Captain Steele decided it was time to move on, because a very large iceberg was what we were looking for. The decks were ordered clear, and the boat was submerged using a stationary dive or descent procedure that we had developed for operations within ice-covered waters. At a depth of 150 feet, propulsion was shifted to the main engines.

The radar operator, Electronic Technician 2nd Class Anthony Balestrieri, reported what might be a large iceberg some fifteen miles to the north. A course toward the radar contact was taken as *Seadragon* continued on to a keel depth of three hundred feet, increasing speed to sixteen knots. The radar contact, however, turned out to be just a bergy bit, drawing no more than fifty-seven feet.

Shortly before lunch, leading sonarman George Harlow reported a loud echo on the AN/BQS-4 sonar, indicating the presence of a massive iceberg approximately four thousand yards dead ahead of us.[9] The iceberg detector, manned by Sonarman 3rd Class Owen Carlson, revealed it to be one of extremely deep draft, possibly reaching as much as 400 to 440 feet beneath the sea.[10]

We closed to a thousand yards. In the course of maneuvering around and acoustically examining it, we found the berg to be indeed massive. It appeared surrounded by pack ice, with no surfaceable polynya in the immediate vicinity. Having determined that we could safely pass beneath it, we moved several miles away, came to all stop, and hovered at three hundred feet as we took time out for lunch.[11]

It was during this first hovering beneath the icepack that many of us discovered the wonders of underwater TV. The monitor in the control room revealed all sorts of fish in our immediate vicinity. We thought we were seeing some cod. Larger dark-gray shapes appeared to be sharks or even small whales. Several of us were sure we had seen a killer whale. Exciting! Subsequently, most of us spent as much time as possible at the monitor looking to see what else might turn up.

Following lunch, Captain Steele took the conn, ordered seven hundred feet, an increase in speed to seven knots, and a course that would take us directly beneath what turned out to be a truly monstrous iceberg. The suspense in the control room intensified as we closed and its great size became apparent. All active sonar contact was suddenly lost several hundred yards short. Then, as we passed under, loud gasps went up as the trace on the upward-beamed fathometer showed a gigantic mass of ice plunging rapidly and sharply toward us and continuing on for another hundred feet, much deeper than predicted. I fully expected the captain to order "Emergency deep!" Suddenly the behemoth's deepest penetration leveled off. It then shallowed as we traversed beneath an ice keel almost nine hundred feet wide.

Captain Steele brought *Seadragon* around on a different heading to make a second pass beneath this monster. All eyes were fastened on the upward-beamed fathometer as we once again closed the iceberg, lost sonar contact, and observed an unbelievably huge amount of ice plunging toward us again. Would an even deeper spur a few feet away have come closer? Not satisfied, Captain Steele brought us around for one final pass beneath. As we again watched in utter suspense, we closed from an entirely different direction. I am sure I was not the only one who prayed that the third time would not be our downfall. The keel depth of the iceberg proved to be about the same. This time, however, we traveled for some 1,470 feet along its axis before we emerged from beneath her. Walt Wittmann later calculated the iceberg to have a mass of some 3 million tons.[12]

Buoyed by our success, Captain Steele resolved, in his own words, to "demonstrate beyond question the ability of a nuclear submarine to enter an area of high iceberg concentration with safety" before we left Baffin Bay.[13] To do this, *Seadragon* had to reposition to an area of much higher iceberg concentration. After a discussion with onboard experts, Waldo Lyon, Walt Wittmann, Art Molloy, and Commodore Robertson, the captain added two days to the expedition and headed us to the northeast for Greenland's famous Kap York in northern Melville Bay.[14]

The Kap or Cape is roughly 150 miles due south of Thule, Greenland. It is in this section of northern Melville Bay that the West Greenland Current carries most of the icebergs that have been calved from the western Greenland glaciers north. They subsequently slowly sweep to the west, just south of Smith Sound, where they are picked up by the south-flowing Baffin Island current and, south of Hudson Strait, the Labrador current. They eventually reach the northern Grand Banks. Here the current divides, with some bergs carried to the east, to the north of Flemish Gap, and out into the Atlantic. There they are picked up by the northeasterly flowing Gulf Stream. The remainder of the bergs are carried southward past Newfoundland, to the area between the Flemish Gap and the Grand Banks, to the area is known as Iceberg Alley.

Early on 13 August *Seadragon* entered open water that contained a large number of icebergs. We surfaced in heavy fog some forty nautical miles off Kap York. By midmorning the fog began to lift and revealed, from the report of our lookouts, more than forty very large icebergs.[15] We spent the next several hours moving slowly among and photographing them, as we decided which might be the most suitable for conducting underwater examinations.

*Seadragon*'s scuba divers, headed by photographer Lt. Glenn Brewer, prepared to enter the subcooled water for some conditioning dives and equipment checkout. A thousand yards away was an interesting iceberg 135 feet high and some 560 feet long at the surface, with a huge hole in the middle. On close examination, we could see a profile on its port side that was the exact image of former president and famous explorer Teddy Roosevelt. Since the seas were quite calm, and there was only open water between us and the iceberg, permission was granted for Brewer, diver Robert Harmon, the exec Jim Strong, and the ship's doctor Dr. Lew Seaton, as extra photographers, to take a life raft and paddle over to the iceberg. There they would take pictures, sketch its spurs, and bring back samples. For fun a diver would climb up into the huge hole in the middle and be photographed as he sat or stood within the hole. These were certain to be spectacular, first-ever photos.

It was not to be. When the party was halfway there, a loud cracking noise was followed by a huge mass of ice crashing into the water. This generated a sizable wave, which sped toward and completely swamped the life raft. All

USS *Seadragon* (SSN 584) encounters gigantic iceberg with Teddy Roosevelt profile, Baffin Bay, August 1960. *U.S. Navy*

within were thoroughly drenched. The iceberg teetered back and forth as more large chunks continued to break off and fall into the water. It finally settled on a new water line, which was considerably closer to the large hole in its middle. The photoreconnaissance mission was regretfully scrubbed, and the party quickly scrambled back on board.

We spent the remainder of the afternoon examining five good-sized icebergs and making a total of eleven passes beneath them.[16] It was at this time that we discovered that icebergs give off a loud seltzer or hissing noise as they melt. The noise could be heard as a fine pinpoint of energy as far away as seventy nautical miles. Much discussion followed in the control room on how we might one day apply what we had learned about icebergs and iceberg-infested waters in actual combat situations with our most likely adversary, the Soviet submarine. Certainly an excellent tactic, upon detecting one, would be to move up as close as possible to the ice canopy overhead to better hide one's presence.

There were frequent opportunities to view the undersea life of Baffin Bay on the underwater TV as we cruised in and around the icebergs of this area. The number and variety of fish and marine mammals were unbelievable, and many of us gave up the daily movies just to see what might appear next. There was much chuckling when a certain type of fish seemed unable to avoid running into *Seadragon*'s sail. I saw numerous killer whales, a beluga whale or two, and at least one narwhal at close range. One of the most startling and unsettling experiences of my life occurred while I was manning the periscope as we cruised slowly just beneath the surface. I thought I saw something pop up and quickly trained the scope in that direction, shifting to high power, and suddenly found myself looking directly into the super-intelligent eyes of a large bull killer whale that was spy hopping. As we held each other's gaze I could feel the intensity of his penetrating stare right down to my toes. It took considerable effort to break away from his hypnotic stare.

During the evening and into the early morning of 14 August we continued to examine the underside of twenty-one very large icebergs before Captain Steele decided to call it quits. I was fortunate enough to be diving officer of the watch for most of the late evening's and early morning's work. As a result, we learned much that had not been known before. Besides being unstable and unpredictable, icebergs are of such varying density that the old rule of thumb that one part above indicates seven parts below did not necessarily apply. The ratio of iceberg above the surface to that below could, in fact, range anywhere from 1:3 to 1:23. We learned further that

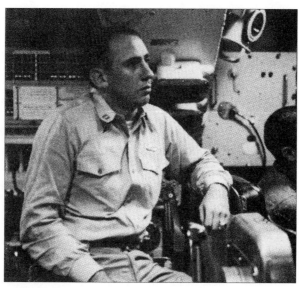

Lt. Alfred S. McLaren, diving officer of the watch, Baffin Bay, August 1960.

many dangerous, steel-hard spurs could extend well beneath the water's surface for tens of feet away from the berg. Most could not be seen from the surface and were quite difficult to detect with the under-ice sonar. The lesson to be learned here was that it would be wise for any ship or submarine to give all icebergs a wide berth. This was solidly brought home to me when I had the dive during our last pass beneath a deep-draft iceberg. The captain decided to do it at a higher speed than before. Just as we cleared its ragged bottom, a huge mass of ice became detached, probably as a result of our wake. At the first sign of what was happening, I well remember the captain opening his mouth to say, "Emergency deep!," but it was too late: hundreds of tons of ice came crashing down immediately astern of us. Fortunately, no damage was done.

Completely satisfied with what we had learned about icebergs and what would be required to operate safely in their near vicinity, *Seadragon* set a westerly course for Lancaster Sound and the Northwest Passage. Later on the morning of 14 August, as we crossed Baffin Bay on the surface en route, a very large iceberg suddenly loomed out of the fog. Captain Steele couldn't resist examining it and then passing beneath it, to the great amusement of Commodore Robertson, who remarked to Captain Steele that he was "exactly like an alcoholic with icebergs!"[17]

# CHAPTER 9

## Through the Northwest Passage

**W**e entered Lancaster Sound, 650 nautical miles long, during the evening of 14 August.[1] It was quite deep and almost forty miles wide in some places. The next day we spent submerged, pushing slowly westward along the main channel en route to Resolute on the southern tip of Cornwallis Island. We surfaced south of Devon Island shortly before noon and fixed our position. We then established communication with the Royal Canadian Air Force (RCAF) station at Resolute. After informing them of our expected arrival time, our captain invited the squadron commander and two of his staff to join us for dinner.

We remained on the surface the rest of the afternoon as we proceeded toward Cornwallis Island. It was a beautiful but chilly sunlit day, beginning with excellent views of the bleak and seemingly endless mountainous southern coast of Devon Island. We arrived just off the small bay at Resolute at approximately 6:00 p.m.. *Seadragon* carefully maneuvered its way through an increasing number of small ice floes as she approached the seaward edge of the anchorage recommended and dropped her mushroom-shaped anchor. We were the first submarine to visit Cornwallis Island.[2]

A boat soon delivered Squadron Leader S. E. Milikan, commanding officer of the RCAF contingent, Flight Lt. W. Owstan, RCAF, and Mr. Paul Adams of the U.S. Weather Station to us. Honors were rendered, and they and their boat crew were ushered below to join the wardroom and crews mess, respectively, for dinner. Our guests presented us with the latest meteorological and ice information for the route we would be following through the Northwest Passage. They had no more information than we had, however, concerning depth soundings along the way.

Since they were all special guests, the captain, at *Seadragon* doctor's suggestion, spliced the main brace with medicinal brandy as we junior officers looked on with envy. As they talked we wondered irreverently what these two RCAF officers might have done to warrant such an arduous duty station, but didn't dare ask.

Dinner was served amid the exchange of lively sea stories around the table. Our guests were as amazed at our description of life on board a continuously submerged submarine as we were at their harsh life at such a bleak, northern outpost. The continuous threat of polar bear attack certainly caught our attention. We traded gifts over dessert and coffee, and *Seadragon* received a beautifully carved seadragon of walrus tusk ivory as imagined by a local Inuit carver. Captain Steele, in turn, presented the squadron leader with our bronze plaque, which portrayed a fierce, fire-breathing dragon angrily emerging from the depths with an atom in one claw. On the rim of the plaque were the words USS *Seadragon* (SSN 584) and the boat's motto in Chinese translated as, "From the Depths I Rule."

Wishing us good luck, our visitors took all our mail in several large bags and reluctantly left us about 10:30 p.m. We retracted our anchor to its stowed position flush with the underside of *Seadragon*'s hull and slowly eased our way through ice floes to an area sufficiently clear and deep for us to safely submerge.[3]

Once submerged, we set course for the narrow eastern entrance to the Barrow Strait, located between Cape Hurd on Devon Island to the north and Prince Leopold Island to the south. It was approximately thirty miles wide and less than eight miles away. It was here where we would resume our survey of the Northwest Passage. The strait overall was approximately 170 miles in length from its eastern junction with Lancaster Sound to its junction with Viscount Melville Sound to the west. The strait separated several large islands in the Canadian Arctic Archipelago—Devon and Cornwallis Island to its north and Somerset and Prince of Wales Islands to the south. If there were to be difficulties in finding a safe, deep, submerged route through the Northwest Passage, it would be within this largely uncharted and relatively unknown segment. Although we entered with some degree of trepidation, we knew that if we were successful in finding the passage it would be one of the major achievements of the entire expedition.

The first to discover and navigate the Barrow Strait was Sir William Edward Parry, leader of the British naval Northwest Passage Expedition, in HMS *Hecla* during the summer of 1820. Sailing close to the northern shore of the strait, he discovered and surveyed the south coasts of Cornwallis and Bathurst Islands. He continued on into Viscount Melville Sound, where he discovered the south coasts of Byam Martin and Melville Islands. Heavy ice conditions prevented him from proceeding farther west into the McClure Strait; otherwise, he might have been the first to discover and transit the Northwest Passage almost a full century before the famed Norwegian explorer, and first to reach the South Pole, Roald Amundsen.[4]

Our plans upon entering were to determine the deepest and safest passage through the four known islands in the area: Griffith, Young, Garrett, and Lowther. A suspected fifth island, Davy (reported by Parry in 1820), was also plotted to the west, along our intended route. Its position was marked as doubtful, however.

Excitement rose throughout the boat as Captain Steele announced we were about to enter largely uncharted waters, where the U.S. Hydrographic Office had stated, "Depths are shallow, and this area is poorly surveyed. . . . Pinnacles have been reported." It was thus no surprise that the latest charts *Seadragon* had of this region showed nothing but large blank areas.[5]

## A New, Safe Passage

Our official orders did not, in fact, require a survey of the Barrow Strait. *Seadragon* was directed only to "investigate the feasibility of a submarine passage through the eastern segment of the Northwest Passage, the Parry Channel."[6] During a lengthy evening conference with Commodore Robertson and Waldo Lyon, and follow-on discussions drawing on the commodore's knowledge of the geological morphology of the area and the lines of glaciation, Captain Steele made his decision: the most valuable thing *Seadragon* could accomplish would be not just to find a narrow opening to pass through the Barrow Strait, but also to try to "find a deep-water pass in the channel that could be used by a nuclear submarine under the worst conditions in winter's darkness." Ruling out a far northern track followed by Canadian icebreakers through the strait, Captain Steele aimed first to make a series of four survey runs between Lowther and Garrett Islands to find the most likely deep-water passage—the northern part of the strait. We would follow these runs by a series of three runs in the less likely southern portion between Lowther and Young Islands.

*Seadragon* surfaced early on 17 August and obtained a radar fix in choppy seas generated by a stiff wind from the east. She then submerged to 120 feet and commenced the first survey run at seven knots, becoming, as Captain Steele later put it, "the first ship ever to take extensive soundings of this little-known corner of the world; in a modest fashion, we were now entering the great company of explorers."[7]

We proceeded without incident in what proved to be surprisingly deep water for most of the day. Ice-chart reports from Resolute indicated that we could expect to encounter a sharp ice boundary beginning about longitude 96° W, just beyond Griffith Island along our intended route. Total ice coverage of the strait was expected to begin shortly thereafter. To everyone's amazement, we did not encounter any sea ice when we reached this meridian. It was thus deemed prudent to return to the surface around 6:30 p.m. and take another radar fix so as to solidly anchor our track, soundings, and position relative to the nearest islands. We would also visually assess our surroundings before we reached the heavy sea-ice boundary expected to lie farther to the west.[8]

Our navigator, Al Burkhalter, soon reported that he could not obtain a good fix from the islands within view. They appeared to be as much as four miles farther apart than indicated on our chart. Needless to say, an error of this magnitude could easily result in our going aground following resumption of the submerged survey. Accordingly, Captain Steele concluded that the safest strategy would be to determine our location relative to the islands ahead of us, as they were the only ones that posed a danger.[9]

The remainder of this first survey leg, during which I was diving officer of the watch for at least four hours during the night, proved to be anything but tranquil. The water beneath us began almost immediately to become more shallow, forcing Seadragon to decrease depth, to slow, and to adjust her course as necessary to remain above whatever appeared to be the deepest canyon. Complicating the situation was that our under-ice piloting sonar, or iceberg detector, was indicating heavy ice ridges ahead of us. Either a collision with ice or a bottoming of the boat was imminent if we were not careful. But then, thanks to the discovery that our upward-beamed fathometer was not registering any ice overhead, we concluded that the iceberg detector was actually picking up reflections from the bottom ahead. From this, we realized that the iceberg detector could be used as an under-ice obstacle-avoidance sonar as well, for example picking up shoals and seamounts that could threaten the safety of the boat.[10]

Once we were certain there really was no chance of colliding with ice along our intended track—because there was none—and the bottom began to recede fortuitously into a seemingly deeper valley, we finally began to relax. It was at this time that Captain Steele pulled out the huge leather-bound first volume of Parry's 1820 journal and began reading aloud what Parry and his crew of the sailing ship *Hecla* had encountered in roughly the same area some 140 years earlier. It was a magical, almost *Twilight Zone* moment. It was if we were in direct communication with this renowned explorer of a much earlier era.

At 4:15 a.m. on 18 August *Seadragon* passed through the Barrow Strait and was back in the seventy-fathom water of Lancaster Sound.[11] Reversing course, we headed back into the strait, taking a survey line about a mile and a half to the northwest of our original track. At 7:30 a.m., while approaching Garrett Island from the east, the water beneath our keel began to shoal rapidly from 106 to 26 fathoms. We quickly headed for the surface and into turbulent seas. Our radar revealed that we had been swept off course by an unexpected current and that we would have run into the island if we had remained on our track.[12]

The less-than-tranquil survey runs between Garrett and Lowther Islands in the Barrow Strait were completed late that same day. The captain, navigator, and Waldo Lyon concluded that, although the bottom topography was irregular in the northern portion of the Barrow Strait, and although a submarine would find this first route or passage tricky, it could be used year-round. The boat would have to have the proper charts, however, and a necessary modification to the iceberg detector, enabling it to better delineate deep-draft ice directly ahead.[13]

Shortly after midnight on 19 August, Captain Steele, with Waldo Lyon, Commodore Robertson, and Lieutenant Burkhalter, discussed the possibility of discovering a better route through the Barrow Strait south of Lowther Island. The commodore thought it likely that we would encounter shoal water but agreed that it would be worth a try.[14]

*Seadragon* took a southwesterly course at seven knots at a depth that would be certain to provide us safe clearance beneath the sea ice. Our sea ice expert and hydrographer Walt Wittmann continued to marvel at how ice-free the passage had been thus far and stated, "We've never seen the Barrow Strait like this in our generation."[15] Captain Steele informed the crew over the 1MC what it was we were embarked upon, producing a perceptible wave of tension in the control room. There was little doubt in anyone's mind that, during the next several hours, we would be running into the shoal water forecast by Commodore Robertson. The captain resumed reading aloud portions of Parry's 1820 journal that he deemed of general interest. I was privately struck by the difference in the degree of control and overall safety between our respective ships: sail power versus nuclear power, the former greatly affected by weather and environmental conditions, the latter hardly at all.[16]

Several long and uneventful hours passed, and although the bottom rose gently, we remained in very deep water without the slightest indication of the expected shoaling. Our ships inertial navigation system, reported Electronic Technician 1st Class John E. Pendleton, indicated we had already gone aground, but that was because, as we already knew, the islands in this area were not charted correctly.

By 2:45 a.m. the suspense had built to the point that we had to come to the surface to fix our position. The bottom was still irregular and relatively deep. The navigator's fix confirmed our dead-reckoning position, and we continued. We soon passed through the expected shoal water without a hitch. To our surprise the bottom began to grow slowly deeper: so much for the commodore's dire prediction. Robertson shook his head in disbelief when by 6:00 a.m. we had successfully and quite easily transited the Barrow Strait once again.[17] The crew was jubilant when the captain announced this over the 1MC. There was no doubt now that *Seadragon* and her crew had discovered a completely safe, new passage through the Barrow Strait—one that avoided all the problems of the more northerly one surveyed earlier.

Our next task was to determine how wide our newfound passage might be. Course was reversed, and *Seadragon* followed a parallel track three thousand yards to the north of the survey run just completed. The iceberg detector soon revealed an isolated seamount dead ahead that the fathometer confirmed during several close passes. We made a quick excursion to the surface to fix our position as well as that of the seamount. A series of passes over the seamount subsequently revealed it to be small and forty fathoms deep. We resubmerged, completed the run, and then reversed course for a third and final survey to delineate the width of the passage running to the south, which paralleled the previous two.[18]

By early afternoon we had come to the end of this last survey line. Captain Steele announced that the new passage was "wide and deep with a single shallow spot that will serve as a convenient landmark for future submarines coming here."[19] In his book, *Seadragon*, the captain was to write of our accomplishment:

A sense of history gradually came over me. Sir John Barrow, so many years ago, was sure that a way lay through here to the Far East. How startled he would be to see us probing the cold depths of the strait he imagined in London. What would the world see here one hundred and forty years from now? I seemed to see Arctic communities, furnished heat and power by nuclear reactors, busily engaged in exporting the mineral wealth of the Canadian Northwest Territories. The Barrow Strait and the Parry Channel would then be a great Arctic waterway for the commerce of the world, served by nuclear submarine cargo vessels and tankers. One day this very passage that we were the first to examine might be a principal thoroughfare of the world.[20]

The captain announced to the crew, "We are now bound for the Arctic Ocean via Viscount Melville Sound and McClure Strait!"[21] He increased speed to sixteen knots and the depth to two hundred feet and ordered me to turn over the dive to the chief of the watch and assume the conn. This was a special occasion for me, because Captain Steele now considered me a qualified officer of the deck and submerged conning officer. We entered the next portion of the Northwest Passage, Viscount Melville Sound. The water was much deeper there, with the fathometer indicating some one hundred fathoms beneath the keel.[22]

Basing his decision on the superb and accurate performance of the ships inertial navigation system, sonar, and iceberg detector, Captain Steele considered the desirability of completing our survey and transit of the classic Northwest Passage with a high-speed run through the approximately four hundred nautical miles of the Viscount Melville Sound and McClure Strait that remained between the Arctic Ocean and our position. Although both the navigator and the exec expressed their concerns about the possibility of unknown currents, compass error, heavy ice overhead, and the still poorly charted route ahead, the captain made the decision to proceed. A speed of sixteen knots, in the captain's opinion, would emphasize the advantages of the Northwest Passage over the Panama Canal for submarines passing between the Atlantic and Pacific Oceans.[23]

We were now more than halfway through the Northwest Passage but had yet to encounter the sea ice that normally blocks its more western portions. The real risk for *Seadragon* would be coming to periscope depth or surfacing in heavy ice for the first time. This would be particularly dangerous if the ice ridges and floes were in motion and colliding and grinding together due to the strong winds typical of the area.

A major event occurred at 5:12 p.m. on 19 August when we became the first submarine to pass close aboard the North Magnetic Pole, while still navigating Viscount Melville Sound. British explorer Commander John Clark Ross had discovered this much sought-after pole some three hundred miles southeast of our position on 1 June 1831.[24] *Seadragon* followed a zigzag course at a depth of three hundred feet through Viscount Melville Sound so as to chart as much bottom topography as possible in an area that had never been surveyed before. The passage was an easy one because, to our relief, the bottom remained quite regular and the water deep throughout.

We finally encountered the ice pack at 3:45 a.m. on 20 August at longitude 110° W. Walt Wittmann in his initial report to Captain Steele stated that this much open water in the Northwest Passage had not been seen in modern times.[25] There was no doubt that we were well into it now, as indicated by the upward-beamed fathometer. Ten-foot block and brash ice overhead quickly became deep draft ridges every five hundred yards, reaching as much as eighteen to twenty-one feet beneath the sea. Sea ice of six feet in thickness then gradually filled in the space between these ridges such that only occasional open water was seen overhead as a twenty-four-hour rotating ice watch was set. "An impenetrable, stone-like roof blocking us from access to air," as Captain Steele put it, would, in all probability, be our operating environment until just north of the Bering Strait, several weeks distant.[26]

Deep-draft ice keels sixty to seventy-five feet beneath the sea lay overhead as we changed course to the northwest and entered the deeper water of McClure Strait. If calculations were correct, we would pass safely between Melville Island to the north and Banks Island to the south as we headed toward the open Beaufort Sea and the Arctic Ocean. As all in the control room figuratively held their breath for the next several hours, Captain Steele began to read aloud from the story of the investigator and commander Robert McClure.[27]

After two hours it appeared certain that the danger of a head-on collision with Banks or Melville Islands had passed. Captain Steele congratulated Al Burkhalter and asked that he let him know when *Seadragon* had reached longitude 125° W, a line that passed just west of Prince Patrick Island, the northwestern island of the Parry Channel. It was here that our orders called for sending a message changing from the operational control (CHOP) of the commander in chief of the U.S. Atlantic Fleet (CincLant) and ComSubLant, at Norfolk, to that of commander in chief of the U.S.

Pacific Fleet (CincPac), at Pearl Harbor. Our trip would be made public on receipt of this report. Most importantly to us, our families would finally learn what we had been doing since we left Portsmouth.

The navigator reported that we would clear the McClure Strait and reach the point at 2:15 a.m. the following morning, 21 August. The captain put the officer of the deck on a three-hundred-yard execute effective at that time. This was a technique developed by the commanding officer of USS *Skate*, Cdr. James F. Calvert, in 1958 as the first step in surfacing within the Arctic pack ice. It called for being alert for any open water or thin-ice openings: polynyas, leads, or skylights at least three hundred yards long.[28] When one was encountered, the officer of the deck was to put *Seadragon* into a Williamson Turn, designed to return us to the center of this possible surfacing area, and station the polynya-plotting party.

A long lead was located at 3:40 a.m., and the boat smartly returned to a surfacing point well within it. Captain Steele took the conn and carefully eased us up into a polynya with sharply defined edges. As soon as *Seadragon*'s sail was awash, Steele raised the periscope, confirmed that all was clear, and ordered the requisite antenna raised. He then gave Chief Radioman John K. Evans permission to inform CincPac at Pearl Harbor that *Seadragon* had completed the first submerged transit of the Northwest Passage and was "reporting for duty."[29]

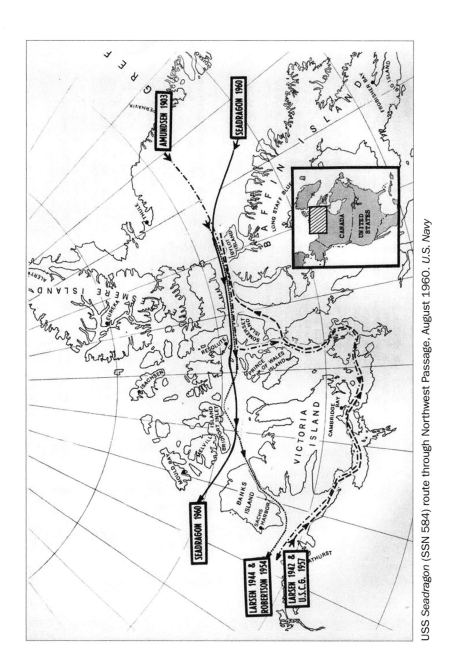

USS *Seadragon* (SSN 584) route through Northwest Passage, August 1960. *U.S. Navy*

# CHAPTER 10

# Surfacing at the Pole

S*eadragon's* next objective was to achieve the North Pole some 840 nautical miles to the north. Before we could submerge and set course, however, she had to remain on the surface within a quite sizable, 350- by 400-yard polynya for another five hours following the exchange of messages with CincPac. Our task was to install protective steel bars over the cavity in the sail into which the radar mast with its delicate antenna was lowered. Additional bars were also bolted over the bridge cockpit in order to protect the compass repeater and its fittings within. Once completed, we would be fully prepared to avert damage from any heavy ice as we approached the surface or when actually surfacing through or within the ice-filled leads and polynyas en route. The navigator and his team took advantage of a near-perfect day to take a series of sun lines to determine latitude and to firmly fix our position. At the same time, Captain Steele allowed members of an excited crew to come on deck to view, take pictures of, and, most importantly contemplate the magnificent, heavily hummocked ice stretching to the horizon in all directions that we would be operating beneath during the weeks to come. There was no doubt in my mind, as I noted their expressions, that all got the basic message that we needed to ensure that *Seadragon* emerged safely in the Chukchi Sea on the other side.[1]

Once the work was completed, all hands were sent below, deck hatches were shut, and the bridge was cleared. All MBT vents were opened, and *Seadragon* slipped quietly beneath the ice. We proceeded to a depth of three hundred feet and set course for the North Pole. A course north along longitude 117° W was taken initially. This was followed by a super-imposed broad zigzag course that covered the least known parts of the Arctic Ocean. It was, at the same time, well away from the tracks followed to the North Pole by our predecessors, *Nautilus* and *Sargo*.[2]

At noon on 21 August, we were well beneath the permanent Arctic pack ice. By the time the off-going officer of the deck, Lt. (jg) Vince Leahy, had reported his relief to the captain, *Seadragon* was already passing beneath deep-draft pressure ridges, or keels, that reached almost a hundred feet beneath the sea. This exceeded not only the maximum predicted by Walt Wittmann for this area, but also for the Arctic Ocean as a whole. Even-deeper-draft ice keels were encountered as the afternoon progressed. Captain Steele prudently ordered the officer of the deck to proceed to four hundred feet. This gave us a greater safety margin from the very heavy ice overhead should we unexpectedly lose depth control at our present speed of sixteen knots.[3]

Visibility was estimated to be on the order of several hundred feet in the pale blue and quite clear polar water. On the bow-mounted underwater TV in the control room, we were continuously treated to a spectacular panorama of the underside of the sea ice that we were the first in history to see. Individual keels like huge claws seemed to probe, one after another, deeper and deeper toward us. The continuous flow of undulating ice as it passed overhead reminded me of low-lying stratus clouds. The thicker portions were blacker and more ominous, except that the outlines of individual floes were much sharper than those of clouds, adding to their sinister aspect.

Some couldn't help but think of Sir Hubert Wilkins and his converted U.S. World War I diesel electric submarine, *Nautilus*, which reached latitude 84° N almost thirty years before, in 1931. It now seems unbelievable that, well into the twentieth century, anyone could have thought that the underside of the Arctic ice pack was perfectly flat, much less believe that a submarine such as Wilkins' *Nautilus* would head north for a first transit beneath the Arctic ice pack with much of her topside configured like an inverted sled runner. Just a glance at *Seadragon's* upward-beamed fathometer recordings showed that Wilkins' submarine would have been hopelessly trapped within the irregular and quite thick under-ice topography of the Arctic ice pack if she had managed to force her way completely beneath the nearest ice floe on that expedition.

As *Seadragon* proceeded farther north, the ice cover overhead gradually approached 100 percent. The number of open-water leads and polynyas noted on the upward-beamed fathometer steadily decreased, as did the depth of pressure ridges. To our surprise, however, at about noon on 22

August, *Seadragon* entered an area where the sea ice seemed to have completely disappeared. This continued for over three miles before the ice pack was reengaged. Investigation at slow speed on another, near perpendicular, axis confirmed that we were beneath a gigantic polynya that was as wide as it was long.[4]

We proceeded to the surface at approximately 12:20 p.m. and found ourselves in what could best be termed a large lake that was completely clear of ice. With the exception of a low mist, visibility was good thanks to a brisk northeast wind that generated slight waves.[5]

Captain Steele decided to take advantage of what appeared to be near ideal conditions to check out *Seadragon*'s ability to moor to the thick first-year ice that ringed the polynya, which was approximately six feet thick overall. He ordered Lt. Robert D. "Bob" Doelling, the first lieutenant, to break out two six-foot steel mooring spikes of three-inch pipe and sledgehammers and ferry them over to the ice edge via rubber life raft.[6] In the meantime, the chief of the boat, Philip Le Clair, cut loose the mooring lines from the topside lockers where they had been tightly lashed to prevent them from streaming loose and getting entangled in the propellers.[7]

The iron mooring spikes were carefully lifted from the life raft and dragged a hundred feet or so onto the ice floe to which we planned to moor. Once in their respective positions, the captain ordered them driven into the ice. This turned out to be a near impossible task, sledgehammers notwithstanding, since the ice was as hard as concrete. After the better part of an hour amid loud cursing and grumbling, the men had driven spikes to a depth of approximately two feet. Light, weighted heaving lines were tossed from the boat to those on shore and used to pull our heavier nylon mooring lines onto the ice where they could be secured to our new mooring posts. Captain Steele brought *Seadragon* gently alongside the ice edge. The lines were doubled, and the underway watch was secured.[8]

Shore leave, as it were, was now granted to all hands not on watch. The crew was told we would be moored for at least six hours. Orange life jackets were required for all going onto the ice. We were instructed to remain within sight and hailing distance of the boat and not to wander off alone at any time.

As the crew prepared to go out on the ice, a few Arctic-experienced hands had fun cautioning those going ashore about the threat of polar bears. "You won't be able to see one until it opens its mouth," they said, supplying vivid descriptions of how a polar bear can quietly sneak up on the unwary by holding one paw over its black nose and mouth, close to within thirty feet, and then suddenly pounce on its intended victim. Human beings, they said, were a favorite food, and a polar bear could smell a human from miles away. Furthermore, they could run at speeds up to thirty miles per hour, so it was wise to go ashore with someone slower than you were.

Captain Steele noted in his book, "The surface of the ice field was irregular, generally rough, and covered with what seemed to be old snow crystals that crunched when stepped upon. Great lines of upended ice floes over eight feet high marked the pressure ridges/ice keels that we had seen from below."[9] The rafting of one ice floe over another that created these ridges was a result of the unusually high winds that characterized this harsh environment. In addition, refrozen melt ponds and dark pools of water dotted the surface in all directions. Beneath each lay an icy water column that descended some 11,000 feet beneath the sea.[10] These partly hidden crevices would pose the most immediate danger for the unwary crewmember if he accidently stepped into one.

As members of the crew wandered over the ice, the captain gave Lt. Glenn Brewer and his scuba team permission to make their first dive in the near vicinity of the polar ice pack, restricting them to one of familiarization and instructing them, to their disappointment, not to go under the ice at this time.

Before going out on the ice, I spent a good deal of time in the control room using our new 70-mm periscope camera to record the fantastic scene that surrounded us. The photos I shot that day and other photos taken during the remainder of the voyage were used in the media during the next several decades. Afterward I joined my shipmates in an all-hands snowball fight that erupted during our remaining hours on the surface, soon to degenerate to an inevitable crew-versus–officers and chief petty officers melee. The officers' side got the worst of it.

Tired and happy after our lengthy excursion on the ice, the sea and anchor detail was set, the mooring lines were taken on board, and *Seadragon* got under way. The polynya was so enormous that after a brief detour to the south the captain ordered a course change to due north and increased speed to fifteen knots, certainly the highest speed ever attained on the surface within the polar ice pack. As we proceeded forward with still no ice in sight, we joked about continuing all the way to the North Pole on the surface. The edge of the vast ice pack soon reappeared, however, and we made a normal quick dive to test depth in order to check and record the characteristics of the water column beneath us. We recorded a water temperature of about 38° Fahrenheit at the surface, which decreased steeply to slightly less than 30° at twenty feet beneath the surface. The temperature then remained a steady 30° to test depth.

Shortly after breakfast on 23 August, the officer of the deck in the control room reported that visibility under water was exceptionally good with extraordinarily clear detail. Deep-draft keels could be seen on the TV reaching down to as much as ninety feet beneath the surface. The movie camera and tape recorder were ordered started to catch as much of this unearthly and strikingly beautiful image as possible.[11]

Captain Steele later ordered the officer of the deck to slow to seven knots and ease the boat up to a depth of 150 feet. Once there, speed was reduced to three knots, and the captain slowly raised the periscope. He was immediately heard to gasp and exclaim as he observed gigantic blue-black masses of ice rush toward and then pass above and over the periscope. Those watching the TV monitor had much the same reaction. It would appear as if we were in imminent danger at first, but the iceberg-detector watch continually

USS *Seadragon* (SSN 584) crewmembers explore ice pack in Arctic Ocean, August 1960. *U.S. Navy*

Heavy sea ice above USS *Seadragon* (SSN 584) near North Pole, August 1960. *U.S. Navy*

reassured all that we were well clear of the massive procession of huge ice boulders that passed rapidly overhead. The captain next called the exec, Lt. Cdr. Jim Strong, to the periscope to observe. He too was startled by the continuously evolving ice display and could only murmur, "What a sight, what a sight!"[12] Called to the periscope, our senior scientist, Waldo Lyon, had the same reaction. This veteran of essentially all earlier voyages by U.S. submarines under ice had never seen anything like it, for the simple reason that none of these submarines had been equipped with underwater television.

The captain took the time to permit each of our crew of 102 men to observe the unbelievably harsh yet beautiful under-ice topography that continually passed over us. The inevitable submariner's rough joke was played halfway through when our underwater photographer, Lt. Glenn Brewer, took the periscope. He had no sooner put his eye to it than the whole submarine shook with a heavy, thudding shock, followed by several more shocks in rapid succession. With his eyes wide in horror, Glenn quickly lowered the periscope and almost fell to the deck. He had a near heart attack as the rest of us roared with laughter. The captain had given the weapons officer, Lieutenant Doelling, permission to fire water slugs, using high-pressure air, from the forward torpedo tube just as Glenn put his eye to the scope.

Once all of the crew and officers had had a good look, we settled into a more normal watch routine as we sped toward the North Pole at a depth of four hundred feet.

*Seadragon* continued transiting at deep depth for the next several days. The vast polar ice pack that passed overhead seemed much like a never-ending grayish white blanket of malevolent-looking clouds. Its general undersea topography was extremely rugged. We encountered many deep-draft keels of over sixty to eighty feet along our route, thrusting downward like sharp talons, ever ready to catch the unwary. We also passed beneath a surprising number of open-water polynyas and leads. One could easily conclude from the latter that a submarine would have absolutely no difficulty locating open water during the summer months should it come to the surface in the event of an emergency.

## Baseball on the Ice

On 25 August 1960 USS *Seadragon* reached the North Pole. We were the fourth nuclear submarine to achieve the Pole and the third to surface there. We were now midway geographically through the first transpolar submarine voyage from the Atlantic to the Pacific, and to *Seadragon's* new home port in Pearl Harbor. Our slogan for the voyage was, appropriately, "Under the ice to paradise!"

*Seadragon* surfaced early morning within a medium-sized polynya that was surrounded by thick sea ice as far as the eye could see. The skies were clear and the air temperature a bracing 28° Fahrenheit. Only a light cover of snow blanketed the ice. Scattered throughout were small pools of meltwater that had refrozen into clear glass-like ice and huge ridges throughout like seams on a baseball.

A number of memorable events took place during our brief visit to the North Pole. Captain Steele talked over the radio with the U.S. Amundsen-Scott South Pole Station located at the geographic South Pole in the Antarctic.[13] We also sent scuba divers under the ice at the North Pole for the first time ever. We sent a survival party off to set up camp several hundred yards away from the boat as an exercise in determining how quickly crewmembers could exit the boat in the event of an emergency. The most indelible memory, however, was the first game of baseball ever played at the North Pole.

For days beforehand officers and crewmembers talked about the game, which promised to be a heated contest between the engineers aft, the most

USS *Seadragon* (SSN 584) scuba divers at North Pole, 25 August 1960. *U.S. Navy*

vocal of whom were Ronald J. Waldron, Edward Briggs, and Philip Philipps Jr., and those who worked and stood watch forward of *Seadragon's* reactor compartment, such as Grady E. "Two-Gun" Roberts, Earl J. Crowley III, and John K. Evans. Boasts and threats were traded as we geared up. The engineering department team was made up of enginemen, machinist's mates, electricians, and radio chemists. The forward end team was made up mainly of torpedomen, sonar men, radiomen, auxiliary men, yeomen, and cooks. Interspersed throughout both teams were key division officers, department heads, and the captain. The chief hospital corpsman, Richard A. Morin, was to serve as umpire.

It was an ideal afternoon for baseball. We were blessed with a clear blue sky overhead, warm sunlight, and little or no wind. The large ice floe on which we would be playing contained Al Burkhalter's best estimate of the closest we could get to the geographic North Pole. This would enable the crew to locate the pitcher's mound directly over the Pole and orient the base-ball diamond such that a straight line from home plate through the pitch-

First pitch in historic first baseball game at North Pole, 25 August 1960. *U.S. Navy*

er's mound to second base paralleled longitude 000°, or the Greenwich Meridian. As it continued through center field, it coincided with longitude 180°, or the International Date Line.

The stage was set: If a lucky batter on either side hit a home run, he could circumnavigate the globe and pass through some twenty-four time zones as he circled the bases on the way to home plate. If he hit the ball into right field, he would be hitting it across the International Date Line into tomorrow. If the right fielder caught it as a fly ball, he caught it the next day. Hence the batter could not be considered out for another twenty-four hours. However, if he hit a line drive into right field and the ball was successfully fielded and thrown to either second or third base, it would have been thrown back into the day of play, or yesterday. A ball hit to left field would remain within the same day. If it was caught and then thrown to first base, it could enter tomorrow, depending on just where the first baseman was standing. Double and triple plays could take several days to complete. Base stealing or a slide into base took on a whole new meaning during *Seadragon's* contest. Action in the vicinity of second base could again take several days to complete, and a slide into any base could take a runner straight to the ice edge. A second-base slide could be quite hazardous to whoever was playing

"Batter up!" Baseball at the North Pole, 25 August 1960. *U.S. Navy*

shortstop. On the other hand, it made the runner easy pickings, because if a baseman with the ball missed him on the first go-around, he would get a second chance. Finally, the batter, catcher, and umpire had best get well out of the way during a slide into home base.

Both teams had great fun with all of this. Disputes over just what day and time anything had occurred contributed to frequent and often utter confusion of the base and field umpires, not to mention the game recorder. No one remembered the final score or even the day on which it ended for sure. We do know the exact date, though, when the umpire yelled, "Play ball!": 25 August 1960.

The baseball (really a softball) used during the game was dried out and, following our arrival in Pearl Harbor, presented to the Baseball Hall of Fame on behalf of the U.S. Navy submarine force. What a day!

Once all hands were confirmed below decks, the maneuvering watch was set. *Seadragon* made a stationary dive down to two hundred feet, and the boat was slowed and trimmed for neutral buoyancy. Once completed, depth was increased to 350 feet and speed to approximately eighteen knots. The course was set to the southwest for the Bering Strait. An hour later we all sat down to a fabulous celebratory dinner of our best real steaks, baked potatoes, and vegetables—nothing ration-dense here. For dessert, the cooks unveiled a huge, beautifully iced North Pole three-layer cake. It was cut by Captain Steele and *Seadragon's* youngest crewmember, and generous pieces were passed out to all hands.

Later that evening we turned our full attention to safely navigating our way, as sea-ice conditions permitted, to the Bering Strait and Nome, Alaska, via the shallow Beaufort and Chukchi Seas.

# CHAPTER 11

# The Bering Strait and Nome

O n 25 August 1960 we reached the famed Lomonosov Ridge, first discovered by the Soviet high-latitude air expeditions in 1948.[1] The ridge was named after Mikhail V. Lomonosov (1711–1765), Russian poet, scientist, and grammarian. He made substantial contributions to the natural sciences, reorganized the St. Petersburg Imperial Academy of Sciences, and established the Imperial Moscow University in 1755, now known as the Lomonosov Moscow State University, whose research priorities are science and the humanities.[2]

A steep, sill-like ridge dividing the Arctic Ocean into two major basins, the Lomonosov Ridge extends from Ellesmere Island on the continental shelf of North America, north to a point near the North Pole, and south to a point near the continental shelf of the New Siberian Islands. The basin on the Atlantic side, called the Eurasian Basin, is more than 13,000 feet deep. The adjacent Amerasian Basin is about 11,050 feet deep. Between the two basins the ridge crest at its highest point is at a depth of 3,169 feet from the surface of the ocean.[3]

The abrupt decrease in depth was a real shocker, occurring at approximately latitude 88° 50' N, from over 13,000 feet beneath our keel to slightly over 3,250 feet in just a mile or so of forward travel. It was more than sufficient to cause us to abruptly slow, decrease depth, and prepare to reverse course. Once the depth of water beneath our keel appeared to steady, we increased speed and gingerly made our way across the ridge for fifty miles or so.

Early the next afternoon *Seadragon* surfaced within a medium-sized polynya and placed Lt. Glenn Brewer and our doctor, Lt. Cdr. Lew Seaton, on the surrounding sea ice. They were tasked with photographing and making a film recording of *Seadragon* during a subsequent surfacing.

When all was set, *Seadragon* submerged and headed a couple of hundred yards away from the polynya. She then made a Williamson Turn and steered course for the center of the polynya that we had just left. She missed the center, probably due to the constant movement of the ice pack above us, forcing us to slowly and carefully attempt to relocate the polynya that we had just left.

If there was rising anxiety in the three men left on the ice when they heard us repeatedly pass beneath them, it was even more tense in the control room. We relocated the polynya within a half hour, however, and all ended well with no polar bears sighted, to everyone's relief. Once the photographers and doctor were back on board, we made a stationary dive beneath the ice and resumed our transit south. Captain Steele ordered the main brace spliced with a shot of medicinal brandy to settle the badly frayed nerves of the three who had begun to fear they might be left on the ice. The photographic party brought back some wonderful stills and the first-ever movie footage of *Seadragon* surfacing in an Arctic Ocean polynya.

We entered the Beaufort Sea and neared Alaska on 28 August. *Seadragon* surfaced and tried to visit Ice Island T-3 for scientific operations: Ice Island T-3 is a floating ice island that originates from the Ellesmere Island Ward Hunt Ice Shelf in the Arctic Ocean and on which a permanent campsite was erected in 1952. It was thirty-one miles in circumference and a minimum of five miles across at the narrowest part. The scientists manning the island obtained a tentative ice thickness of about 160 feet through seismic sound-ings of the ice and the ocean bottom.[4] To our disappointment and that of the scientific personnel on the ice island, the island was found to be aground off the north coast of Alaska. The waters around it were too shallow and it would have been hazardous for us to come any closer than a few miles.

We passed through the Bering Strait on the surface early on the morning of 5 September and by early afternoon reached Nome for a brief port visit. We had been at sea, mostly submerged under the Arctic pack ice, for over a month and were starved for some diversion. Interestingly, an artist among our crew designed a USS *Seadragon* First East-West Polar Transit–August 1960 tattoo that proud crewmembers could get inscribed on their bicep at the first opportunity. After mooring alongside the U.S. Coast Guard's icebreaker *Northwind* about a mile or so from town, *Seadragon's* crewmembers went ashore courtesy of the *Northwind's* liberty boats. Captain Steele had encouraged us all to thoroughly enjoy ourselves, but under no circumstances to get drunk or disorderly or in any other way bring discredit to our boat or to the submarine force. Nonetheless, young sailors and officers took their chances. So as we wandered from one bar to another, a good and well-lubricated time was had by all, despite the captain's warning.

USS *Seadragon* "First East–West Polar Transit—August 1960" insignia. *U.S. Navy*

Nome at that time was still a picturesque frontier town with board sidewalks, not much changed from the gold rush days of the late nineteenth century. The citizens of Nome in this new forty-ninth state had never before seen a submarine and went all out to welcome *Seadragon*'s crew. They set up tours, with the most popular being to a working gold mine. Midafternoon *Seadragon*'s captain and officers gorged at a sumptuous banquet at the old Bering Sea Hotel, hosted by a beautiful Eskimo woman who was the "queen" of Nome, the mayor, and Nome's other leading lights. In addition to Alaskan king crab, halibut, and Arctic char, we enjoyed such local delicacies as whale steak and seal. The latter were oily and strong-smelling—definitely an acquired taste. Wine and beer in copious amounts were also served, and toasts were exchanged from every direction. The local bakery provided a huge Arctic cake iced in pale shades of blue and white that typified the frozen environment. The banquet ended with Captain Steele and the Eskimo queen cutting and distributing pieces to all present. We each came away with small vials of gold dust as a souvenir of our visit, gifts of our hosts.

Afterward we repaired to a local Eskimo village for a special ceremony that featured strange and affecting throat singing.[5] Our hosts tossed the captain high into the air with a large sealskin as though he were an Eskimo hunter attempting to see as far as possible over the horizon. To his credit and the cheers of the village, the captain remained on his feet throughout a half dozen vigorous tosses.

Unfortunately I missed all the fun because, following the cutting and distribution of the cake, Captain Steele charged me, as the newest officer, with the responsibility of transporting what was left of the cake out to *Seadragon* for the duty section still on board. I gave a cheery "Aye, aye, sir!," and somewhat dejectedly struggled back to Nome's boat landing with the still-sizable, heavy, and awkwardly shaped remains. My mood rapidly picked up within minutes of leaving the hotel, however, when two attractive Wien Air Alaska flight attendants who had been at the banquet joined me and asked if they could be of help. They could, of course, and the three of us made light work of the task as we talked and laughed and carried our burden a hundred yards to the boat landing, loaded it on one of the *Northwind*'s liberty boats, and got it on board *Seadragon* and safely below decks to the crews mess.

I treated the young ladies to a cup of hot coffee in the wardroom after touring them through the boat. They in turn suggested that the least they could do was take me on a tour of Nome's nightspots. Naturally I accepted, and we forthwith left the boat and went ashore to the chagrin of *Seadragon*'s duty section, which had been deprived of female companionship for almost five weeks.

As the three of us toured the bars, singing and exchanging toasts and generally having a roaring good time, I started to realize that the town's citizens mainly made their money selling liquor to each other. I had never seen so many saloons, virtually side by side, even in a big Navy town like Norfolk or San Diego. After saying goodbye to the locals, I had the luck to be escorted safely back to the boat landing by one of the flight attendants.

### A Whalebone for the Duty Section

It was late on our last night of freedom in Nome and turning a numbing cold. As the visit drew to a close, a small group of us rushed to catch the last Coast Guard liberty boat back to the submarine at anchor. Running along a wooden boardwalk to the town wharf, somebody spotted a huge whale rib lying nearby. It was slightly curved and was at least eight feet long—the perfect gift for the forlorn duty section left on board. It took three of us, aided by my Wien Air Alaska friend, to hoist it into the air and onto our shoulders. Once secured, we took off running through the dark toward the boat landing, laughing and yelling like maniacs.

Arriving at the landing, we overrode the objections of the boat coxswain to gleefully toss our prize on board the small launch. My flight attendant friend presented me with a special Alaskan Statehood Dollar, and we hugged as we said goodbye. After I boarded the boat, we continued waving until we disappeared from each other's sight.

As the boat approached *Seadragon,* we were gratified to find the forward torpedo room hatch open. Pulling alongside the starboard bow, several of us jumped to the main deck and, with the aid of the topside watch and boat coxswain, wrestled the huge whalebone on board. It was much bigger than we had thought! The main access hatch into our boat was located amidships, some fifty feet astern. None of us wanted to carry it back there only to have the topside watch call the duty officer to tell us we had to throw our trophy overboard.

So, peering down the forward torpedo room hatch into the compartment below and noting that all lights were out in what also served as a major berthing area during the voyage, we decided to dump the whalebone straight down the hatch. Three of us lifted it off the deck, and carefully positioned it on the edge of the hatch so that when released it would slide straight down and into the center of the torpedo room. When all was ready, we let go. The whalebone slid, scraped, and banged its way to a resting position exactly where we wanted it, amid sleeping crewmembers and spare torpedoes. As the lights came on, accompanied by shouts of alarm, we fled aft, laughing hysterically, and made good our escape down the midships compartment hatch.

To the men below the racket must have sounded like a depth charge as the huge artifact bounced and rolled around, until one man more sensible than the others discovered the cause of it all. An informal investigation by the exec Jim Strong the next day, after *Seadragon* was submerged and many miles south of Nome, failed to discover the guilty parties. A command decision was eventually made to take it to Pearl Harbor and present it to the Submarine Force Museum. Meanwhile it was stowed beneath one of the torpedoes.

# CHAPTER 12

# Pearl Harbor at Last

W e transited through the Bering Sea, the Aleutians, and the Pacific north of the Hawaiian Islands without incident. After a long final week at sea, we entered the Pearl Harbor Channel on the morning of 14 September 1960. Water-spouting tugboats filled the channel; helicopters dropped orchids, and one lowered a huge flowered lei directly over *Seadragon*'s sail. It seemed as if every ship in port was welcoming us by sounding its whistles. As we proceeded to our berth in front of ComSubPac's headquarters, a U.S. Marine Corps band played lively

USS *Seadragon* (SSN 584) arrives in Pearl Harbor following historic transit from the Atlantic to the Pacific via the North Pole, September 1960. *U.S. Navy*

marches, and family members who had been waving from the banks earlier excitedly rushed forward.

We had no sooner moored than all hands not on watch were mustered on the pier alongside. CincPac Adm. John H. Sides and ComSubPac Rear Adm. Roy S. Benson stepped forward to greet and congratulate us all on our successful passage from the Atlantic to the Pacific via the North Pole. ComSubPac read a formal citation from the U.S. Secretary of the Navy and presented Captain Steele with the Legion of Merit and USS *Seadragon* with its first Navy Unit Commendation. Admiral Benson announced that we were now ComSubPac's new flagship, his lead ship in the Submarine Force Pacific. It was a proud moment for us all. Liberty immediately commenced for all hands not on duty, and we eagerly embraced our family members whom we had not seen in almost two months.

*Seadragon*, the fourth nuclear submarine to join the Pacific Fleet, had logged 8,800 nautical miles since leaving Portsmouth, New Hampshire, on 1 August 1960.[1] She now entered a much-needed, extended in-port upkeep of almost three weeks. Not only did we have many important voyage repairs to accomplish, but we also had to prepare for what would prove to be an intensive local operations schedule, providing services for the rest of the year to a wide variety of ASW units as one of the Pacific Fleet's first nuclear attack submarines.

## Getting Wasted

We prepared for the ASW services, but then were diverted to conduct what turned out to be a series of Cold War operations that took a great deal out of both boat and crew. The latter had to do primarily with monitoring Soviet long-range ballistic missile tests. We were operating during an era when, as one of the few nuclear attack submarines then in existence, we were subject to being ordered off on missions of indeterminate length, often at a moment's notice, not having enough time to complete routine upkeep. As a result, both officers and crew were frantically busy throughout the boat whenever we were in port. Since we might have to live with whatever didn't get fixed for extended periods of time at sea, we worked hard to ensure that all equipment and systems were, or would be, up and running 100 percent of the time before we were next scheduled to get under way.

*Seadragon's* sanitary system was a case in point: She was equipped with two sanitary tanks to receive waste from the galley, sinks and showers, and the laundry room, and all discharge, liquid and solid, from the heads (toilets). One tank was located forward and the other aft. Both filled fairly rapidly during the course of any given day and had to be evacuated by being blown to sea, using low-pressure air, at least once every twenty-four hours. This was an essential system, and had to be fully operational at all times. A clogged drain pipe or jammed valve from sink, shower, or commode could be hugely inconvenient because our crew of more than one hundred members already had to stand in line to use the few we had. The heads, moreover, required copious amounts of salt water from sea to flush each time they were used, which could be thirty or forty times a day each.

The sanitary system was one of many essential fluid and air systems maintained by a team of auxiliary men within the engineering department. Other systems for which they were responsible included freshwater, hydraulic, air conditioning, refrigeration, ventilation, and various other equipments associated with atmosphere control such as oxygen generators, carbon dioxide scrubbers, carbon monoxide–hydrogen burners, and percipitrons that removed hydrocarbons from the atmosphere. All were very important for crew comfort, well-being, and morale.

Several sanitary system drain pipes had gradually become clogged. One of the worst was the pipe from the officers' head. It was a great source of frustration and grousing, particularly by the captain. This particular head was located at the forward end of the officers' berthing compartment on *Seadragon's* second level.

Directly below the officers' head, on *Seadragon's* third level, was the miniscule chief petty officers' lounge area, which consisted of a small table, surrounded on three sides by a banquette. The drain pipe from the officers' head passed directly through the ceiling or overhead of this area, angled down well above the small table, and then ran down the forward bulkhead en route to one of the sanitary tanks.

Well into the first week of our upkeep, we tackled the problem of the clogged drain pipes. Uppermost on the list was the pipe from the officers' head. On this particular day, the entire sanitary system was out of commission, and all hands were instructed to use the nearest facilities off the boat. All the heads throughout the boat were then red tagged to prevent inadvertent operation, all head doors were shut, and "DO NOT USE OR OPERATE" signs were hung on the outside of the doors where they could be clearly seen.

The section of drain pipe that angled down from directly above the chief petty officers' table had already been carefully removed and drained midmorning. It was now at the machine shop in the submarine base in Pearl Harbor, where internal scaling was being thoroughly reamed out. Reinstallation was planned for later in the day.

I happened to have assumed duties as in-port duty officer that morning and had not been told, or had missed the fact, that the forward sanitary system would be out of commission for the rest of the day. Sometime during the late morning a serious call of nature resulted in my mindlessly rushing to the officers' head. I rejoiced to see the door wide open and dashed right in. Closing and locking the head door after me, I quickly sat down and alleviated my own internal plumbing with a sigh of relief. I even took a few minutes to pick up a handy magazine and begin to read.

Afterward I filled the toilet bowl with flushing water and opened the large flushing valve at the base of the bowl, using a large lever to its right. Within seconds there was a loud and frantic pounding on the head door before I had finished shutting the valve, much less unlocked the head door to exit. "*Bang! Bang! BANG!*" The door jerked this way and that as several people outside sputtering loud curses tried to yank it off its hinges. As I fearfully unlocked the door, I came face to face with three infuriated chief petty officers so agitated as to be almost incoherent. Two of them grabbed me by the arms and rushed me aft and down the stairway to the third level where they propelled me into the chief petty officers' lounge area. A fourth chief petty officer, splattered with toilet paper and much else, met me as I entered.

An acey-deucy game that had been in progress on the table was covered with water and . . . what looked like . . . "Oh my God," I exclaimed. The overhead directly above the table and from which the piping that normally angled above the table had been removed was still dripping. My profuse apologies were to no avail. Facing what appeared to be a small lynch mob, I frantically attempted to calm them down, calling for the duty section to bring lots of rags, cleaning gear, and water to the chief petty officers' quarters pronto.

Using a scoop, bucket, and soap, I set to work, surrounded by four glowering chief petty officers, and finished up in record time with all as good as new. As a final gesture of appeasement, I emptied my wallet to pay what were certain to be big cleaning bills plus enough for several rounds of beers. Then I made a rapid exit, or rather escape, as far away as was possible on this cramped sub.

How did this embarrassing incident happen in the first place? And why didn't I notice the "DO NOT USE" sign located on the front of the officers' head door? Someone, for his sake never identified, had left the head door all the way open, preventing anyone from seeing the warning sign suspended on the other side. Also, the flushing water valve itself had not been red tagged. Maybe the whole thing was a genuine oversight, or a prank, and most would consider me guiltless. On the other hand, I had assumed duty that day without learning, and carefully observing, all that was going on on board *Seadragon*. I would not let that happen again.

It took the four chief petty officers a few weeks to forgive me. Then, during our next lengthy operation, the incident became a source of jokes and took its place in the lore and history of *Seadragon*.

### An Early Passive Trailing Exercise

One thing Captain Steele was good about was providing his junior officers with regular opportunities to learn the fine points of operating a nuclear attack submarine—techniques that would be fully required of them as commanding officers one day. He was also always receptive to trying out a new idea or new method of doing something operationally. I was lucky enough to have him as a commanding officer early in my career. What he taught was to stand me in extremely good stead during my remaining years in submarines. This was to be especially true during my subsequent tours of duty on USS *Greenling* in 1968 and as commanding officer of USS *Queenfish* from 1969 to 1973.

One night in the spring of 1961, *Seadragon* spent an entire night with a sister nuclear attack submarine, USS *Swordfish* (SSN 579), devoted to submarine-versus-submarine tactical exercises. Both commanding officers elected to develop techniques for trailing another nuclear attack submarine—something that had not yet been employed by any nuclear attack submarine during a Cold War operation but that would become necessary and well developed in the U.S. Navy. It would be of importance in keeping close tabs on deployed Soviet ballistic missile submarines, both diesel and nuclear powered, or on nuclear attack submarines that might be searching for one of our own ballistic missile submarines.

The submarine-versus-submarine exercise began shortly after 8:00 p.m. and lasted until almost sun-up the next day. Each watch-standing team on its respective submarine would attempt to trail the opposing submarine for approximately two hours, with any given session ending earlier if the trailing submarine lost its quarry for longer than thirty minutes. If this occurred, both submarines were to hold their depths and slowly circle on station as they attempted to locate each other via active sonar and underwater telephone. If contact could not be reestablished, they would proceed carefully to periscope depth and establish contact via radio. In either case, when contact was reestablished *Seadragon* and *Swordfish* were to position themselves within a thousand yards of each other, with a depth separation of at least one hundred feet, and the next session would commence.

Each watch section elected to trail the target boat using active sonar, which seemed to work very well. However, the use of active sonar not only made one's boat detectable to the submarine being trailed, but also, in the event of an active trail, it would most certainly be regarded by the adversary as an overt, aggressive, and threatening action. It might, furthermore, in certain circumstances, result in a torpedo or two coming our way, depending on where we were geographically and the political situation at the time. In addition, the active-ranging trailing submarine would be making itself highly detectable to ASW forces, whether another submarine, surface warship, aircraft, or fixed sonar array might be in the area. It could also make our submarine more vulnerable to any acoustic-triggered mines, including those left over from previous wars, such as the Korean War.

As the newest officer of the deck on board *Seadragon*, I was not in line to trail *Swordfish* until the wee hours of the morning. I asked Captain Steele if I could attempt to maintain continuous trail by using passive sonar only, and at the same time attempt to remain undetectable by presenting as little bow aspect as possible to *Swordfish*. Captain Steele answered, "Sure, go ahead and let's see what happens." His only provisos were that I remain at least one hundred feet below *Swordfish*'s specified depth of two hundred fifty feet and at least one thousand yards from *Swordfish* at all times. I assumed the conn and briefed all compartments, and in particular the control room, the sonar team, the fire control tracking party, and the maneuvering room on just what we would be doing. Critical to our success would be sonar's ability to inform me instantly of any changes in *Swordfish*'s course, speed, and depth. Our success would also depend heavily on the fire control tracking party's ability to continuously determine the range to *Swordfish* using passive ranging methods only.

*Swordfish* started off at ten knots and I maneuvered *Seadragon* directly astern of her so that we would be well within her baffles, making us undetectable to her passive sonar. My plan was to increase *Seadragon*'s speed sufficiently to enable us to maneuver back and forth in *Swordfish*'s wake so that the fire control party could continuously refine its solution, using passive methods, with regard to *Swordfish*'s range, course, and speed.

Swordfish did her best to shake us by using sudden changes in course and speed, including reversing course to better detect and evade us. I soon found that an excellent tactic for combating the latter and staying on her trail was to increase speed sufficiently to remain within her baffles as *Swordfish* made the turn, so that we could follow her right through the course reversal. As we became more confident in our ability to remain in contact by means of our passive sonar, I found that we could continuously trail at greater and greater ranges without losing contact. This also led to our discovery that, whenever *Swordfish* made a rapid excursion to either port or starboard, our best tactic was to immediately slow and present minimum aspect toward her, the better to evade detection as she tried to pick us out of her baffles.

Swordfish maneuvered back and forth during the next hour or so as her efforts to shake us became more violent and unpredictable toward the end of my trailing session. She never succeeded in getting away from us. At the end of the exercise, her skipper, Cdr. Ross S. Leddick, who would later be my first squadron commander during my command of USS *Queenfish* in 1969–70, sent his congratulations on the underwater telephone to whomever had the conn on *Seadragon* during the past several hours. Captain Steele immediately informed him, "It was Lt. Fred McLaren trying out a new technique for trailing." He was later to mention in my Fitness Report of 27 May 1961, "Recently Lieutenant McLaren developed a tactic hitherto believed impossible, by tracking another nuclear submarine submerged without the use of active sonar."[2] This method of trailing another submarine passively was to become, with further refinements, standard practice by the time I reported to USS *Greenling* for a several-month Cold War operation during the summer of 1968.

# CHAPTER 13

# A New Commanding Officer

We had completed a historic transpolar voyage and a series of short Cold War missions during a significant portion of the fall of 1960 and winter/spring of 1961 with an exceptional captain, Cdr. George P. Steele, whom we were all very sorry to lose. The change of command was scheduled for 27 May 1961, and officers and crew awaited the approaching date with trepidation. Our new skipper, Lt. Cdr. Charles D. Summitt, seemed pleasant enough, but no one on board had ever served with him or knew much about his reputation. We learned that he had served on the Atlantic diesel boats USS *Sea Poacher* (SS 406), USS *Ray* (SSR 271), and USS *Tirante* (SS 420), and that he had been the exec of a sister boat, USS *Sargo*, for the past year, although to the best of our knowledge he had never deployed with her or taken part in any Cold War operations.

USS *Seadragon* as one of the Pacific Fleet's newest nuclear attack submarines was scheduled to depart for a six-month deployment to the WestPac on 1 June, just four days after the change of command. With the deployment would be sure to come several two-month Cold War missions. How this new commanding officer would handle himself and a presently superb boat and well-trained, high-morale crew was foremost in our minds. I had already taken part in a number of well-conducted missions.

From waterfront talk in Pearl Harbor and in the Far East while on *Greenfish* I had learned that attack submarine captains could range from the extremely aggressive to the extremely timid. I had served with the former on *Greenfish* and with one who was aggressive but prudent on *Seadragon*. Both captains knew their boats and crews thoroughly and were competent and cool-headed in tight situations. They were skippers in whom the crew could take pride and who were pleasant to work with besides. By contrast, judging from statements by U.S. Naval Academy and Submarine School classmates, there were a few others in the Submarine Force Pacific who were overly cautious and hesitant in almost all operational situations, especially during special operations. The officers and crews of the submarines they commanded would just roll their eyes and shrug when asked, "How did it go?" upon their return to port. It was thus no surprise that both morale and the reenlistment rate were lower on these boats. What would our new commanding officer be like? Only time and events would tell during the coming year.

Our exec, Jim Strong, also slated to leave, remained on board for several more weeks. His relief, Lt. Cdr. John W. "Wes" Harvey, had just reported and needed some time to get oriented. As I recall, Jim departed during our first stop in Guam. He was another true gentleman and we hated for him to leave.

We departed for the WestPac at 10:00 a.m. on 1 June 1961. The projected return to our home port was early December, providing there was no national emergency at that time. This was my third six-month deployment in less than six years of married life and, if anything, the most difficult of the three so far. It pained me deeply that I would not only be leaving Mary, but also our five-year-old son, Fred Jr., and our seven-month-old daughter, Margot Anne. The months to come would be precious ones in their growth and development and I would be missing it all.

Leaving port and home at an unnecessarily slow speed of advance on the first day, to the tune of a Navy band, and at the beginning of another beautiful day in Hawaii, was especially hard. The midmorning hour of departure was more show for our superiors than anything else. The remaining daylight hours would then pass excruciatingly slowly as we watched Oahu and its magical mountains gradually disappear en route to our diving point. It caused me to think about what I might do one day as commanding officer to make this dreaded day somewhat easier for both the crew and their families.[1]

There was little change in established routine during the initial transit. Our new commanding officer and exec-to-be appeared to be more than happy with this. The transition from one captain to another therefore appeared seamless to both officers and crew, and we looked forward to a continuation of the partnership that Captain Steele and Exec Strong had forged.

The Steele-Strong method had been to share all pertinent information with the wardroom, senior chief petty officer, and crew, and to consult with us all when *Seadragon* was to be tasked with an unusual operation or Cold War mission. The boat was, as a result, always well prepared for the assigned mission each time we departed for sea. This method of communication with the crew was a great learning experience for us all, and especially so for us young officers who aspired to command one day.

Wes Harvey, a former U.S. Naval Academy football player, at first seemed much more extroverted than his predecessor Jim Strong. Strangely enough, though, this did not convert into improved communication between the commanding and exec and the officers, senior chief petty officers, and crew. A "gotcha" system of interacting with each officer, and with the most senior chief petty officers, came into play. The exec alternated between good guy and bad guy, while the captain became increasingly more remote and inscrutable. The effect was to create anxiety over just where we stood with each as we carried out our respective duties. The fact that there was rarely any positive feedback from the captain was in sharp contrast to what had been routine with our previous captain. I was *Seadragon's* electrical and reactor control division officer and assistant engineer officer at the time. Thankfully, my immediate superior, the engineer officer, Lt. Cdr. Al Burkhalter, shielded me from most of the consequences of this decreased communication.

The long submerged transit to Subic Bay in the Philippines was broken up by a short stop in Guam where a group of Navy nurses hosted us at several parties and seemed to enjoy singing off key together, especially "On the Road to Mandalay." Noticeable during this time in port was the captain's congeniality and sociability with all, particularly with the more senior officers. He laughed a lot and in many ways came across as a completely different person.

On arrival at Subic Bay, *Seadragon's* crew had a lengthy upkeep and a most pleasant time on shore, either at the base enlisted club, chief petty officers club, and officers club, or out in the town of Olongopo. Subic Bay was to serve as our initial WestPac home port as we rendered several-day local ASW target services on an almost continuous basis to various units of the Seventh Fleet. I can't say that we did much for the units' morale. Rarely did they ever detect us, and even then not until we were in the final stages of a simulated attack on the defended primary target, usually an aircraft carrier. Our speed, maneuverability, and quietness as one of the latest class of nuclear attack submarines were just too much for our own ASW forces of that era.

I had become aware during these local operations out of Subic Bay that the morale of *Seadragon's* more senior officers who were department heads was low. One incident stands out: We departed for sea one Monday morning without our navigator, Lieutenant M, who was a friend of mine from the days when we both served on diesel boats out of Pearl Harbor.

He had gone ashore with us the previous afternoon and spent some time with us at the Subic Bay officers club. On this occasion, however, he was uncharacteristically quiet and uncommunicative. Eventually, after more than a few drinks, he began muttering complaints about our new captain and exec, swearing that he had "to get off this boat." We tried to talk him into returning on board to get a good night's sleep. He would have none of it and, saying that he was going to go out in town, left us.

Lieutenant M did not make it back to the boat, although he was there to meet us when we returned to Subic Bay a day later. He was promptly ushered into a private meeting with the captain and exec. We never learned why he chose to miss the sailing and what might happen in the way of discipline. We did note that he was not allowed to go ashore again in Subic Bay or to join the rest of us in Hong Kong. During his remaining days on board he was rarely seen and left us permanently midway through the deployment. We were never to hear from him again. It was a sad and unnecessary occurrence in my opinion. He had been a good friend and shipmate. I believe strongly that either the captain or the exec should have detected whatever problem he was having and provided the necessary help to him before he ruined his career.

Although U.S. nuclear submarines were not themselves permitted to visit Hong Kong at that time, *Seadragon*'s crew became the first to be flown by a naval transport plane to what was then a British Crown Colony for a few days' liberty. Before departing we were all thoroughly briefed by the U.S. naval attaché, who flew over to brief us in Subic Bay on such cheery subjects as the possibility of getting kidnapped. He even told us what some of us in key jobs would be worth on the open market. I was amused to learn that, as *Seadragon*'s reactor officer, I might be worth as much as $900. We were instructed to stay in groups no matter where we went and not to strike off on our own under any circumstances. We were also discouraged from crossing over to Kowloon, which was on the Chinese mainland, and forbidden to go to the Portuguese colony of Macao. Finally, we were instructed to wear civilian clothes at all times.

A number of us had been to Kowloon before. A favorite place for a young officer to spend his time was at the magnificent old Peninsula Hotel, which probably had the most elegant high tea service in the entire world. Several hundred well-heeled Westerners, including a great number of attractive young women, frequented it. Suffice it to say, several of us ignored the instructions and spent most of every liberty hour there. The rest of our time we went shopping for tailor-made clothing for which Hong Kong was famous. We could get a Brooks Brothers–like suit or sports jacket made of the finest British fabrics in twenty-four hours, and at an unbelievably low price.

We all returned safely to our boat in Subic Bay, and those who had remained on board to stand duty in our absence were then flown over for an equal amount of time. I think most would agree that Hong Kong was every sailor's favorite liberty port during a lengthy WestPac deployment.

*Seadragon* conducted two Cold War missions of approximately eight weeks each during our deployment, one of which resulted in our completing a fifty-eight-day submerged endurance operation. Neither was memorable with regard to reconnaissance or intelligence collection. What does stand out in my memory is that our captain seemed anxious to stay as far as possible away from any Soviet naval units, whether they were submarines or surface ships. One of my primary duties during these missions was that of photographic officer, an assignment that proved unrewarding under this captain because he would never have us approach any vessel closer than 12,000 yards. As a result, my photos revealed nothing more than the basic outline of a particular submarine or surface ship—good enough to determine its class but not hull numbers, armament, antennas, or any other distinctive features. Our sonarmen were equally frustrated, for we never closed any target of significant interest sufficiently to gather acoustic information of intelligence value.

Both missions, in short, were long and boring. Although crewmembers were careful not to express their disgust out loud, word did leak out that they had given our captain a nickname, not revealed here, that aptly expressed their derision. To the best of my knowledge, neither the captain nor the exec was aware of it.

### Aircraft Reconnaissance Mission

Between *Seadragon's* two Cold War missions, while I was at sea in the Northern Pacific with Seventh Fleet ASW units, I transferred to the aircraft carrier USS *Midway* (CVA 41) for several days to take part in a flight operation. A helicopter hovered above our sail, lowered a harness, and, once I had secured myself within it, lifted—or rather yanked—me up into the air and reeled me to an open door in the side of the helicopter where several crewmembers grabbed and hauled me inside. We flew to the *Midway* and landed on her flight deck, and I exited to be met by Cdr. Frank S. Haak who would be my host during my visit. I was quickly shown where I would be berthed and given a brief tour of "officers' country" and the bridge area, where flight operations were in progress.

When mealtime came, I was turned over to two junior naval aviators who would take me to dinner in what was called the alligators mess, where all the junior officers—mostly ensigns, lieutenants junior grade, and junior lieutenants—ate their meals. It was well named, because the huge dining area seemed to be packed with ravenous junior officers. One of my escorts was a Lt. Robert J. Craig, a fellow U.S. Naval Academy graduate, class of 1956, with whom I had run the high hurdles on the track team. He was flying the Vought F8U "Crusader" on night missions at the time and confided to me how much he disliked making carrier landings at night with that aircraft. He also expressed his concern that he might not make it one night. Sadly, just three months later, his premonition was to prove true.

Following dinner, Commander Haak, who was the squadron commander of VAH-8, a heavy attack squadron, invited me to join him on a night mission in his Douglas A3D-2 Skywarrior, or Whale as it was termed by carrier aircraft handling crews because of its large size compared to other carrier aircraft and its heavy weight of up to 80,000 pounds.[2] The aircraft was a four-seat version that normally carried a pilot, copilot/navigator, radio-electronics operator, and a crew chief who handled the tail guns when installed. I would be taking the crew chief's place. The mission was to be a radar stimulation one off the coast of North Korea, and we would be collecting/recording search and fire control radar emissions plus attendant communications.

I was provided with proper flight clothing and a parachute. I changed clothes and took part in the preflight briefing, which outlined the route that would be followed, the altitude, and the possible reaction by North Korean forces that we might encounter. The briefing also included the survival procedures we should follow if we went into the water or made an emergency or crash landing somewhere. We all climbed on board the aircraft shortly before 8:00 p.m.. The A3D lacked ejection seats, and as a result A3D had come to mean "All three dead," since the only exits in the event of an emergency were a laundry chute under the fuselage, the outer door of which required manual pumping of a considerable number of strokes before it opened, and a narrow slot or escape hatch, about three feet by one foot located directly behind the pilot and copilot. I was told not to consider it, because the pilot and copilot would be using it.

The aircraft had already been preflighted, so once we were all secured in our seats and the pilot, Commander Haak, was ready, we were towed out to a launch position on the flight deck. Once securely positioned on the steam launch and ready, Haak gave a saluting signal and off we went. It was quite a jolt forward and I felt as if my stomach was back on the rudder somewhere. The aircraft took a slight dip toward the water and then began a rapid ascent toward the southeast coast of North Korea. As I recall we were there in about an hour and then flew steadily northward off the coast as various search and fire control radars acquired and tracked us and we, in turn, recorded their emissions. I have no idea what our altitude or speed was, but we must have been pushing the aircraft's ceiling of 41,000 feet and flying at something over five hundred knots. I also can't say with absolute certainty, but it seemed as if several missile batteries were launched at us. Whatever they were, their bright contrails passed well below us. It was pretty exciting as we, at times, rapidly maneuvered this way and that, and I wondered more than once just what I had gotten myself into. I would like to have asked a question or two, but it was not a time to distract any of the flight crew. Interestingly, no North Korean aircraft attempted to intercept us.

We completed the mission assigned around midnight, and headed back to the *Midway*. She certainly looked small, especially the flight deck, as we circled in preparation for landing. The sea state was not too bad, but I could see the flight deck pitching up and down. As we approached, Commander Haak, who sat directly in front of me, told me that carrier aircraft make from time to time something called a bolter, which means an aborted landing because the tail hook didn't catch or the aircraft was too high, or not lined up correctly, for a safe landing, or other scenario. If such occurred, the pilot would give the aircraft full throttle, climb away, and circle for another attempt.

Then it happened: Our A3D Skywarrior seemed to make a perfect landing, but its tail hook didn't catch any of the three arresting wires that crossed the flight deck. Commander Haak applied full throttle, and we blasted off and circled for another try.

Our second landing again seemed perfect, but before the tail hook caught a wire, the copilot yelled, "Power! Power!" to Commander Haak, and we blasted off again. The ensuing discussion between the pilot and copilot indicated serious disagreement over the need to abort the landing.

I found myself eyeing the escape chute, wondering how it would work under water as the aircraft was slowly sinking. Not very well, I decided. I completely unbuckled my chest-mounted parachute and decided that, if need be, I would follow the pilot and copilot through the escape hatch behind them.

We lined up for a third try, and Commander Haak made a perfect landing on *Midway's* flight deck with the second arresting wire catching the A3D's tail hook. The sighs of relief within the cockpit were audible. Commander Haak then shared the information that we did not have enough fuel for a fourth try, and a water landing would have been our only option if the tail hook had not engaged. I later learned that a final arresting barrier could have been used, but this was never mentioned.

We were welcomed back by a crowd of concerned officers and crewmembers, including *Midway's* commanding officer and several other senior captains. They soon went off with Commander Haak and the copilot/navigator to talk privately, while the rest of us went down below for something to eat and drink. I was not to see Commander Haak or the copilot again before I left via helicopter the next day to return to *Seadragon*, but I would have given anything to have attended the debrief of that mission.

Within minutes of boarding the helicopter next morning, we were hovering above *Seadragon's* sail. Returning on board was not as simple as leaving, however, since the seas had picked up and the boat was rolling approximately 10 degrees from port to starboard. As the helicopter continued to hover, I was gradually lowered in a harness to a position just above the bridge cockpit and then suddenly dropped into the arms of several lookouts when the cockpit passed directly beneath me. My harness was quickly removed and reeled back into the helicopter as it gained altitude and moved away. Relieved to be safely back on board, I had no further interest in learning what life on an aircraft carrier was like during that or any future deployment.

## Subic Bay and the Long Transit Home

We made two more brief upkeep and liberty stops in Subic Bay during the late summer and fall. These were interspersed with more ASW services, this time as a submarine target to Seventh Fleet units, before we headed for home and our families and friends after almost six months.

As we began the long transit to Pearl Harbor, *Seadragon's* captain and exec came up with the questionable idea of delaying our return home by upward of three days so that we could undergo some additional training during the long voyage home. The request to our squadron commander and to our overall boss, ComSubPac, was kept secret from the crew and all but the navigator and the engineer. Nonetheless, rumor of what was planned quickly spread through the boat as it invariably does on any submarine. I was shocked that the captain and exec would even contemplate such action, and I asked the exec privately if there was anything to it. He confirmed that the request had been made and further stated that the time would be devoted to the much-needed engineering drills that we had not had time to accomplish during the WestPac deployment. I whistled and shook my head in disbelief. I pointed out the negative impact this was certain to have on the morale of a crew anxious to get home to their wives and families after such a long separation. The exec shrugged and waved me away, signaling that our conversation was at an end. Boy, did that cause my own morale to sink. Our only hope now was that our bosses, World War II submarine aces and veterans who well understood the importance of keeping crew morale high, would say, "Hell no, come home at best speed!" The gods surely smiled on us, because this is exactly what happened several days later. Word leaked out of radio the minute the message came in from ComSubPac, producing universal smiles of relief.

Several of us surmised that our request was seen as an ill-thought-out attempt on the part of our captain and exec to ingratiate themselves with their superiors, including Admiral Rickover, at the expense of the crew. The whole matter greatly eroded our trust in the captain and exec, who should have had the well-being of the crew and their families foremost in their minds.

We made it home safe and sound in late November 1961 and had it easy as the boat entered a three-week-long upkeep. I was made acting engineer at this time, while the engineer, Al Burkhalter, went on leave. All hands were allowed some much-needed time off to relax and spend with their families. Following the upkeep, we once again engaged in local submarine-versus-submarine operations and the rendering of target services to ASW units stationed in the area.

## Seadragon's Officers and Crew Put to the Test

An unpleasant surprise was to greet us shortly after Thanksgiving when we learned that a group from Naval Reactors in Washington, DC, would be arriving in early December to give *Seadragon's* nuclear-trained officers and crewmembers one of the first reactor safety exams by Naval Reactors. All of us were to be subjected to rigorous oral examinations pertaining not only to basic nuclear power plant theory, but also to all aspects of safely operating our S-4-W nuclear reactor. The exercises would cover all supporting systems, such as primary and secondary water, steam generators and turbines, electrical, primary water chemistry, and radiation protection. Our retention of everything we had learned earlier in Nuclear Power School and at the land-based nuclear power plant prototype on which we each trained would be subject to scrutiny. I don't think any of us would have argued against the exams. The time proved, however, to be difficult and frustrating for all. None of us did very well. The fact that we had forgotten a great deal became obvious to the examining team. No doubt this was quickly relayed back to Admiral Rickover who, I am sure, wasted no time in conveying his displeasure to our captain.

We learned during the following months that the officers and crews of all fully operational nuclear submarines had undergone similar examinations, with results that were pretty much the same throughout the Atlantic and Pacific. Admiral Rickover and his staff thus rightfully concluded that all nuclear submarine crews should be periodically examined, both with regard to basic theory and in the demonstration of safe nuclear power plant operation in port and at sea, including demonstrated safe response to and recovery from a prescribed series of casualty drills. It would be a number of years before a formal operational reactor safeguards examination was put into place. Strangely enough, I was not to experience another such examination until early 1970, when I was already in command of USS *Queenfish*.

The first months of 1962 kept *Seadragon* participating in a series of prospective commanding officer exercises during which each group of commanding officer trainees was required to fire a number of exercise torpedoes with plaster/dummy warheads that were not explosive-loaded. Mk-14-5 steam-propelled torpedoes were fired at surface targets, and electrically propelled Mk-37-0 acoustic-homing torpedoes were fired at other submarines during the course of their at-sea training.

I had just become weapons officer at the time, and I recall that, although the Mk-14-5 torpedoes performed reliably, we seemed to have endless problems with the electrically propelled Mk-37-0 torpedoes. Besides having a relatively slow speed and limited range both geographically and acoustically, this torpedo either failed to start up and swim out of the tube on firing, or failed to acquire the target acoustically during what appeared to be a perfect fire-control solution and torpedo run. This led to frustration and finger pointing: *Seadragon* was faulted for probable poor torpedo maintenance and checkouts. The prospective commanding officers were criticized for poor target motion analysis and inappropriate torpedo settings.

We on *Seadragon* soon discovered, and reported, that the anticircular run shutdown, which is designed to prevent a submarine from being hit by its own torpedo, on many of the Mk-37-0 exercise torpedoes we received activated as soon as the torpedo was powered up. This plus the deficiencies cited earlier were proving to be a major problem in all Pacific and Atlantic submarines. Ours was not the only one reporting. This and many other frustrations, such as slow speed and limited range both geographically and acoustically, were to take another decade to resolve.

### One Helluva Close Call

It was early in the evening during the late spring of 1962, and *Seadragon* was submerged in deep water in one of the more distant Hawaiian submarine operating areas. We were there for the sole purpose of testing a prototype passive low-frequency sonar suite, called the sound data gathering equipment (SDGE). This system would enable nuclear attack submarines to detect and track very distant contacts of interest. Navigationally and tactically, we couldn't be better positioned for this exercise, since we were in the near proximity of several major shipping and military traffic lanes across the Pacific Ocean.

At the time I was the weapons officer and the only officer who had been with *Seadragon* since her final months in Portsmouth during the early summer of 1960. I was also the only officer remaining who had taken part in her Atlantic-to-Pacific voyage via the Northwest Passage and the North Pole. At this point, therefore, I was the most experienced officer, having served as supply and commissary officer, missile guidance officer, reactor officer, electrical division officer, damage control assistant and diving officer, main propulsion assistant, and acting engineer for several months. I had additionally participated in an almost-six-month deployment to WestPac during the summer and fall of 1961 and had taken part in Cold War operations assigned to *Seadragon* since the fall of 1960.

*Seadragon* was on station and essentially at all stop. The diving officer was in the final stages of trimming the boat for neutral buoyancy at a depth that would be optimum. Were we on Cold War patrol using SDGE, the fit would have been perfect for passive acoustic detection of low-frequency emissions—broadband, narrow band, and transient—from both surfaced and submerged targets of interest. The battle stations watch section, made up of our most experienced crewmembers, had completed relieving the regular submerged operations watch section, and a condition of patrol-quiet pertained throughout the boat. Ultra-quiet was to follow once the diving officer, Lieutenant P, felt he had achieved a state of buoyancy such that *Seadragon* could hover at a depth of 350 feet for lengthy periods without the need to initiate noise-generating actions like pumping or flooding water from and to the boat's variable ballast tanks. The goal tonight was to ensure that no shipboard noise of any sort was generated that might interfere with optimum performance of the equipment to be tested. Ideally, we wanted a condition where, by not radiating noise of any sort, *Seadragon* would be quieter than the surrounding sea state.

The diving officer reported, "Three hundred and fifty feet, trim satisfactory!," to the officer of the deck, who responded, "Very well." "Rig for ultra-quiet! Rig for ultra-quiet!" was then passed over the sound-powered phones to all compartments.

For a sonar test of the kind *Seadragon* was about to conduct, it was necessary to fully shut down the nuclear reactor. Essential rotating equipment, such as the priming pumps for the trim and drain systems throughout the boat, had to be secured.[3] All nonessential equipment was to be shut down as well. Crewmembers not on watch or test-monitoring positions were to repair either to their bunks or to the crews mess. They were to remain there until further ordered. They could not even use one of the boat's three heads. All hands, of course, remained free to move and take whatever action was necessary if an actual emergency suddenly developed like flooding or fire.

Once ultra-quiet was achieved, all compartment bilges were confirmed dry or pumped dry, and *Seadragon* was at a very stable degree of neutral buoyancy, we were ready to take the next step. The command watch officer, who was the exec, would be supervising the operation. He directed the officer of the deck to establish an even more austere condition of quietness throughout the boat, called super-quiet, to support the SDGE sonar test.[4]

Once the foregoing had been completed, the diving officer had the difficult task of maintaining the boat in a neutrally buoyant condition and on depth for whatever length of time was required, ordinarily two to three hours, to test the capabilities of the SDGE system. If suction was lost on the trim and drain pumps, and depth control was subsequently lost, only *Seadragon*'s two battery-powered emergency propulsion motors would be instantly available to drive both propeller shafts to regain depth control. This was with the understanding that an overall speed of no more than four to five knots could be attained. If more speed were required, either upward to the surface or downward through test and crush depths, serious loss of depth control could be countered only if the diving officer recognized the situation and took quick action. He would call for immediately flooding the variable ballast tanks or he would initiate a partial or full blow of high-pressure air to all MBTs to prevent what could be a catastrophic depth change. The great danger of loss of depth control is that it can rapidly accelerate, possibly leading to collision with a ship on the surface or, conversely, passing through crush depth and imploding. In summary, *Seadragon*, or any other nuclear submarine of that era, was in an exceedingly vulnerable and potentially unsafe condition whenever tests of the SDGE and similar experimental sonar equipments were conducted.

The condition of super-quiet and near-perfect neutral buoyancy at a depth of 350 feet was achieved by approximately 9:30 that evening. The SDGE sonar test was commenced and so reported by the officer of the deck to the command watch officer (exec) on the scene and to the captain who, mysteriously, was in his stateroom with the door closed, just forward of *Seadragon's* control room.

Although the captain had been in command for well over a year, his knowledge of *Seadragon's* capabilities and limitations, not to mention his expressed knowledge of submarine operations in general, had not inspired a great deal of confidence in his abilities or in his determination to ensure our general well-being and safety should we suddenly find ourselves in an operational emergency or a Cold War suddenly grown hot. Our lives were in his hands, yet he remained largely an enigma. We were about to conduct a completely unfamiliar and high-risk operation. Certainly the captain's reputation with the crew was not helped on this particular evening by his already being in bed, or so we assumed.

With the exception of the chief of the boat and a number of senior chief petty officers who had chosen to hang around the control room, those men not needed in their particular battle stations position were either in their bunks or in the crews mess. So too were several officers not on duty, with the exception of a few of us in the wardroom.

About an hour and a half into the test, a messenger rushed in and whispered to me excitedly, "Lieutenant, lieutenant, the chief of the watch requests you come to the control room immediately!" I hurried after him. As I entered the control room, I saw alarm on the faces of all the enlisted watch standers, particularly the chief of the watch and the auxiliary man of the watch, who was operating the high-pressure air manifold.

The chief of the watch, with a gesture, directed my attention to the depth gauge above the planes and helmsmen. It indicated we were well below the 350-foot depth called for by the test and just twenty feet short of *Seadragon's* test depth of seven hundred feet. It was obvious the boat was sinking at an accelerating rate of descent. The auxiliary man of the watch already had his hands on the high-pressure air valves as he anxiously awaited a command from someone to "Blow all main ballast tanks!" The diving officer, the officer of the deck, and the exec, who was acting as command watch officer, on the other hand, appeared eerily calm considering the condition of extremis that *Seadragon* was rapidly entering.

The diving officer was attempting to use the drain pump, ordinarily used as a back-up to the trim pump, to pump water from the trim tanks to sea in order to check the boat's downward descent and regain positive buoyancy. As I moved into the control room, he looked at me saying, "The trim pump doesn't work either!" I immediately reminded all within earshot that suction had in all probability been lost on both these critically important pumps because their respective priming pumps had been defused as part of the rig for super-quiet. I turned toward the exec and officer of the deck and said, "I strongly recommend that you blow all main ballast tanks *now!*" At the same time I recommended they immediately inform the commanding officer of the situation.

Amazingly, there was no reaction or response from either officer. They appeared to be mesmerized by the increasingly dangerous predicament that *Seadragon* was in. In the meantime, the expressions on the faces of the chief of the watch and the auxiliary man of the watch were agonized, pleading for some forceful corrective action to be taken at once.

Since there was no time to lose, I stepped in as *Seadragon's* senior watch officer and ordered, "Blow all main ballast tanks!" I picked up the 1MC mike and ordered, "Maneuvering, conn, make maximum turns on the EPMs [emergency propulsion motors]!" I followed this with, "Maneuvering, conn, commence emergency reactor startup!"

The engineering officer of the watch in the maneuvering room acknowledged and repeated both orders to the engineering watch who instantly responded. Even so, *Seadragon* continued to sink below test depth.

I then used the 1MC to pass the word: "Captain to the conn! Captain to the conn!" We were now at a depth of almost seven hundred fifty feet, fifty feet below test depth, with no indication that the actions I had ordered were going to arrest, much less reverse, our rapid descent. *Seadragon's* hull was beginning to make loud cracking and groaning noises. Small seawater leaks were being reported from throughout the boat. As we continued to descend, I made status reports to the captain via a messenger and another urgent request, "Captain to the control room! Captain to the control room!" over the 1MC system.

As we passed seven hundred eighty feet, en route to our still-classified crush depth, *Seadragon*'s descent began to slow ever so gradually. Finally, at just short of eight hundred feet, or one hundred feet below test depth, we briefly paused and then began to ascend very slowly. By this time everyone's knees were shaking. Still, to my utter consternation, the captain had yet to make an appearance. Moreover, neither the exec nor the officer of the deck had moved or even made a sound up to this point. They seemed not to have emerged from their mesmerized state. As we slowly passed through 730 feet on the way up, the engineering officer of the watch reported, "Reactor critical!" He further reported that the engineering watch had commenced an emergency warm-up of the ship's service and main propulsion turbine generators and that he expected maneuvering would be ready to answer all bells (main propulsion orders) in a few minutes.

I then ordered, "Secure from super-quiet! Secure from super-quiet!" I further directed the engineering officer of the watch to restore all equipment and systems secured for the SDGE sonar test to full operation as soon as possible. The diving officer was ordered to take charge of the dive and to do all he could with the bow and stern planes to slow our ascent.

"Take charge of the dive! Make your depth 150 feet!" I ordered. "Take charge of the dive! Make your depth 150 feet!" the diving officer responded. The diving officer of the watch now had speed control and initially ordered maneuvering to make turns for sixteen knots as soon as possible. Maneuvering acknowledged the command and began to provide a steadily increasing amount of main propulsion power.

The dire operational situation up to this point had not afforded us an opportunity to launch a series of emergency red flares to warn off any ships that might be in the vicinity. The key question of concern now was whether we would have main propulsion power back in sufficient time to level *Seadragon* off at a safe depth of at least one hundred feet below the surface. Sonar had been actively searching for indications of close contacts and reported none. We still could not be sure that the surface was completely clear above us, even so, since we were not yet able to safely change course and to clear our baffles to check for contacts astern of us. My concern about the possibility of inadvertently colliding with a contact on the surface above us intensified as *Seadragon* began to ascend more rapidly.

Shortly after beginning the ascent I directed an officer, who had entered the control room a few minutes earlier to assist, to check on the status of the captain. I asked him to determine, if he could, why the captain had not been able to come to the control room during the emergency. The officer soon returned, reporting that the captain was still in bed.

I glanced at the exec to note his reaction, but he just shrugged his shoulders and looked away. In the meantime, with the steadily decreasing water density and the regain of main propulsion power, *Seadragon's* ascent finally began to slow. As we approached a depth of two hundred feet, I felt confident enough to order the MBT vents cycled several times and then left open. It was clear it was not going to be possible to level off at one hundred fifty feet, so I next ordered, "Make your depth one hundred feet!" "Make your depth one hundred feet!" the diving officer responded.

A subsequent burst of speed thanks to our newly regained main propulsion enabled the diving officer to level the boat off smartly at one hundred feet. The diving officer now proceeded to trim the boat to achieve neutral buoyancy in combination with judicious decreasing of speed as we remained at depth. We cleared baffles to ensure that the surface overhead was all clear prior to continuing on to periscope depth.

"No close contacts!" reported sonar several minutes later. "Up periscope!" called the exec, who had been taking a more active interest in our recovery since we had begun our ascent. I continued in the role of officer of the deck, which I had so abruptly taken over earlier. The diving officer soon reported, "Trim satisfactory!"

The exec searched the surface overhead for signs of nearby contacts or obstacles with which we might collide. As we continued to clear baffles to search astern, sonar confirmed his earlier report of "No close contacts!" The exec next ordered, "Six five feet smartly! Make turns for three knots!"

*Seadragon* proceeded to plane smoothly up to periscope depth without incident. The exec made a series of rapid 360-degree low- and high-power periscope searches and reported, "No surface or air contacts!" He then turned the periscope, and watch, over to me and proceeded out of the control room to confer, for want of a better term, with the captain. Radio began to copy our broadcast as we continued to complete securing from an unusually exciting SDGE sonar test. The boat was restored to patrol-quiet normalcy. We remained at periscope depth at minimum turns in our assigned exercise area until early morning. How the overall results of the special sonar test were going to be reported to our superiors was anyone's guess.

The captain had yet to appear in the control room, much less do anything more than just acknowledge, without question or comment, the continuous stream of reports he had been receiving via the sound-powered telephones since the emergency first developed. He had offered nothing at any time in the way of advice or orders. Certainly the more senior of us wondered if he had had a stroke or similar debilitating medical emergency.

He did not appear again until breakfast, looking perfectly normal, as if nothing undue had happened. It was quite evident, however, that he had no interest in talking about the previous evening's events. One would do so only at his peril. Since the subject remained uppermost in everyone else's mind, the wardroom atmosphere was subdued as we officers quietly finished breakfast. En route to Pearl Harbor, the exec made it clear to all that upon our return to port, absolutely nothing was to be said about what had transpired during the SDGE sonar test.

We remained in port for another week or so of routine shipboard maintenance, and life went on as before. What we had just gone through was truly the stuff of nightmares, and definitely trauma producing, yet we all acted as if none of us had come as close as we had to losing our boat and our lives.

Four days after the event, a messenger informed me that the captain wanted to see me in his stateroom immediately. I knocked and, upon his response, entered. He asked me to close the door and then, to my utter astonishment, proceeded to dress me down severely for, as he termed it, "arbitrarily taking over the watch" during the course of the SDGE sonar test. I listened incredulously and with mounting outrage as he continued to chew me out for saving *Seadragon* from complete disaster. Wisely I kept my tongue and temper. As soon as the captain had finished, I left his stateroom and the boat and walked several piers down to where *Seadragon's* previous exec, Jim Strong, had recently taken command of a diesel boat. He was awaiting orders to a new nuclear attack submarine being constructed at Portsmouth Naval Shipyard.

Fortunately, he was on board. A crewmember topside ushered me down to the captain's stateroom. Once the door was closed, I poured out all that had occurred during *Seadragon's* recent period at sea. I concluded with the statement that I wanted to get off the submarine as soon as possible and asked if he could help me. Strong was a true professional and a gentleman. After asking a few questions, he said he would see what he could do and I was not to worry or do anything rash. Within a week I received dispatch orders to the submarine *Jack* (SSN 605), that our old exec, Jim Strong, was to take command of. I was to be detached the following month and, following thirty days' leave, join her new construction crew.

Not surprisingly, this did not sit well with either my commanding officer or the exec. Despite their best efforts to get them rescinded, the orders appeared firm and unchangeable. To the best of my knowledge, the two never found out how this sudden receipt of orders came about.

My family and I departed *Seadragon* and Pearl Harbor as scheduled in late May 1962 via the wonderful old Matson luxury liner *Lurline*, en route to San Francisco. There, we picked up a new car and leisurely drove across the continent to Portsmouth via Bangor, Washington, where my father, Dad McLaren, commanded the Naval Ammunition Depot and the Naval Torpedo Station at Keyport, and then via the Trans-Canadian Highway.

### *Seadragon's* Demise

On her second Arctic expedition during the summer of 1962, *Seadragon* was joined by USS *Skate*, coming from the Atlantic. They rendezvoused under the vast Arctic Ocean ice pack on 31 July, and both boats surfaced together at the North Pole on 2 August. *Seadragon* returned once more to the Arctic Ocean for classified operations in 1973.

*Seadragon* was to make twelve more six-month deployments to the WestPac. During this time she was to become the first U.S. nuclear submarine to visit Hong Kong, enter Japanese home waters to visit Sasebo and Yokosuka, and visit Hobart, Tasmania. She also earned a Meritorious Unit Citation for Cold War operations during 1975.[5]

By the time she was decommissioned on 12 June 1984, she had steamed over 200,000 nautical miles and conducted some 1,800 dives and surfacings.[6] *Seadragon* was stricken from the Navy list on 30 April 1986 and then languished for eight years at the Puget Sound Naval Shipyard at Bremerton, Washington, until she entered the Navy's Nuclear Powered Surface Ship and Submarine Recycling Program on 1 October 1994. This beautiful boat finished the program and ceased to exist on 18 September 1995.[7]

# PART III

## USS *Skipjack* (SSN 585)

### Root of the New Sea Power

Launch of USS *Skipjack* (SSN 585). *U.S. Navy*

# CHAPTER 14

# First Months on Board

The third attack submarine I was to serve on board, from the summer of 1962 until the late spring of 1965, was USS *Skipjack* (SSN 585), named for a fierce, deep-water, steel-blue game fish known for its speed and aggressiveness. How did I end up on *Skipjack* when I previously had orders during the spring of 1962 to report to the new-construction submarine, *Jack?* *Jack* was a later *Permit*-class nuclear attack submarine, slated to be under the command of the former exec of *Seadragon* and my good friend, Cdr. Jim Strong. As summer approached, my family and I were in the final stages of preparing for our move from Pearl Harbor to Portsmouth. Within days of my detachment from *Seadragon*, however, I received a call from the submarine officer detailer. He told me that the construction and subsequent launch date of *Jack* were to be delayed significantly. I was, therefore, to "skip the *Jack* and report to USS *Skipjack* (SSN 585)." Conveniently, *Skipjack* was also in Kittery where she was midway through an extensive overhaul.

Three U.S. Navy submarines that bore the name lived up to the *Skipjack's* reputation: The first, also known as the *E-1*, was commissioned on 14 February 1912, with Lt. Chester W. Nimitz in command.[1] The first submarine to use diesel engines, she made a transatlantic crossing en route to her World War I patrol area off the Azores to test submerged radio communications. The second *Skipjack* (SS 184), commissioned in 1938, was in Manila Bay at the advent of World War II. She made ten war patrols under eight commanding officers, earning seven battle stars and sinking six Japanese ships, including a destroyer with a "down the throat shot" for a total of 43,738 tons. Her most famous captain was James W. Coe, who was awarded the Navy Cross.

The modern *Skipjack* was the first of a new class of six single-screw nuclear attack submarines that included *Scamp* (SSN 588), the ill-fated *Scorpion* (SSN 589), *Sculpin* (SSN 590), *Shark* (SSN 591), and *Snook* (SSN 592). Her overall characteristics were as follows:

- Displacement: 3,124 tons surfaced, 3,569 tons submerged
- Length overall: 251.7 feet
- Beam: 31 feet 7 inches
- Draft: 29 feet 5 inches
- Propulsion system: One Westinghouse S-5-W nuclear reactor plant
- Propeller: One five-bladed
- Speed on surface: 20+ knots
- Speed submerged: 33 knots
- Range: Unlimited
- Endurance submerged: Unlimited
- Armament: Six 21-inch torpedo tubes, all forward
- Crew: 8 officers and 85 enlisted[2]

This new class combined the tear drop–shaped hull of the experimental USS *Albacore* (AGSS 569), which significantly reduced underwater resistance with a third-generation Westinghouse nuclear power plant.[3] The power plant's two steam turbines were able, with a single, massive, fifteen-foot-diameter, five-bladed screw, to produce a maximum of 15,000-shaft horsepower. The usual forward-mounted bow planes were moved to her sail, and subway straps were mounted in her control room for us to use during high-speed turns and depth excursions. All told, *Skipjack* was a highly maneuverable nuclear attack submarine with a submerged speed that far exceeded her *Nautilus*-, *Seawolf*-, and four *Skate*-class predecessors.

*Skipjack*, in effect, was a high-speed underwater airplane that seemed to be able to fly through the water and reverse course almost within her own ship length. Most of us in the submarine force were aware that she had made the fastest submerged transit of the Atlantic on record, en route to the Mediterranean during her shakedown cruise in 1959, but no one really knew at exactly what speed. I fully believed that *Skipjack* was capable of making speeds in excess of forty-five knots.

*Skipjack*'s keel was laid at General Dynamics Corporation, Electric Boat Division, Groton, Connecticut, on 29 May 1956. She was launched on 26 May two years later and commissioned on 15 April 1959. With her superior hydrodynamic shape, devoid of any superstructure except for a huge sail that protruded like a shark fin from the hull, *Skipjack* was soon setting all kinds of undersea speed records, beginning with her initial sea trials in March 1958. Her actual top speed, however, has remained a secret known only to her crews. By the time I reported on board in July 1962, during her extensive overhaul in the Portsmouth Naval Shipyard, Kittery, Maine, she was already the first nuclear submarine to have passed through the Strait of Gibraltar to operate in the Mediterranean. In addition, she had earned a Navy Unit Commendation and her first Battle Efficiency "E" awards for a mysterious and apparently successful Cold War mission, accomplished under her first skipper, World War II six-war-patrol veteran and Silver Star holder, William W. Behrens Jr.

Admiral of the Fleet, the Earl Mountbatten of Burma visits USS *Skipjack* (SSN 585) accompanied by Vice Adm. Hyman G. Rickover, Rear Adm. Frederick B. Warder, and Lt. Cdr. William W. Behrens Jr., commanding officer of *Skipjack* (SSN 585). *U.S. Navy*

*Skipjack*'s second commanding officer, relieving Lt. Cdr. William W. Behrens Jr. (later rear admiral) in December of 1960, and the one to whom I reported, was a former Vanderbilt and U.S. Naval Academy football player, Cdr. Leslie D. "Les" Kelly Jr. A tall, genial, and powerfully built man, he was one of the first three officers that Admiral Rickover chose for the nuclear power program. Commander Kelly had previously commanded USS *Trigger*

(SS 564) and been chief engineer during the construction and commissioning of what was then, at an overall length of 447 feet, the world's largest submarine, USS *Triton* (SSRN 586). *Triton* was the only U.S. submarine to be powered by two nuclear power plants; it had originally been intended to serve the fleet as a radar picket submarine.

During 1961 *Skipjack* took part in a series of exercises, both independently and with surface antisubmarine units. These exercises were aimed at evaluating rapidly evolving nuclear submarine tactics and doctrine, and at teaching ASW forces how to combat a high-speed nuclear submarine. As can be imagined, *Skipjack* with her high-speed advantage and extreme maneuverability proved herself invulnerable to a successful attack of any type. I was told of an occasion under Captain Behren's command where an acoustic homing exercise torpedo had been launched against *Skipjack*. Behrens allowed the torpedo to acoustically acquire the boat. He then immediately increased speed to flank, and the torpedo led right back toward the original firing U.S. ASW ship. The torpedo subsequently acquired and struck that ship. *Skipjack* had been deployed on a second Cold War mission for several months during the early summer of 1961. She finished the year taking part in further, more-advanced exercises with antisubmarine units of the Atlantic Fleet.

I was initially disappointed at being diverted from *Jack*, but soon became intrigued, if not downright pleased and awed, to be ordered to an operational high-performance attack submarine like *Skipjack* as prospective auxiliary division officer and diving officer. More exciting was the prospect of becoming part of *Skipjack*'s legendary crew. Her radio call sign was a sexy "Starfire," and her motto a most appropriate Radix Nova Tridentis (Root of the new sea power).

As it turned out, I was one of four new officers to report on board this nuclear sub at the same time. The others were Lt. William T. "Ted" Hussey (later commander) and Lt. Ronald M. "Ron" Eytchison (eventually vice admiral), followed by Lt. Bernard M. "Bud" Kauderer (later lieutenant commander, eventually vice admiral), who would relieve the chief engineer, Lt. Robert W. "Bob" Chewning (later lieutenant commander, eventually rear admiral). Bob immediately fleeted up to exec, relieving a real character, Lt. Cdr. Robert H. Weeks, nicknamed Crusader Rabbit, for reasons that can only be guessed at. Weeks, interestingly, would then depart for *Seadragon* where he would relieve Wes Harvey, who would become commanding officer of USS *Thresher* (SSN 593), also in Kittery for overhaul, once he had completed Admiral Rickover's prospective commanding officers course at his headquarters in Washington, DC. We remaining three lieutenants relieved officers who were scheduled either to leave the submarine force for the civilian world or to go on to various new-construction submarine billets.

I had the pleasure of relieving an old friend and fellow 13th Company U.S. Naval Academy classmate, Lt. William E. "Bill" McCarron Jr., as auxiliary division and diving officer. These would prove to be the most challenging jobs on such a high-performance and complex submarine as *Skipjack*. The auxiliary division was essentially responsible for all the ship control equipments and hydraulic systems relating to operating her, both submerged and on the surface. In addition, the submarine's air conditioning and refrigeration systems, and all atmosphere-control systems, including two new oxygen generators, were to fall under my purview. Bill had already been admitted to medical school and was eager to be on his way, but he took the necessary time to ensure that I had a thorough grasp of my new responsibilities. We then reported to *Skipjack*'s commanding officer, Captain Kelly, to inform him I was ready in all respects to relieve Bill.

We had no sooner knocked on the door and stated the purpose of our visit than the captain began to ask me a number of detailed questions. He wanted to know whether I truly understood my responsibilities as auxiliary division officer and *Skipjack*'s diving officer. The questioning ranged over the many equipments and systems in various states of overhaul and repair. I recall that my two greatest concerns, and the questions that I had considerable difficulty answering, were those pertaining to the two new oxygen generators. No one on board, including me, had ever had any operational experience with them. The other was ensuring that a very toxic, experimental hydraulic fluid was successfully replaced with the standard fluid used by the rest of the submarine force.

As *Skipjack*'s diving officer, I would be responsible for her safe and completely in-control handling during high-speed maneuvers and depth excursions. I would also have to ensure that when we returned to sea for our first test dives, the boat would be ballasted such that we were neither too heavy nor too light. *Skipjack* had to be capable of safely submerging and being brought to a neutral buoyancy condition very quickly. How was this to be achieved? By keeping close track of the weight and effect, fore and aft, of everything that was removed or added to *Skipjack* during the course of the yard overhaul. Since she had already been in the shipyard for over five months, I had to start with the essentially unverifiable ballasting or weight and balance records that had been kept up to that time. I not only had to backtrack looking for errors or omissions, but I also had to keep up-to-date on a day-to-day basis. A worst-case scenario would be to depart for sea trials tens of thousands of pounds heavy and not know it, in which case *Skipjack* would probably plow into the bottom during the initial test dive. The converse would be to depart for sea in a too-light condition and not be able to submerge. That would be profoundly embarrassing. It would not, however, be as potentially fatal as the former, particularly if the depth of the sea-trial area exceeded *Skipjack's* crush depth.

Since I had been diving officer on both *Greenfish* and *Seadragon*, I was experienced to the degree that I was probably a little cocky upon reporting on *Skipjack*. I will never forget the mortifying exchange that happened several days after I assumed my new duties. Commander Kelly invited me into the wardroom for a cup of coffee and asked some thoughtful questions concerning the settlement and comfort of my family in the Kittery area. He then suddenly asked me, "Fred what are your plans for our initial test dive? How do you plan to ballast the boat?"

Like an idiot, I confidently stated something to effect that I planned to go as our initial ballasting calculations indicated. This would have been with no additional or precautionary ballasting just in case our figures were off. The captain just smiled, and the conversation wandered on to other subjects.

I had no sooner departed the wardroom than I said to myself, "What utter stupidity. What is to be gained by not taking additional precautions when it is completely appropriate? On what basis can anyone ever be completely sure of the accuracy of ballasting figures kept by both shipyard and ship during a lengthy shipyard overhaul?" So, hat in hand, I returned to the wardroom area and knocked on the captain's door. When Captain Kelley opened it, I blurted out, "Belay my last, captain. We will ballast *Skipjack* at least 20,000 pounds light before we make our first dive." The captain grinned broadly, slapped me on the back, and said, "Good!"

I walked away feeling like a complete ass but vastly relieved, knowing I had done the right thing. At the same time, I had more properly set the tone for my working relationship with my new captain. Submarining has never been a profession where chances or shortcuts of any sort are appropriate just for the sake of expediency or pride. There was clearly no operational need for pride and the stakes, beginning with the basic safety of the crew, were too high. The pressures of a Cold War operation or combat at sea were one thing, but our present job was to get *Skipjack* to sea in such condition that we could later confidently push her to the limits operationally whenever the occasion demanded.

*Skipjack's* overhaul proceeded like most: slow, tedious, frustrating, and exceedingly demanding of both officers and crew. In addition to maintaining complete control of the nuclear power plant and all related systems in a shutdown condition, our job was to monitor and work closely with Portsmouth Naval Shipyard personnel on all tasks. This was to ensure that all of *Skipjack's* myriad equipments and systems were repaired, modified, or upgraded as appropriate and as safely and expeditiously as possible. Offices, communication facilities, and berthing were set up for us on a nearby barge such that ready access could be had to our boat at all times. The crew and officers operated on a twenty-four-hour watch and monitoring schedule seven days a week during the overhaul.

Once all required shipyard work had been accomplished on a particular equipment or system—air, liquid, hydraulic, or electrical—it was ready for testing. After completing the tests successfully, we accepted and took control of that equipment or system. Its safe operation was then our responsibility for the remainder of the overhaul and at-sea operations thereafter.

My family and I passed a pleasant couple of months in Kittery, which included some enjoyable wardroom social events. When the overhaul was completed later in the fall of 1962 I planned to relocate my family to Navy housing in Groton, Connecticut, near *Skipjack's* home port of New London. After two years in Hawaii, we had become thoroughly acclimated to island life and had forgotten how muggy it was during a typical summer in New England. We very much missed the tropical beauty and cool breezes of Hawaii, and the more casual and leisurely lifestyle.

During the week, when not slated for the watch or a special testing schedule, most of the crew and officers lived and slept on the barge moored alongside the boat at Kittery, then drove south to New London or Groton to spend the weekend with our families. My memories are those of a completely torn-up submarine interior, constant machinery and mechanical tool noise, dust everywhere, and the overwhelming smell of oil, paint, and human sweat. We were treated to portable radios endlessly blaring music, mostly the two pop songs "Monster Mash" and "Witch Doctor." I recall with amusement how our exec, Bob Chewning, when sleeping on the barge, would get up in the middle of the night to use the head and invariably run into the adjacent bulkhead with a loud *thud* and groan. We had a ship's picnic or two and enjoyed an occasional lunch or happy hour at the officers club, but all in all the period was constant and seemingly unending drudgery. We couldn't wait to get back to sea.

It was under Captain Kelly's superb mentorship that I began to mature and truly thrive as a submarine officer, subsequently qualifying as command of submarines and as engineer. He was later, as submarine detail officer in the Bureau of Personnel, U.S. Navy Department, in Washington, DC, to have a profound effect on my future as an exclusively nuclear attack submariner: in 1963 he positioned me to become *Skipjack*'s engineer officer and later the commissioning exec of the first of the new *Sturgeon*-class nuclear attack submarines to go to sea, USS *Queenfish*.

### The Cuban Missile Crisis and Another Near Miss

The original best estimate for *Skipjack*'s final departure from the Portsmouth Naval Shipyard was sometime before Christmas 1962. The schedule was changed abruptly, however, when U.S. intelligence began to get hints, that had begun in late July, of the Soviet Union's increased military assistance to Cuba. Air defense missile sites were observed in late August, followed by Cuban-bound ships that were determined in early October to contain crates of IL-28 medium-range bombers. By mid-October the United States had conclusive proof that the Soviet Union was secretly building medium-range missile installations in Cuba.[4]

The rapidly developing situation in Cuba hastened efforts on the part of both shipyard and crew to get *Skipjack*'s overhaul completed and our boat ready for sea, and we wrapped up the overhaul by late September. Following a somewhat abbreviated series of sea trials, *Skipjack* moved to her home port of New London. She then began preparations for deployment in response to the ever-mounting crisis.

During these initial sea trials I was put to the test as the diving officer. *Skipjack* had not been to sea in over seven months. In the shipyard, much equipment and many components had been removed, repaired, modified, or replaced as new equipment and components of various weights were added. It was up to shipyard and crew, working together, to keep an accurate accounting of all weights added and removed, their exact location, and the resultant changes in *Skipjack*'s state of ballast, both overall and fore and aft, once she returned to sea. It was desirable for *Skipjack* to leave the shipyard in either a neutral or a slightly positive ballast condition. As I indicated above, if the boat was too light, or positively ballasted, it could prove difficult for it to submerge beneath the surface; if the boat was too heavy and thus in a state of negative ballast, depending on depth and degree of control, she could plow into the bottom, or exceed crush depth, with disastrous results. As the boat's diving officer I ordered that *Skipjack* be ballasted at least 20,000 pounds light before we made that first dive. During our initial dive to periscope depth, as diving officer I discovered the boat to be too light and ordered the chief of the watch to begin flooding variable ballast tanks from the sea. We reached neutral buoyancy after flooding in approximately 15,000 pounds. As it turned out, the initial ballasting record had been quite accurate—only five thousand to six thousand pounds light. I was thus able to report to the commanding officer, "Six five feet, trim satisfactory!" within ten minutes of proceeding beneath the surface.

Once a satisfactory trim was established, sound-powered phones were manned in all compartments, and we proceeded slowly down to our test depth of seven hundred feet in one-hundred-foot stages, as the crew carefully checked for leaks in all compartments. In that era many seawater systems had sil-brazed (silver soldering or hard soldering) rather than welded joints. Since they were not as strong as welded joints, they sometimes weeped or leaked, and then could rupture at depths of four hundred feet and below, presenting an ever-present danger. It was incumbent on us to keep our eye out, particularly throughout the engineering spaces.[5] Upon completion of our dive to test depth, Captain Kelly put *Skipjack* through her paces. It was during these first sea trials that those of us who were new to the boat gained a full appreciation of *Skipjack*'s extraordinary maneuverability and speed. We were mighty glad to have those subway straps to hold on to in the control room, as the boat rapidly changed up and down angle and depth, and when she heeled almost 50 degrees in a flank speed, full rudder turn. We confirmed that *Skipjack* could come very close to turning within her own length should an operational situation demand it.

On the transit back to the Portsmouth Naval Shipyard, Captain Kelly demonstrated what *Skipjack* could do on the surface in calm seas. I was fortunate enough to be officer on the deck on the bridge when Kelly came up to join me. After we had completed a good low-pressure blow of all MBTs, he directed me to order the stern planes put to full rise and speed increased to flank. As we sped through the water, *Skipjack* begin to squat, or settle, by the stern. The captain then guided me through a process of gingerly decreasing rise on the stern planes until we had only a 3-degree rise. As speed increased, more and more of *Skipjack*'s hull rose up and out of the water. Upon reaching maximum or flank speed with a slight rise on the stern planes, *Skipjack* hydroplaned on the water surface at more than twenty-two knots. It

USS *Skipjack* (SSN 585) under way on surface. *Photo courtesy of General Dynamics Corporation*

was spectacular. The stern planesman below and I had to work very closely together. If the stern planes should suddenly go below 3 degrees, or worse, fail in the full-dive direction, the boat would abruptly "fall off the step" and plunge beneath the surface at high speed. That would be a dangerous situation for those on the bridge and for the control room, particularly if the lower trunk hatch was not shut. Such an event would call for immediately ordering, "All back emergency!" with both sail and stern planes placed on full rise and confirming that the bridge access hatch was shut.

As we continued intensive at-sea operations off New London during the first weeks of October, it became evident that we might be deploying to the eastern Mediterranean rather than to the Caribbean as originally expected. The last few days prior to departure were difficult ones emotionally, for we had to keep our families in the dark, for security reasons, about the direction of our impending deployment. They were not to be told until the last day or so. We knew that, in the event of a nuclear exchange between the Soviet Union and the United States, our families and loved ones would be in mortal danger.

Our hull number of "585" was painted out on both sides of the sail late evening before an early-morning departure in late October. That particular day began very early for all. After kissing their families or loved ones a final goodbye at State Pier, New London, crewmembers proceeded on board and were at their underway stations by 7:00 a.m. Those eating breakfast earlier were greeted with a bizarre sight as they entered the crews mess: scattered across the top of each dining table were what appeared to be thousands of M&M candies. Junior Quartermaster C had left them there, stating that he had always wanted to see what twenty-five pounds of M&Ms looked like. Even after the massive cleanup, we continued to find stray M&Ms all over the mess hall deck for weeks. Thus began of a series of incidents involving this young man that would soon come to the attention of all.

Captain Kelly came on board following a final briefing by the Commander Submarine Squadron Ten, shortly before 8:00 a.m.[6] He met briefly with the exec and navigator and then went to the bridge. We took in all lines, backed clear of the pier, and headed down the Thames River. We then transited across Long Island Sound at best speed on the surface. Once in sufficiently deep water, *Skipjack* submerged and raced across the Atlantic at flank speed, test depth. We were bound for Piraeus, Greece, and duty with the Sixth Fleet in the Mediterranean. The objective was to protect allied forces from Soviet submarines and surface warships that might be present, including those that might egress from the Black Sea.

The Cuban Missile Crisis was evolving rapidly as we sped across the Atlantic. On *Skipjack* we expected to be diverted south at any time to take a steadily growing number of Soviet ships and submarines under surveillance and attack them if need be. During the course of each day, we frequently exercised at battle stations, including practicing both single, ready torpedo snapshots at a suddenly detected, simulated Soviet submarine close aboard, and spreads of two and three torpedoes at simulated surfaced Soviet submarines and ships. It was a tense time, especially when we slowed and came to periscope depth to copy our radio broadcasts. On our minds at all times, as we transited east at high speed, was the very real possibility of encountering an enemy submarine that might anticipate the direction of our deployment and be lying in wait for us as we approached the Strait of Gibraltar. We frequently slowed and altered our course at irregular intervals to conduct thorough passive sonar searches for any Soviet submarines that might lie ahead or deep within our port and starboard baffles. All of us believed we might soon be engaged in combat against units of the Soviet navy, or even more horrifically, that we might be engaged in an exchange of nuclear weapons between our two countries

The U.S. Navy had no nuclear submarine opponents at that time. It was known, though, that the Soviet Union was in the process of building and testing a new *November* class of nuclear attack submarine at sea.[7] Our most likely adversaries were certain to be an unknown number of diesel electric-powered *Whiskey*-, *Foxtrot*-, and *Zulu*-class attack submarines, which could have been used to saturate all approaches to Cuba, Murmansk, and the Mediterranean.[8] All these submarines were of fairly recent vintage and had been built in quantity. By the fall of 1962 two hundred fifteen *Whiskeys*, twenty-two *Foxtrots*, and twenty-six *Zulus* were in service.[9] They had been patterned after the German high-performance Type XXI class, which had first gone to sea during the closing years of World War II. All were snorkel-equipped and very noisy while charging their batteries submerged. They were capable of patrolling in an extremely quiet condition, however, at all other times. Hence, each could be considered a potentially dangerous adversary, particularly if *Skipjack* was running at a high speed, since this speed negated our normal acoustic advantage.

### An Electro-Hydraulic Failure

It was well into the mid-Atlantic during our transit that I first experienced how *Skipjack* might respond to a sudden failure of its electro-hydraulically controlled dive planes due to a blown fuse. We knew full well that if the sail planes failed to full dive at high speed and test depth, we would have just nine seconds to bring the boat under control before exceeding crush depth.

Suddenly just before noon in late October in a fraction of a second, the sailplanes went to full rise. *Skipjack* angled sharply upward and went rocketing toward the surface amid a deafening cacophony of crashing, clanging, banging, and breaking noises of mess hall dishes, glasses, cutlery, and everything throughout the boat that wasn't firmly bolted down. I was officer of the deck or conning officer at the time, and as I fought to remain standing I ordered "All stop, back full!" to reduce our speed as rapidly as possible, and I ordered the stern planesman to go to full dive. The sail planesman shifted to manual control and began frantically cranking the sailplanes to full dive.

*Skipjack's* upward ascent was checked in the vicinity of two hundred feet from the surface. I ordered the sail and stern planesmen, "Take charge of your planes and level the boat off at a depth of one five zero feet!" At the same time I ordered, "All stop, ahead two-thirds!" followed by "Ahead one-third!" as we gradually leveled off and brought *Skipjack* back under control. Whew! I then returned control of the dive to the diving officer of the watch. Even the most experienced on board were shaken at what had just occurred. The unplanned depth excursion also played havoc with the crews mess, the wardroom, and what was to have been our lunch.

What had caused the incident? An electro-hydraulic failure, as I recall— probably a blown fuse.

# CHAPTER 15

# In the Mediterranean

The remainder of our high-speed transit to the Strait of Gibraltar and the Mediterranean was relatively uneventful. To our disappointment mixed with relief, we didn't detect or encounter a single Soviet naval vessel or a warship of any nation. During the last week of October we surfaced in the early morning hours under a beautiful star-filled, crystal-clear sky. *Skipjack* slowly approached and silently glided through the strait just as the sun was rising over the Mediterranean Sea. In almost glass-calm seas, the Rock of Gibraltar to port and the coast of Africa to starboard was a magnificent and unforgettable sight. I remember Captain Kelly excitedly saying that it was a scene he had wanted to see all his life. We on the bridge atop the sail couldn't help but think of how many mariners, going back to the time of the ancient Phoenicians, Greeks, and Romans, had shared this same sight.

## La Spezia

We "chopped" (changed from the operational control) to the Commander Sixth Fleet upon passing through the Strait of Gibraltar and learned that our first port of call had been changed. Instead of Piraeus, Greece, as originally slated, we were to set course for the Italian naval base at La Spezia, Italy. Submerged, we proceeded at a speed of advance that would get us there by late morning the following day. Obvious to us all, both visually on the surface and via passive sonar while submerged, was the tremendous amount of ship traffic in the Mediterranean, the vast majority of it composed of merchant ships of all nationalities and of every size and shape. The risk of collision was high, particularly in conditions of reduced visibility such as in rain, fog, and high sea states. We had to be constantly on our toes whenever we

USS *Skipjack* (SSN 585) moored in the Mediterranean during the Cuban Missile Crisis. *U.S. Navy*

came up to periscope depth to fix our position and copy our radio traffic. When submerged, of course, we remained on the alert for Soviet submarines and ships.

*Skipjack* reached La Spezia in the late morning and berthed just down the pier from the Italian diesel attack submarine *Leonardo da Vinci*, whose brother submariners gave us a rousing welcome. We were no sooner tied up than those officers not on watch were ordered to change into dress whites and hustle over to the Italian naval officers club where we were to be hosted at lunch by the wardroom officers of the *Leonardo da Vinci*. What an afternoon: copious amounts of fine Italian wines were served before and during a lavish spread of pasta plus many dishes with octopus and squid, which none of us had ever tasted before. None of *Skipjack's* officers spoke Italian, nor did any of the Italian submarine officers speak much English, the only exception being the captain who knew a few words of our language, enough to toast *Skipjack* and the U.S. Navy.

The language barrier made no difference. The more we drank, the better we understood each other. Our own captain, unfortunately, had to make an abrupt departure in order to meet with higher command representatives who had traveled to La Spezia from Sixth Fleet headquarters to brief him on what was planned for an as-yet-indeterminate stay in the Mediterranean. The luncheon rapidly evolved into a riotous affair that lasted well into the afternoon. It was punctuated by numerous exuberant toasts, with enthusiastic gestures and much laughter becoming a universal language that we all understood. Some of us thought later that such an afternoon with our Soviet submariner counterparts might go a long way toward defusing the very serious international situation that had brought us into the Mediterranean.

We staggered back to our boat just before sunset, most of us too wiped out to do much more than collapse into our bunks. Any rest was cut short, however, as we were soon unceremoniously rousted out and handed a cup of hot black coffee. Our skipper, Cdr. Les Kelly, mustered us in the ward-room for dinner on board and an important briefing on what he had learned that afternoon.

The captain, seated at the head of the wardroom table, regarded us sternly, making it unmistakably clear that we'd better sober up and pay close attention. He told us that we were there because of the fear that the Soviet Union might deploy its Black Sea surface and submarine forces if the Cuban Missile Crisis escalated into a full-blown conflict. Our primary mission would then be to interdict and destroy them. He also told us we had not been routed to Greece because our deployment that far in the east-ern Mediterranean might be considered provocative by our adversary and its Eastern bloc allies—not a wise thing to do in the midst of an already severely tense situation. The latest development was that at least three Soviet sub-marines had been detected some hundred miles to the east of Cuba.[1] What their interaction might subsequently be with our blockading naval forces already in place was anyone's guess.

Until then, we could expect to be employed in various exercises with NATO and U.S. surface forces in order to peak up and maintain our over-all readiness for combat in the event that units of the Soviet Black Sea Fleet suddenly deployed. When deemed necessary, we might also be assigned to patrol certain critical choke points in the eastern Mediterranean.

In the middle of this meeting we learned that the wife of one of our officers had just arrived in Naples, and he would be granted leave beginning that evening to join her. Unusual, to put it mildly, and not well received by his brother officers. There must have been some prearranged senior officer pressure on our captain to grant the leave. The effect was to increase the at-sea and in-port watch-standing load on us all significantly. We would also be minus a key division and battle stations officer at a time when there was a very real possibility we might soon be involved in combat action. I scratch my head to this day in wonderment as to what that officer and his wife must have been thinking of.

Finally, the captain made clear that if we were to be routed to another port for a short upkeep and liberty, we were not to go on shore power, even if available. We would, rather, maintain the engineering plant on line with the reactor critical and ships service turbine generators providing all electrical power. *Skipjack* was to remain capable of getting under way in less than an hour. This meant, of course, that at least two-thirds of the officers and crew would have to be on board at all times. So much for whatever we envisioned in the way of liberty. The captain then went to the control room, had all hatches shut and secured and telephone lines disconnected and, using the 1MC system, informed the crew of what we in the wardroom had been told earlier.

No further shore liberty being granted, those not on watch retired for the night to see what the next day might bring. To the great credit of *Skipjack*'s wardroom and crew, there was no grumbling. We were all professionals, and understood why we were in the Mediterranean. We knew what might be required of us in the U.S. national interest as a well-trained and combat-ready team.

## An Unexpected Distinguished Visitor

I took over as duty officer in port at 8:00 the following morning, with one of my fellow officers as engineering officer of the watch. We learned at breakfast that the crisis remained stable, with no new developments of any significance. It was expected, therefore, that we might remain in port for only several days more. A liberty routine was established for all hands such that we were placed on an eight hours on, sixteen hours off duty routine. Along with it came the strict requirement that whatever our rank or rate, we arrived on our assigned watch rested and sober, or else. I was elated, because it meant I would be able to leave the boat shortly after 4:00 p.m. and have the entire evening, up to midnight, to enjoy myself on shore. What there was to do beyond visiting the elegant Italian naval officers club, I had no clue.

The morning was routine. Those on board stood normal in-port watches topside and below decks. The engineering department stood their watches as if we were at sea. Since the reactor was critical, all engineering plants systems were fully operational, and our ships service turbine generators were supplying all of *Skipjack*'s electrical power needs.

I roamed the boat restlessly during the course of the morning until my boredom was suddenly broken up by the topside watch calling, "Officer of watch topside! Officer of watch topside!" over the 1MC system. I rushed up on deck to see what was going on. The topside watch directed my attention to what appeared to be a very high-ranking Italian naval officer on the wharf, walking rapidly toward *Skipjack*. Fortunately, I was properly attired in a clean, pressed khaki uniform and was wearing my tie.

As the individual closed the boat, it appeared he must be someone of great importance. He was dressed in a crisp white uniform with a red stripe running down each leg of his trousers, a bright crimson sash wrapped several times around his waist, through which passed an unsheathed saber, and a most impressive hat from which a bright white feather plume projected.

As it happened, neither the captain nor the exec was on board. It was up to me to offer the official welcome to our unexpected distinguished guest. I called "Attention on deck!" All topside and on the pier saluted as he crossed the gangplank. He returned the salute, taking my extended hand and shaking it warmly as he stepped on board. I greeted him politely in English, signaling him with gestures to follow me below decks. This he did without uttering a word. As we proceeded to the wardroom, everyone we encountered froze to attention against the bulkheads as we passed. At the end of the wardroom table I took the captain's seat and invited him to sit on my right hand. The duty steward's mate immediately offered our visitor a cup of coffee, which he accepted with a *"grazie"* and a broad smile of thanks. I too took a cup of coffee, and as we each stirred in sugar and cream, we looked at each other with friendly expressions. I had no idea who this gentleman was or why he had come, but assumed he intended to meet with the captain.

Our initial attempts to communicate were an utter failure. I drew on my Naval Academy Spanish, but that only added to the confusion. We continued to gesture and smile, but were obviously getting nowhere. Recognizing the problem, the duty steward's mate went looking for an Italian speaker among the duty section. He returned with a senior petty officer who spoke fluent Italian. The petty officer politely addressed the gentleman and more or less asked what we could do for him. It turned out our visitor was not a high-ranking Italian naval officer at all, but a senior chief petty officer from our Italian host submarine, the *Leonardo da Vinci*. He had come to invite our chief petty officers to lunch on board his boat.

Up to this point, I had thought I was dealing with an Italian admiral. The chief of the boat was summoned to the wardroom and I introduced him to our visitor. Our Italian-speaking petty officer did the interpreting and, following smiles and a departing handshake, escorted our distinguished visitor to the chief petty officers' quarters. There, with his assistance, an invitation to lunch on the *Leonardo da Vinci* was extended to all *Skipjack*'s chief petty officers. At that I shook hands with our departing guest and returned his salute.

I had done the right thing, of course, but probably left our Italian chief petty officer guest thoroughly confused with regard to U.S. Navy protocol. One can only imagine the stories that his visit must have engendered when he was back on his own submarine.

## Sunday Afternoon at the Opera

The nuclear standoff between the United States and the Soviet Union was seemingly resolved by early November 1962 after frantic diplomatic negotiations. We on board were only told, however, that the crisis had passed, and *Skipjack* ended up spending as much time in port as at sea. None of the at-sea periods was particularly memorable, beyond proving once again that current NATO and U.S. surface ASW forces were no match for a high-performance nuclear attack submarine. The Soviet navy had yet to acquire any that were deployable during the present crisis, so we took advantage of the time to make port visits to several cities in Italy and France.

After a short transit at sea, our next port was Toulon, France, where we moored our boat toward the end of a long mole or pier built up from the bottom of the sea. Our orders were to remain in a state of manning and readiness such that we could deploy on war patrol at a moment's notice. As at the Italian navy base at La Spezia, this state of readiness required that our nuclear reactor be kept critical. It further required that at least half of the crew and officers to be on board at all times. Since we were not allowed to wander beyond our immediate berth alongside the mole, arrangements were made with port authorities for liberty boat service for the duration of our stay.

Toulon, although a friendly city, still reflected much of the anti-Americanism that prevailed throughout France. We could never be sure when encountering people on shore whether we were going to be smiled at or spit at. *Skipjack*'s crew was not considered altogether safe anywhere in the city or its suburbs while on liberty or shore leave. We learned, from indirect experience, that an American sailor with a few drinks under his belt was at serious risk of injury if he wandered into the wrong neighborhood. The sum total was that there was a good chance of inadvertently creating an embarrassing international incident at a time when tensions were already high worldwide.

The French naval authorities consequently requested that *Skipjack* post a permanent shore patrol. A minimum of one officer and one chief petty officer plus three additional lower-rated petty officers was required. All were to reside on shore at the French naval base. As a senior lieutenant, I was delighted to be designated *Skipjack*'s senior shore patrol officer for the entire period that we were scheduled to be in port. It meant I would be berthed at the French naval officers club, a not-too-onerous assignment.

Our primary duty as the U.S. Navy shore patrol was to work closely with both the French navy's own shore patrol and Toulon's police force, which was not noted for its gentle treatment of anyone taken into custody. All three entities were divided into teams and charged with keeping the peace. Each team was tasked with patrolling the various areas most likely to be frequented by our sailors from early afternoon until midnight, when all were required to be back on board. Of greatest concern was the prevention of even the most minor incident or disturbance.

It proved to be a generally uneventful week. No incidents or unpleasantness of any sort occurred, and *Skipjack*'s crewmembers received high marks for their conduct on shore. I enjoyed repairing to another, nearby French armed forces officers club upon going off duty shortly after midnight each night. Arriving in a crisp tropical white uniform bedecked with ribbons and submarine Gold Dolphins, I was welcomed with open arms by one friendly group after another and treated to all the fine wine and champagne I could possibly drink. It was a lot of fun communicating with brother French naval officers and their more-often-than-not lovely companions. Our lingua franca combined Spanish, English, and French with many gestures and smiles. Amazing how well we understood each other.

Sunday 18 November was the last complete day of liberty on shore, as *Skipjack* was scheduled to get under way early the following morning, Monday. Members of the crew were again cautioned to maintain their excellent conduct record on shore and not to drink too much during the last day of our visit to Toulon. Since this had not been a problem so far, we all anticipated a quiet, normal Sunday.

I had just finished a late lunch at the French naval officers club and was relaxing with a newspaper. It was midafternoon on a perfect and wonderfully pleasant day. This idyllic state of affairs was not to last. Representatives of the French navy and Toulon police suddenly arrived to inform me that one of our crew had just collapsed. It seemed he might be dead. "Good God!" was my reaction. I quickly donned my uniform and rushed with them to the Toulon Opera House.

The Opera House was a magnificent building not more than a mile away. It was the second largest in France and could seat almost 1,800 people on five levels. It was also a national historic monument of the country. Verdi's *La Traviata* was being performed that afternoon. As we rushed into the building, I reflected that this was the last place I would have expected to find any of *Skipjack's* crew. Several ambulances pulled up, with paramedic personnel rapidly emerging, carrying stretchers and medical emergency equipment of various sorts.

The auditorium was filled with hundreds of well-dressed opera lovers. To their obvious annoyance, *La Traviata* had been abruptly stopped in the middle of an act. As medical personnel, uniformed representatives of the French navy, Toulon police, and I tramped down the center aisle, we were met by hostile stares and mutterings. The performers were standing silently on the stage, glaring at us. I had a sinking feeling in my stomach when it became clear that a small group of our sailors, all in uniform, had purchased tickets on the first row.

As we approached, we could see the supposedly dead sailor sprawled on the floor. A French doctor was kneeling beside him, directly in front of the stage and between the orchestra and the audience. Talk about high visibility! It was evident from the alcoholic fumes emanating from *Skipjack's* opera-fan contingent that all were well lubricated. As a uniformed representative of the U.S. Navy, I would have given anything to vanish from sight at that moment.

A stretcher was quickly placed alongside the sailor, whom I recognized as the notorious petty officer, C, of the twenty-five pounds of M&Ms caper. As he was gently lifted onto the stretcher, the opera house doctor looked at me with concern and whispered in perfect English, "I am very sorry to tell you this. He is alive, but he is in serious condition from drinking and may also have had a heart attack."

What an ending to a perfect week, I thought, as we slowly progressed up the aisle with our downed sailor, followed by three of his companions and the hostile stares of the audience as we passed row upon row to the lobby. We were definitely "Ugly Americans" in their eyes.

Just as we reached the top of the center aisle, our fallen crewmember suddenly sat up. "Hello Mr. McLaren. What are you doing here?" were the first words from this modern-day Lazarus, before he collapsed again. We all realized to our collective chagrin that we were engaged in medically evacuating not a dead sailor, but a dead-drunk one. We picked up the pace and quickly exited the opera house to a chorus of hisses and boos.

The errant sailor was unceremoniously loaded into one of the waiting ambulances and transported back to *Skipjack* and the not-so tender mercies of his superiors and the commanding officer. The aftermath from both French naval authorities and our own naval and state department superiors was anything but pleasant. Our opera-loving sailors were permanently restricted to the boat for the remainder of our Mediterranean deployment.

### George's Excellent Adventure on Shore

In late November *Skipjack* departed Toulon for another week of ASW exercises with French and Italian NATO units. The Cuban Missile Crisis had ended on 28 October 1962, to our collective relief, and we expected to be returning home in time for Christmas. Morale was high. We were in an exuberant mood, too, because we had once again proved our virtual invulnerability to both detection and attack by air and surface ASW units. Upon completion of the exercises, we headed for Naples, Italy, and one final liberty over the Thanksgiving holiday before returning to the United States.

A group of us celebrated with a huge spaghetti dinner and copious amounts of Chianti at a wonderful outdoor restaurant in Pompeii. Only one officer on *Skipjack*, a Lt. George H, had steadfastly refused to leave the boat to go anywhere during the entire Mediterranean deployment. Being newly married, he had up until that time spent almost all of his in-port time on *Skipjack* in order to save money.

It was our final day ashore. We were scheduled to get under way to return to the United States the next morning. All on board were full of excitement at the prospect of returning to our home port in New London.

The boat had been moored for several days in the sewage-laden Bay of Naples, at the end of a long mole that promised robbery and assault to the unwary soul on foot during the hours of darkness. The U.S. Naval Activities Command in Naples required the crew to use a specially scheduled liberty boat to go to and from the mole. Most off-duty personnel had already left the boat to savor one last time all that the city had to offer a healthy young American sailor.

The engineering department and all officers had a different duty schedule from that of most of the crew. The nuclear reactor had to be kept critical in order to supply all our electrical power needs, requiring us to maintain a full engineering-spaces watch twenty-four hours a day. *Skipjack's* officers, therefore, were filling both in-port officer of the deck and engineering officer of the watch assignments on an eight hours on, sixteen hours off schedule around the clock. We were free to go ashore during normal liberty hours— 8:00 a.m. to midnight—when not on watch, however.

Lt. George H and I had just completed our appointed duty stints. George had been aft in the engineering spaces and I in the forward part of the boat as in-port officer of the deck. Rather than eat supper on board, I was eager to go ashore for one last meal at the excellent NATO officers club. A fabulous full-course dinner with wine could be obtained for a modest price ($5.00, at the time). Although George had brought an expensive new British-tailored wool suit with him for a special occasion or two while in the Mediterranean, such occasions never materialized, and he had never worn it.

Preferring not to go ashore alone, I spent the better part of an hour in the wardroom trying to convince George to join me at the NATO officers club.

"Come on, George," I said to him, "This is our final night in port and your last chance to get away and relax. You owe it to yourself to have an elegant yet inexpensive dinner at the officers club."

"George," I went on, "the floorshows at the club are terrific, and this being Sunday evening, we're certain to be treated to a colorful evening of Neapolitan song and dance."

Finally, I said, "Come on George, you won't regret it, I promise. I'll even pay for the taxi there and back."

After what seemed an eternity, George reluctantly agreed to accompany me ashore.

We quickly donned our best suits, George in his new one, and took the next liberty boat ashore. Upon landing, we hailed a taxicab and headed for the officers club. Entering the spacious and beautiful dining room, we were seated at a perfect table for viewing the scheduled floorshow.

The menu of Italian cuisine was fabulous, as were the low prices. We each ordered multiple-course, typical Neapolitan dinners with accompanying wines and settled down to relish dinner and the evening. After several glasses of wine, George was completely relaxed. He thanked me profusely for persuading him to join me on shore. The more we ate and drank, the more ebullient we became. The superb floorshow put us in even higher spirits.

Around 10:00 p.m. we decided to head back to the submarine for a good night's sleep. In the vicinity of the mole where we were moored, we stepped out of the taxi into a clear, star-filled night. I spotted a small, inviting-looking waterfront *taverna* and suggested we stroll over. We could check it out for a few minutes, take in some local color, and then head for the boat. As we walked, George kept thanking me for convincing him to join me on shore. He even told me he wished he'd had the good sense to join us at the other ports *Skipjack* had visited.

The closer we got to the little *taverna*, the more interesting it appeared. At the entrance we heard lively Italian popular music and noted more than a few attractive young women seated, without escorts, at various tables inside. "Let's go in for a quick drink," George suggested, to my surprise.

We found ourselves ushered to a cozy little booth where we ordered two of what we thought were the least expensive white wines. Our drinks arrived and we settled back, taking in the picturesque scene and its inhabitants.

Within minutes two tall, stunning Scandinavian young women had joined us. Drinks in hand, they told us they were tourists as well. We soon got into animated conversation since they spoke English very well. We asked what they wanted to drink. They answered champagne. By then in an expansive mood, George said, "Why not?" to my inquiring glance. He ordered champagne for us all. We danced, talked some more, danced, and soon finished the bottle. Well after 11:00 p.m. I suddenly remembered we had to be at the boat landing at the foot of the mole by 11:30. If not, we would miss the last boat to our submarine. "We better get going," I said, starting to get up. But George wasn't ready to leave. "Come on," he begged. "We've got time for one more," and he ordered our glasses refilled.

We were running out of time. If we missed the last liberty boat, we would have to walk the entire length of the unlighted mole, risking God knows what dangers to life and limb. We gulped down the last of our champagne and called for *il conto* (the bill). Our new friends with sweet words and caresses, however, urged us to stay, "Just a little longer . . . please!"

The bill arrived and George and I went into shock: in U.S. dollars the bill amounted to over $70, more than $500 today.[2] We protested angrily, arguing with the waiter, then with the manager. Meantime, our companions had abandoned us without as much as a goodbye or word of thanks. As the discussion, or rather confrontation, got more heated, other waiters approached. Among them were two that could only be described as thugs. We quickly realized that it would be wise to shut up, pay the bill, and get the hell out of there. Emptying both wallets and pockets of everything we had, we still came up a few dollars short. The manager snatched the money away from us, pointing to the door.

Once outside with our hides intact, we raced back to the boat landing, only to find the last boat had already left and was almost halfway to our submarine.

George's previously near-euphoric mood evaporated. He was not only drunk, as was I, but angry about all the money he had thrown away in the last five minutes. "I wish to hell I had never listened to you," he railed at me. "You purposely led me astray." As his litany of complaints continued, I was busily trying to decide just where we entered the mole and what route to our boat might be the best lighted and safest.

Suddenly a large naval motor launch appeared, from a U.S. aircraft carrier anchored out in the bay. It pulled alongside the boat landing and discharged a sizable group of shore patrol. They were rounding up the last group of American sailors still on the beach. If history was any guide, this was bad luck for anyone still on shore from any vessel, including *Skipjack*. We could be taken back to the aircraft carrier and forced to stay there until it returned to the States. Those of us not belonging to the aircraft carrier would be considered deserters from our own ships. There was a time in French ports, following World War II, that the healthiest of these late hell raisers, both officer and enlisted, might well have found themselves taken into custody by the Foreign Legion, which was always on the lookout for recruits.

We explained our plight to the boat coxswain, and to our relief he agreed to transport us out to *Skipjack*. We boarded the launch, pointed out the location of our boat, and were on our way. In less than ten minutes we were alongside and abreast the topside watch standing on deck. "See, George," I said, "We made it! Everything is going to turn out all right." George responded with an unhappy grunt.

I spoke too soon. The only way we were going to get back was to stand on the rocking gunwale of the launch and jump to the top of the rounded hull of our submarine. This would only work if the topside watch was poised to grab our hand and to pull us as high as possible up the side of the hull. If either of us miscalculated, we would slide down into the murky brown water.

Offering to show George how easy it was, I jumped first. I caught the topside watch's extended hand and made it safely on board. After considering the situation for several long minutes, George jumped too. However, he fell short, missing our extended hands, and slid slowly, crawling, scratching, and cursing, down *Skipjack*'s hull into the murky, brown waters.

"Man overboard portside! Man overboard portside!" called the topside watch over the 1MC. I threw George a nearby life preserver. Crewmembers rushed topside to haul him, soaked from head to toe, with his new wool suit a wet, soon-to-shrink remnant of its former self.

We scurried down midship's hatch and into *Skipjack*'s warm interior. With a parting curse, George hurried off to remove his clothing and get into the nearest shower. The hospital corpsman followed him armed with a special cleansing soap and ear swabs, to make sure the microorganisms populating the water did not infect George. He bagged up George's suit and took it away to be disinfected and dried.

*Skipjack* got under way as scheduled next morning, on time and with all hands on board. By then news of his dunk in the bay had spread throughout the boat and become the source of much jollity at his expense. By noon, George had pretty much recovered his composure, but he avoided speaking to me except on official business for the remainder of the voyage home. The slightest smile on my part had the effect of pouring kerosene on a fire. Many months were to pass before he could begin to see the humorous side of our excellent adventure on shore.

# CHAPTER 16

# Home Port in New London

Skipjack was detached from the Sixth Fleet in early December 1962. Upon exiting the Strait of Gibraltar and the Mediterranean, we descended smartly to test depth. We then increased speed to our maximum and set course for New London. The transit across the Atlantic was rapid and uneventful, with one notable exception. On surfacing in Long Island Sound it was determined that we had made the fastest transit ever across the Atlantic Ocean. This was a new record to add to *Skipjack's* growing collection of laurels. The record still stands and remains classified information.

We surfaced off Long Island Sound in early December and proceeded up the Thames River. By late morning we were safely moored at our usual berth at State Pier, New London, where we were met by our families and loved ones. Following a joyful reunion, all but the duty section departed for some well-deserved leave and relaxation.

*Skipjack* remained in port and tied up at State Pier until late January 1963. Both boat and crew had been run hard since leaving Portsmouth Naval Shipyard the previous September, and we all needed a good rest.

I took only a few days leave over Christmas, however, because Captain Kelly had recommended me for qualification for submarine command immediately upon our return home. I had much to accomplish in a short amount of time. I wanted very much, if possible, to complete my command thesis and all aspects of the in-port and at-sea examination by our squadron commander before Lt. Cdr. Shepherd M. Jenks relieved Captain Kelly toward the end of January.

We settled into our normal in-port watch-standing routine with two officers at all times—one as engineering officer of the watch, the other assuming officer of the deck in-port duties. Since we were all qualified to do both, we altered between the two as we stood a normal one day on, two days off in-port routine.

## Swimmer in the Water

The submarine force was a key factor and active player in U.S. Cold War strategy, and much effort and money was spent to heighten and strengthen its overall security while any boat was in port. USS *Skipjack* being a front-line nuclear attack submarine and the world's fastest was considered a prime target for Soviet bloc espionage. All in-port topside watch standers were, as a consequence, qualified and armed with .45-caliber pistols and several clips of ammunition.

Well into the holiday season, *Skipjack* was moored at State Pier, along with another half-dozen or so diesel and nuclear submarines. Some were also moored across the pier alongside the submarine tender *Fulton*, home of our immediate superior, Commander Submarine Squadron Ten. Both submarines and the tender were thus much more accessible from the Thames River and its shore than they would have been if moored farther upriver at the submarine base in Groton. All Squadron Ten commanding officers were constantly cautioned to ensure that their duty officers and in-port watch standers exercised special vigilance. They were to be hyper-alert for underwater swimmers and overland intruders both day and night.

*Skipjack* was a beautifully streamlined, almost football-shaped subma-rine. Centered on the top of her hull was the large fin-like, hollow structure called the sail. The sail was some eighteen to twenty feet in height, approximately six feet wide, and was free-flooding while submerged. Its main purpose was to provide a rigid, protective housing in which to position a vertical bridge access trunk from the control room, two periscopes, the snorkel mast and head valve, and all electronics masts and radio antennas. Each of these was quite lengthy and penetrated the pressure hull at a point at its base. The sail enabled *Skipjack* to position her hull at a depth well below the sea surface when using these periscopes and masts. This lessened the boat's susceptibility to heavy wave motion from rough seas and high winds and significantly decreased the possibility of her being sucked to the surface and broaching under such conditions.

*Skipjack*'s bridge, from where she was maneuvered while on the surface, was located within a small cockpit located in the upper forward portion of the sail. The bridge was accessed from the control room via the bridge access trunk. This trunk was in fact a cylindrically shaped pressure vessel that was sealed at each end by watertight upper- and lower-access hatches when the boat was submerged.

The forwardmost of the two sets of the boat's diving control planes, or sail planes that replaced the older type bow planes, and that projected from each side of the sail, were like short, stubby wings. The interior of the sail could be entered from either the port or starboard side by doors or from the control room by a watertight hatch located on the main deck, or top of the pressure hull, within the sail. This latter hatch was the usual point of personnel entrance to and from the submarine's interior while in port.

Armed topside security watch standers normally stood their watch out on the main deck, amidships, near the egress from the brow, or gangway. In the event of inclement weather they could also stand their watch within the sail itself. The best and most reliable topside watch standers always remained on deck near the brow. It was from this position that they could best keep an eye on what was going on around the boat. Those less conscientious, however, never missed an opportunity to sneak within the sail's warmer and more protective interior.

After Christmas on a clear, cold evening, Lt. Bud Kauderer and I were sharing duty that night and for the moment were sitting in the wardroom drinking coffee. Both of us were qualified veterans of many years of submarining by now, and we were discussing the sequence of the next morning's reactor training startup. Suddenly we heard a loud, muffled roar from the direction of the control room, located above and forward of the wardroom. We raced out of the wardroom and up a stairway into the control room.

A quick inspection revealed nothing amiss, but several crewmembers were peering up the bridge access trunk with surprised and inquiring looks on their faces. We quickly climbed up the ladder and into the sail. Sprawled on the deck before us was the topside watch, Petty Officer C of earlier fame, with his .45-caliber pistol in hand. Also immediately noticeable were bright, waist-high metallic bands or streaks that circumnavigated the interior of the sail.

I reached down and carefully removed the .45 from C's hand. It was still warm from being recently fired. I checked its condition and unloaded it. Meanwhile, Bud Kauderer attempted to calm the visibly shaken sailor.

"What on earth happened?" was our first question. When C calmed down, he told us he thought he had seen a swimmer in the water just below the open starboard access sail door. His clearly not-well-thought-out action was to retreat within the sail, load his pistol, and then fire a single .45-caliber bullet at the imagined intruder. Unfortunately, C missed the target, and the bullet hit the confined steel interior of the sail, producing the loud, muffled roar and the visible evidence of a high-velocity slug ricocheting around. It was an exceedingly dangerous thing to do. C was lucky not to have been seriously injured.

He was immediately relieved as the topside watch and sent below. In the meantime, some degree of normalcy returned. There was no swimmer in the water. C was disqualified as topside watch stander. I later arranged to retrain him, particularly with regard to the proper handling and use of firearms. This and a number of earlier bizarre incidents involving C, some of which I have recounted, led Captain Kelly to detach him and send him to the Submarine Medical Center at the submarine base in Groton, the following morning. There he underwent an extended mental examination and evaluation.

Petty Officer C returned to *Skipjack* a few weeks later, in mid-January with, to our consternation, a clean bill of health. He was on board no more than a few days when he was heard to announce at breakfast in the crews mess, "I am the only sane member of *Skipjack*'s crew, and I have the papers to prove it."

### "Let's Go Skiing"

For almost a month, from just before Christmas until Captain Kelly's change of command on 25 January 1963, I was to become the despair of the exec, Bob Chewning. Captain Kelly, a passionate downhill skier, learned that I too loved to ski. He took every opportunity during the in-port period to head out to the slopes. We both, in fact, to the disapproval of our superiors, had learned to ski while going through the six-month, land-based nuclear power plant prototype training and qualification period—Kelly learned at Arco, Idaho, and I learned at West Milton, New York.

On my first run down a ski slope at Glens Falls, I injured my left ankle so badly that I had to be taken by ambulance to the naval hospital at St. Albans, New York. There doctors put my leg into a bulky cast. Making it worse for me was that a U.S. Naval Academy classmate and fellow submariner, Dennis J. "Denny" Sullivan, and I had been playing hooky that day during a period of mandatory training. I will never forget the reaction of Cdr. Jeffrey C. Metzel Jr., our officer in charge at West Milton, the next day. He waved his fist at me saying, "Go ahead McLaren, ski all you want, but you better never miss another day of training." I took that to heart, sort of. As soon as my ankle began to feel better, I began purposely stomping around in wet snow until my cast was covered with dirt and debris. As I'd hoped, I was sent down to a naval clinic at Poughkeepsie to have my cast replaced. Once there, I convinced the doctor that my ankle felt so good I was sure I no longer needed a cast. The doctor agreed and, telling me to be very careful with it for another three weeks, sent me back to West Milton with only an ace bandage. I was back on skis by the following weekend. Utterly stupid and unprofessional, but fun. By the time I finished my prototype training and qualified as a chief operator on the S-3-G land-based nuclear power plant, I was a pretty good skier.

So it was that, while in port, I always brought my skis to work with me. Several days a week, not more than a half hour after I had come on board about 7:00 a.m., Captain Kelly would wander out of his stateroom looking for me. "Let's go skiing," he would say as soon as he found me. This was especially true on rainy days, because, as he put it, "If it's raining here in New London, it's bound to be snowing farther north." I would then go find the exec and sheepishly request permission to leave the boat to go skiing for the day with the captain. Bob Chewning used to groan every time he saw me coming toward him with a big grin on my face, which was always just about the time the workday officially started.

The captain and I would secure our skis and poles on the back of his VW bug, and off we'd go, driving through rain, sleet, and eventually snow to reach our destination. By late morning we would be skiing somewhere in northern Connecticut or Massachusetts, or by mid- to late-afternoon in southern Vermont. On many occasions his wife Nancy joined us.

One day it rained and continued to rain, no matter how far north we drove, but Captain Kelly was not to be deterred. By the time we found good skiing conditions, we had driven all the way up into the Green Mountains of Vermont, almost halfway up the state. We arrived at the ski area about 5:00 p.m., skied for three hours, and then headed home, stopping to eat on the way back. Little did we suspect that if we had not returned home by 10:00 p.m., our families and all those on board *Skipjack* would be up in arms. Shortly after midnight, a Connecticut state trooper waved us down asking if we were the missing skiers. We produced our ID cards, telling him we didn't know we were missing. He advised us to call our families and the duty officer on board *Skipjack*. We did so after finding a telephone booth at a gas station and then resumed our journey south. We each drove to our respective homes to be met by outraged spouses. They were certain we had been in a serious accident of some sort. We never traveled that far afield again but probably got in at least ten days of skiing in just one month.

Captain Kelly and I were never to ski together again, following his forth-coming change of command. He went to Washington, DC, for his next tour of duty as the submarine officer detailer at the U.S. Navy Bureau of Personnel, and *Skipjack* began a rigorous at-sea period during the months that followed that precluded any skiing.

## Qualification for Command

It is hard to believe, in retrospect, that I managed to complete my qualification for submarine command thesis and my in-port written examination questions and go to sea for three days during the December–January upkeep period. My lengthy command thesis, in which I developed and explained a method for repairing a seawater-flooded periscope while at sea, was completed in early January 1963. The three in-port examination questions, covering a tactical situation, a disciplinary problem, and an operational planning problem, were provided to me in early January 1963 upon Captain Kelly's recommending me to Commander Submarine Squadron Ten for qualification for submarine command. After completing the thesis and written questions, the at-sea qualification for examination was scheduled. The exam required me to make three successful and undetected attacks, firing at least two dummy torpedoes against an auxiliary ship escorted by two active-echo-ranging destroyers. The submarine division commander (DivCom), Cdr. Shannon D. Cramer Jr., was my examiner. He was a top-notch professional in every sense. Relaxed and friendly, he put me at ease, but made it clear from the outset that he expected a high standard of performance.

Since *Skipjack* was still in upkeep, I went to sea for my examination on another nuclear attack boat within the division, USS *Seawolf* (SSN 575), whose layout and operational characteristics were somewhat different from those of *Skipjack*. Commander Cramer also spot-checked my ship-handling skills, getting the boat under way from State Pier, New London, and making the landing upon *Seawolf*'s return several days later. Accomplishing both was not without hazard in view of the strong currents and tides that were typical for the Thames River. He closely observed as I acted as commanding officer during all diving and surfacing operations. In between operational evolutions and emergency drills, he engaged me in intensive discussion on the various cold war and hot war submarine-versus-submarine tactical situations I might find myself in one day, and on the best manner in which to handle them.[1] For example, he asked, "Your submarine has just slowed from a high-speed transit and detects a hostile submarine close aboard. What should be your immediate action?" Or, "You detect a torpedo coming your way. How do you best avoid being hit?" The at-sea examination included lengthy tours of *Seawolf*'s engineering spaces and torpedo rooms as Commander Cramer probed the depths of my knowledge and experience. It was clear from the start he would have to be completely satisfied that I was truly ready in all respects to take command of an attack submarine before he would give me his certification.

I passed with flying colors in all areas. Each of my minimum aspect approaches and attacks was completely undetected until the torpedoes I launched at a range of approximately three thousand yards from the target were actually in the water. "Minimum aspect" meant that my technique during the course of the submerged approach and attack was essentially to point the nearest escort ASW vessel as I closed the target's track to within firing range of the torpedoes I was using, which were two steam-driven Mk-14–5 "fish." I was equally successful in avoiding acquisition and counterattack by either of the escort vessels. This was because I ordered the boat to go deep following torpedo launch, increase speed, pass directly beneath the nearest escort, and clear the area in a direction directly astern of the target vessel. This tactic plus very poor winter underwater acoustic conditions ensured that any brief contact that had been gained by one or both escort vessels could be quickly broken.

I was formally qualified for command of submarines on 4 April 1963.

## The *Thresher* Disaster

We bid a sad farewell on 26 January 1963 to Commander Kelly at his change of command of *Skipjack* and welcomed Lt. Cdr. Shepherd M. "Shep" Jenks as our new skipper. My eight months with Kelly had been pivotal for my Navy career. He had done everything possible to help me more rapidly develop and mature as a submarine officer. He also proved to be a good friend and mentor during our time together on *Skipjack* and in the years to come.

Commander Jenks came to us fresh from being commissioning engineer of the world's first ballistic missile submarine, USS *George Washington* (SSBN 598), but his fame as navigator of USS *Nautilus* during her 1958 historic first transit of the Arctic Ocean via the North Pole preceded him. We were all quite excited about what the future might hold for *Skipjack* and her crew. Would we soon be off for the Arctic to further test the capabilities of the world's fastest and most advanced submarine off the northern shores of our Cold War adversary? Under the command of the submarine force's acknowledged master navigator, the potential missions for *Skipjack* were limited only by one's imagination.

Our primary task as the first of a new class of nuclear attack submarine that could outrun, outmaneuver, and outperform anything on the ocean was to demonstrate *Skipjack*'s capabilities as an ASW weapon. *Skipjack*, accordingly, was scheduled for one at-sea exercise after another that pitted us against surface and air ASW forces up and down and across the Atlantic Ocean. These exercises often involved warships of our principal NATO allies such as the United Kingdom's aircraft carrier HMS *Hermes*. We operated against ASW-escorted amphibious warfare groups, fast-carrier task forces, and ASW search-and-destroy forces. They were no match for *Skipjack*'s speed and maneuverability.

It was early afternoon on 10 April, during the course of one of these exercises, that we in the submarine force received the worst possible news. A fleet-wide "Event SUBMISS message" reported that USS *Thresher* had failed to return to the surface following the conduct of deep-diving tests some 220 miles east of Boston. She had been in company with the submarine rescue vessel USS *Skylark* (ASR-20). The depth of water chosen for the tests was far in excess of any navy's ability to conduct successful rescue operations, however. *Skylark* had lost all contact with *Thresher* shortly after 9:17 that morning, following the receipt of an alarming series of underwater telephone transmissions from the boat. Beginning at 9:13 a.m., they indicated that *Thresher* was "experiencing minor difficulty, have positive up-angle, attempting to blow." *Skylark* then heard the hiss of compressed air, followed at 9:17 a.m. by a partially recognizable phrase, "exceeding test depth."[2] *Skylark* conducted an expanding sonar and visual search for *Thresher*. She continued to call her on the underwater telephone and to signal her on sonar until late afternoon, with no success. The following day, 11 April 1963, the U.S. Navy officially declared *Thresher* lost with all hands: ten officers, one hundred eight enlisted crewmembers, and twenty-one riders (seventeen civilian technicians and four shipyard/staff officers).

A subsequent court of inquiry, after studying all available data and pictures taken by the bathyscaph *Trieste*, found that the submarine had broken up into six major sections, with the majority of the debris contained within a single area about four hundred yards square on the ocean floor. The court concluded that the loss of *Thresher* was due in all probability to a casting, piping, or welding failure that had flooded the engine room from sea. This water probably caused electrical failures that automatically shut down the nuclear reactor, causing an initial power loss, severe flooding, and the eventual loss of the boat as she descended through her estimated crush depth.[3] Many of *Thresher's* piping joints were sil-brazed, and hence were not as strong as standard welded joints, as discussed earlier.

All on board *Skipjack* were devastated. Most of our crew and officers had come to know *Thresher's* crew and shipyard civilians while we were in Portsmouth Naval Shipyard together during the previous year. Many of us, in addition, had served on other submarines with those lost on *Thresher*. Her skipper was Lt. Cdr. Wes Harvey, the exec when I was on *Seadragon*. The engineer, Lt. Cdr. John Lyman, and I had gone to submarine school and nuclear power school together. Lt. Cdr. Mike J. DiNola had been a neighbor of mine in Pearl Harbor, and I had known Lt. Merrill F. Collier from U.S. Naval Academy days.

The disaster of *Thresher* did not lead any of *Skipjack's* officers or crew to question his choice to serve on submarines. There were no requests to leave the submarine force in the months that followed, to the best of my knowledge. My mother and one sister did call and plead with me to get out of submarines as soon as possible, but neither my wife Mary nor my father, Capt. William F. McLaren, said a thing. I think most of us on *Skipjack* continued to believe that we were invulnerable and that no such accident would ever happen to us.

## Suddenly a Navigator

It was in the middle of the night during one of the fleet ASW exercises in early May 1963 that I was to take on a challenging new assignment. Shortly after 2:00 a.m., not more than an hour after I had gone to bed following a busy evening's conning watch while we were submerged, the messenger of the watch awakened me to say the captain wanted me to come to the control room immediately. With butterflies in my stomach, I raced to the control room. Captain Jenks was standing at the chart table with *Skipjack's* chief quartermaster. Curiously, the hospital corpsman was there as well.

"Good morning, Mr. Navigator," the captain stated upon seeing me. "Sir?" was my astonished reply. I was at the time the main propulsion assistant to *Skipjack's* engineer, Lt. Cdr. Bud Kauderer. I already had considerable time-consuming responsibilities that involved everything associated with *Skipjack's* steam propulsion plant.

As it happened, Lt. Ted Hussey, *Skipjack's* navigator, had come down with the mumps. He had been immediately relieved of all duties and isolated to his bunk until he could be off-loaded on shore. I was to replace Hussey as soon as I had been briefed on *Skipjack*'s current navigational position by the chief quartermaster, confirmed it to my satisfaction, and reported to the captain that I was ready to assume all responsibilities associated with the job. I would also pick up Ted's duties as operations and intelligence officer and electronics material officer. I was in a state of shock. It was not so much that I didn't have a good feel for where *Skipjack* was geographically and what she had been doing; I had, after all, just gotten off the conning watch only a few hours before. But our captain was a master navigator and had already established extremely high standards in this department, among others. How could I match his expertise?

We soon came up to periscope depth during a brief rest period between exercises. I was thus able to fix our position electronically, thanks to excellent Loran coverage within our Northeast Atlantic operating area.[4] Thankfully, my plotted position was within a mile of that indicated by dead reckoning. With the quartermaster's working navigational chart tucked under my arm, I reported to the captain in the wardroom. Lieutenant Commander Jenks, who was always somewhat quiet and austere, examined this latest position closely. He then nodded his head and proceeded to tell me what he expected of the *Skipjack*'s new navigator. He wanted to know just where we were, at all times, whether submerged or on the surface. I was to run my new department, which consisted of enlisted quartermasters and electronics technicians of various rates and degrees of experience, so as to completely support this requirement. Lieutenant Commander Jenks also made it clear that he expected me to personally fix our navigational position every two hours while at sea. Whew! There was definitely no possibility I would be getting too much sleep anytime soon. Thanks to my youth—I was just thirty-one years old—and my good health, I adapted to this new routine without any particular difficulty. I remained on the regular conning officer watch bill as well, although I was able to turn over my myriad duties as main propulsion assistant to another officer within the engineering department.

The next few days were intense. In between navigational fixes, I verified with the chief quartermaster, who was also the assistant navigator, that we had a full navigational chart allowance with all the latest corrections entered. All this went hand in hand with confirming that we had a full allowance of all required equipments, including verifying that all supporting electronic systems such as Loran, Omega, and the Radio Direction Finder were fully operational within required accuracy specifications.[5] I was simultaneously to keep the job of navigator, operations and intelligence officer, and electronics material officer until well into the fall of 1963. During this period, *Skipjack* conducted a two-month summer Cold War reconnaissance and intelligence-collecting operation in the Barents Sea.

### *Skipjack's* Cold War Mission

*Skipjack* departed in dense fog in late June 1963 for the North Atlantic and the Barents Sea from State Pier, New London, on a Cold War mission. All went well until the radar failed as we were navigating through Long Island Sound on the surface. From there on, and until we were well into the Atlantic and able to submerge in deep water, I sweated blood as we carefully navigated outbound using a single Loran line, depth soundings, and intermittent Radio Direction Finder bearings. We doubled lookouts on the bridge, maintained watches on both periscopes, and sounded the required foghorn signals throughout this potentially dangerous, several-hours-long passage. Without operational radar, it was of course impossible to detect and avoid merchant ships, tankers, and small fishing craft along our route until we heard and eventually saw them at quite close ranges. Luckily, we arrived at our diving position outside Long Island Sound without close calls or undue delay.

Skipjack was allowed to proceed to wherever she was ordered at top or flank speed. We were authorized to use what was called an unlimited speed of advance where appropriate, indefinitely. *Skipjack* had the first of the second-generation Westinghouse S-5-W nuclear reactors. Admiral Rickover and his technical staff wanted us to attempt to burn out the uranium fuel core to the maximum extent possible before *Skipjack* entered Charleston Naval Shipyard to be refueled in mid-1965.[6]

The transit to a position well within the southern Barents Sea seemed endless although, in fact, we reached our initial patrol position in a little over a week. Then, en route, our number two periscope (observational and navigation) flooded with salt water while *Skipjack* was running at deep depth, rendering it unusable. This left us with just one usable periscope, our much thinner and more fragile number one attack periscope. Because its smaller cross-section made it much less detectable by radar and visual means, this periscope was normally used in the final stages of an approach and attack at periscope depth. Our particular number one scope was unique in that it came from a German U-boat that had been taken as a prize following the end of World War II. It was a sit-down type—meaning we sat in a special chair to operate it. Through a pair of handles, we could raise, lower, or rotate it, and change its optical elevation and power. We discovered that we could accomplish air, close aboard, and long-range horizon searches much faster with this scope than with the manually operated number two periscope, once we got the hang of it. We loved it, in spite of its reduced-light transmission characteristics.

In the meantime, on a continuous round-the-clock basis, our auxiliary men made every effort to repair number two periscope using the procedure outlined in my command thesis. A powerful vacuum pump was used to drain the salt water, and repeated flushes were conducted with fresh water and high-pressure blows with hot air to remove salt and other foreign matter particles that might be lodged within. At the same time, we checked all possible sources of leaks in and around the periscope head window. The very top, or head window, portion of the periscope was used to capture light images; above and around us as the periscope was continually rotated through 360 degrees, for transmission down the periscope barrel to the observer's eye. This necessitated our having to broach *Skipjack*'s sail above the surface on a number of occasions, when it was safe to do so, in order for us to closely examine and retighten the head window to the maximum extent possible. It was an exceedingly frustrating battle, during the course of the mission, with the periscope successfully returned to full service on a few brief occasions. It would then reflood, probably due to a small crack somewhere. Number two periscope ultimately had to be completely replaced upon our return to port many weeks later.

Our mission was standard reconnaissance and intelligence gathering. We were to stay in international waters at all times and above all we were to remain undetected. The latter task proved to be quite a challenge due to the considerable number of Soviet ships and foreign fishing boats in the Barents Sea at that time. We diligently carried out our mission largely at periscope depth, including frequent repositioning in response to signal intelligence, in the most aggressive manner possible. We were not blessed, however, with any major sightings of Soviet warships or electromagnetic intercepts of any significance throughout the almost six weeks on station.

I found the mission to be a difficult navigational challenge. Flat, calm seas with dense fog characterized the environment no matter where we patrolled, so my navigational team and I had to rely much more on already skimpy Loran and radio-direction finding lines of bearing than on known landmarks. Only occasionally was it possible to take sun lines and/or visual fixes on well-charted landmarks, such as Kildin Island. It was also risky to take fathometer soundings due to the possibility of being detected by a fixed acoustic array or another submarine. We became masters at maintaining a hand dead-reckoning plot. This, in addition to the requirement to personally fix, or confirm, Skipjack's geographical position every two hours, certainly kept me busy. At no time could I be accused of getting too much sleep.

We departed the Barents Sea area later that summer without incident, disappointed that we had nothing special to show for our time there. We did, however, acquire a good feel for the geography, underwater topography, and general environment in what might well be an assigned forward-patrol area in wartime. It was, in addition, an extremely valuable training opportunity for the entire crew. By its end we had definitely jelled as a smooth, competent, and well-disciplined team under our new commanding officer. Our morale, confidence, and ability to operate Skipjack to the full extent of her capabilities could not have been better.

## Seeing Things

On the return passage we encountered an unusual physical or atmospheric phenomenon that I had previously only read about. Skipjack had just proceeded to periscope depth about fifty nautical miles to the northeast of the North Cape of Norway, transiting some six hours at deep depth on a westerly heading. Skipjack had come up to copy our dedicated radio broadcast and to fix our position by Loran and, hopefully, to recognize some physical landmark along the northern Norwegian coast. I had the periscope upon breaking the surface at approximately sixty-nine feet. My initial rapid searches for surface contacts or obstacles close aboard confirmed an earlier estimation that the seas would probably be flat calm. But then my visual search for aircraft contacts revealed some inversions of contacts and land masses due to light refraction that could only be well over the horizon. In addition, it appeared I was passing the sun three times in just one revolution of the periscope. How could this be?

After reporting to the captain, "At periscope depth, no close contacts," I began a series of slower horizon searches. To my utter astonishment, I sighted what appeared to be a long line of steep and quite high brown-colored bluffs to our northwest that extended through some 40 degrees toward a heading of due north. This was impossible. Both the Mk-19 and Mk-23 gyrocompasses indicated we were heading almost due west. Thus, any land within sight could only be the Norwegian coast that was supposedly due south of us. However, it seemed we were too far north to be able to sight any land to our south. "What is going on?" I mumbled to myself. To my further consternation I noted that a sun that should have been shining brightly above the horizon to the southwest also appeared at approximately the same magnitude some 30 degrees to the northwest and again to the southeast. I called the chief quartermaster to the scope to take a look. He immediately confirmed all that I had just observed. I ordered, "Helmsman, steady as you go, make minimum turns!" "Steady on course two six five degrees True," he responded.

I called Captain Jenks to the control room, reported what we were observing, and asked him to take a look through the periscope. I ventured the possibility that we were observing something called parhelia, or sun dogs, which other mariners operating under similar conditions at high latitudes had reported.[7] Sun dogs are manifestations of bright spots of light that can appear at approximately 22 degrees to either side of the sun and at the same elevation above the horizon. They are usually made of plate-like hexagonal ice crystals in high and cold cirrus clouds or, during very cold weather, by ice crystals called diamond dust drifting in the air at low levels. These crystals act as prisms, bending the light that passes through them with a minimum deflection of 22 degrees.

On the other hand, what seemed to be a sizable land mass to the northwest couldn't be explained. Bear Island was over two hundred miles to the north of us and Svalbard was even farther away. It couldn't be these. The captain confirmed our sightings and also informed us that he had seen what looked like several upside-down ships slightly above the horizon during the course of his 360-degrees' search of the horizon with the periscope. We concluded that what we were seeing were severe atmospheric inversion conditions due to the absolutely flat calm seas and bright sunlight. But what could we do about it?

We couldn't help but question our navigational estimate of just where we were. Only our compass headings and a series of secure bottom soundings, which indicated we were in the depth of water expected, corresponded with our best estimate of where we were. We therefore decided to remain at periscope depth and continue to proceed in a generally westerly direction at minimum speed. Hopefully a wind or even slight breeze would soon come up that would help dispel the mirage. Alarming as the sight was initially, we did eventually conclude that what seemed to be land to the northwest was possibly Bear Island.

After what seemed an eternity, a westerly wind came up that restored everything to normal. We changed course to the southwest and closed the

Norwegian coast sufficiently to sight the North Cape and more accurately fix our position.

The transit across the North Atlantic was mercifully swift and uneventful. Once we returned safely home to our normal berth alongside the submarine tender USS *Fulton* at State Pier, New London, we had about a month's stand-down in order to accomplish some much-needed repairs and upkeep. Top on the priority list was to give everybody a few days' leave. During that time we would pull and replace number two periscope, which had caused us no end of annoyance and frustration the entire trip.

My wife Mary used to say that whenever my leave began, hers ended, and vice versa. That was true in spades during this particular homecoming, because she did not get a good night's sleep during the entire time we were in port. I was so used to waking up suddenly every hour and a half to fix *Skipjack*'s navigational position that every night for weeks I would suddenly wake up and jump out of bed, making a lot of commotion.

# CHAPTER 17

# Evaluation of the Nuclear Attack Submarine

The remainder of 1963 was filled with ASW free play operations, with ASW surface units of the Second Fleet, submarine-versus-submarine ASW exercises, and an exercise that involved making simulated attacks on a heavily escorted group of amphibious vessels. The latter were filled with U.S. Marines who would be making landings near Little Creek, Virginia. The primary objective was again to prove the capabilities of the nuclear-powered attack submarine. *Skipjack* could not be touched unless severe exercise restrictions were imposed on her. It was common knowledge that our sister nuclear attack submarines, *Scorpion*, *Shark*, and *Snook* in the Atlantic and *Scamp* and *Sculpin* in the Pacific, were enjoying similar success against surface and air ASW forces.

We did not have the same success against our own diesel submarines during the first, and follow-on, submarine-versus-submarine ASW exercises. It was generally a draw, if anything. *Skipjack* had the speed and maneuverability that enabled her to outrun any electrically propelled ASW torpedo of that day, no matter who launched it, but she did not have the ability to passively detect submerged diesel submarines operating quietly on the battery until they were inside of two thousand yards. Detecting them at longer ranges while they were on the surface, or snorkeling, to recharge their batteries was no problem. On the other hand, we were rarely able to close sufficiently to simulate killing them with a spread of torpedoes, particularly if they were following what was called a combat charging routine—that is, snorkeling for half an hour at a time, suddenly shutting down, and then clearing baffles to determine if anyone was trying to creep up and attack them.

Those in the nuclear attack boats soon realized that the submarine force had to develop and refine a snapshot tactic for close encounters. Such a tactic called for our boat to operate with a fully flooded and ready torpedo tube containing a quiet, electrically propelled acoustic warshot that could be launched against an immediate threat. In those days the Mark-37 acoustic-homing torpedo was the only one available that met this criterion. When launched in the direction of the target it would swim out of the tube within thirty seconds.

The most probable threat scenario envisioned was one in which the nuclear attack submarine had just slowed, either while deep or en route to shallower depth, and had begun to clear and passively examine its baffles acoustically for any threat contacts. The Cold War rules of engagement at the time called for launching a torpedo at an adversary upon detecting the acoustic transient noises associated with a torpedo tube being flooded and/ or the opening of the tube's outer door. Once we had launched the snap-shot, the next move depended on the estimated range to the adversary. We could slow, maintain minimum aspect to prevent detection, and prepare additional warshot-loaded torpedo tubes for launch as necessary. Depending on the target and its capabilities, we might also find it necessary to use maximum speed, maneuverability, and depth to clear the area sufficiently to avoid a counterattack torpedo.

## Submarine Development Group Two

A major problem that came to the fore during these exercises was radiated noise that *Skipjack* emitted no matter what her speed. The noise originated, in large part, from the cavitation generated by her five-bladed propeller, and by rudder and diving plane surfaces, and increased when she used her speed and maneuverability to the fullest extent possible. It meant that a potential adversary, whether diesel or nuclear, had the advantage if patrolling in a silent-running or quiet mode of operation. Hence, if *Skipjack* were to survive and be successful when deployed against enemy forces in a forward area, off enemy ports, and along probable transit routes, she had to operate more quietly than her potential adversaries.

The challenge that presented itself to the submarine force, as well as to the U.S. Navy's Material Command, was how to achieve the degree of sound quieting necessary for all U.S. nuclear submarines, both physically and operationally, without negating the myriad other advantages already gained over potential enemy surface ships or submarines, such as speed, maneuverability, and the ability to remain fully submerged indefinitely. Further required was the ability to avoid or defeat detection by enemy ASW aircraft, or by the sonobuoys they drop, and helicopters with passive and active acoustic-dipping sonar. Such an ability would be essential if front-line nuclear attack submarines like *Skipjack* were to continue to be used on high-priority and sensitive reconnaissance and intelligence-gathering Cold War missions.

In late January 1949 the U.S. Navy and the submarine force had begun to take steps to accomplish the foregoing when the Chief of Naval Operations directed that "Fleet Commanders assign one division in each fleet the sole task of solving the problem of using submarines to detect and destroy enemy submarines. All other operations of any nature, even type training, ASW services, or fleet tactics, shall be subordinated to this mission."[1] This directive led to the establishment of Submarine Development Group Two under the command of Capt. Roy S. Benson (later rear admiral), based at the submarine base in Groton.[2] To assist this newly established command in solving the basic problem assigned, the Chief of Naval Operations subsequently provided a suggested procedure that encompassed the following phases:

- Learn to operate sonar at maximum efficiency, reduce submarine self-noise, develop methods for best maintaining of depth and position, and develop submerged communications and recognition procedures.
- Determine capabilities of installed sonar equipments and best operating depths for various bathythermograph conditions.
- Solve the sonar fire control problem using both passive and active ranging techniques.
- Develop doctrine and tactics for detecting and attacking submerged submarines.
- Develop group doctrine and tactics and evaluate capabilities of submarines versus submarines in all possible tactic situations.
- Determine operational requirements for new and improved equipment to adequately perform the submarine versus submarine mission.[3]

Submarine Development Group Two achieved much on all the foregoing tasks during the 1950s, using the newly constructed diesel submarine, *K-1*, which was later named USS *Barracuda* (SSK1). It was equipped with the first operational large passive sonar array, called the AN/BQR-4, in exercises involving both regular fleet submarines and those that had been modified under the GUPPY program.[4] At the same time, significant

ASW-sponsored research began in U.S. universities, government laboratories, industry, the U.S. Office of Naval Research, a committee on Undersea Warfare of the National Academy of Sciences, and the U.S. Navy's Bureau of Ships. They all worked to determine and then design all that was necessary to cope with the threat posed by a rapidly increasing Soviet submarine force.

The Office of Naval Research itself began extensive work on submarine noise-reduction studies. Civilian scientists such as the physicist Marvin Lasky at the David Taylor Model Basin in Bethesda, Maryland, examined the submarine-quieting possibilities that might be gained from use of a single screw or propeller on the undersea test submarine USS *Albacore*. Lasky was later to be a major player in the Office of Naval Research's successful role in supporting underwater sound-propagation and noise-reduction studies, and introducing the towed acoustic array into both the submarine force and the surface fleet.[5]

From 1962 to 1964 when I was serving on board *Skipjack*, Submarine Development Group Two was under the command of the brilliant, imaginative, innovative, and energetic Capt. Frank A. Andrews. One of his first initiatives was to create the Tactical Analysis Group with a primary task of developing tactics for the submarine weapon systems of the new, follow-on to *Skipjack*, *Thresher-* (later *Permit*)-class submarine. Its first leader was former All-American U.S. Naval Academy football player and colorful submarine commander, Cdr. Donald B. Whitmire. Thus began the appropriately named Big Daddy submarine-versus-submarine tactical exercises that *Skipjack* became involved in during much of my time on board.

The Big Daddy exercise program, working with *Skipjack* and other nuclear and diesel attack submarines of Submarine Squadron Ten, established a series of rigorous at-sea exercises to closely examine the results of (1) submarines (in a barrier) versus transiting submarines, (2) submarines versus intruders, (3) use of nuclear attack submarines as trailers of other submarines, and (4) use of the nuclear attack submarines as carrier task force escorts. This program was subsequently to provide the necessary data for the SSN 594–class ASW performance assessment, which was used in turn to make up the report necessary for selling the need at the very highest levels at the U.S. Department of Defense for a new *Sturgeon* (SSN 637) class of nuclear attack submarine.[6]

I well remember the many hours that *Skipjack* spent playing the transiting submarine against both diesel boats and the new, very quiet USS *Tullibee* (SSN 597). The latter was built to serve as a hunter-killer submarine whose primary mission was to detect, engage, and destroy enemy submarines in her path. She was a test platform for a much quieter nuclear propulsion plan and the first to be equipped with the bow-mounted spherical sonar arrays, the AN/BQQ-2 long-ranging sonar system.[7]

Most of *Skipjack*'s transiting submarine exercise runs were made at high speed, using a zigzag plan of our own design. As I recall, both *Tullibee* and various diesel boats had enjoyed considerable success in detecting us due to our still-high radiated noise, but they were not successful in closing and attacking us. These exercises revealed that the attack submarine's primary weapon, the Mk-37 electric acoustic torpedo, was almost totally ineffective against high-speed targets. This finding was to lead to the accelerated development of the new, and infinitely more capable, Mk-48 torpedo program.[8]

I remember, too, our frustration when *Skipjack* played the intruder, trailer, or carrier task group escort and we were unable to detect either a diesel submarine or another nuclear attack submarine such as *Tullibee* or *Skate* until it was close aboard and well after it had detected us. The limitation further underscored the need for a long-range sonar system like the AN/BQQ to be installed in all nuclear attack submarines. Indeed, the exercises made clear the urgent need to devote the entire bow of future nuclear attack submarines to their sonar systems. The torpedo tubes were moved to an angled, amidships position along the port and starboard sides of the hull, preventing the noise of readying and launching torpedoes from interfering with the sonar detection and tracking of potential adversaries.[9]

## The Seabee Challenge

Following formal written and oral examinations by Admiral Rickover's staff at his Naval Reactors headquarters in Washington, DC, in early fall of 1963, I fully qualified for engineer of nuclear submarines and relieved Lt. Cdr. Bud Kauderer of the position. Relieving me as navigator and operations officer, in turn, was the very capable Lt. Ron Eytchison. The job of engineer officer of the lead submarine of a relatively new class of high-performance nuclear attack subs presented unique challenges. One thing that concerned me when I first reported on board in 1962 was the number of sil-brazed joints that *Skipjack* had throughout her seawater piping. We were almost certain among ourselves that *Thresher* had been lost as a result of a major seawater leak that could not be stopped in one of its sil-brazed joints. All on board *Skipjack* therefore reacted with alacrity to any and all leaks and felt strongly that sil-brazed joints needed to be replaced with welded joints as soon as possible.

Another major concern was that our main propulsion turbines had begun to throw blades. This was due in all probability to metal fatigue as a result of *Skipjack*'s high operational pace, with much of it being at top speed. Each casualty of this sort required time-consuming major repairs involving replacement of the blades and turbine-rebalancing efforts in port at the submarine base in Groton.

Several of the many ASW exercises we engaged in that year took us geographically close enough to enjoy a few days of liberty in Bermuda. *Skipjack*'s exec, Bob Chewning, and I went ashore as often as possible, with our favorite haunt being the bar of the Elbow Beach Hotel. Our purpose was always, of course, to do all we could to further international relations. The only frustration was the lack of taxicabs.

While in Bermuda, a few of the younger members of our crew learned to their grief something that was well known among their World War II and Korean War predecessors: "Don't mess with Seabees"—personnel of the U.S. Navy's construction battalions. They were generally older and tougher than the average sailor or Marine, many having come out of the steel worker and construction trades. On this visit, one of our younger petty officers challenged three Seabees at a local pub. Two fellow crewmembers who were having a good time had no idea what their pal was up to. The Seabees accepted the challenge and moved in on our three guys. The first petty officer broke and ran back to the boat, leaving his unsuspecting two shipmates to take on the Seabees. The outcome was predictable and short: both men returned to *Skipjack* with black eyes, split lips, and a cracked rib or two. The sailor who ran away acquired the name of Speedy Gonzalez from his shipmates, who debated whether he was the smartest or the dumbest of the three.

## The Infamous United Way Drive

We arrived in port at New London a week before the Thanksgiving holiday after a major exercise the previous week. We had been away from home port for most of the past year, and we all needed a rest and time with our families. However, a yearly event in the month that preceded the holiday season was the United Way Drive. The submarine squadron commanders, and deputy ComSubLant above them at that time, placed tremendous pressure on every crewmember of New London–based submarines to contribute to the United Way Fund or suffer the consequences.

*Skipjack* had avoided any repercussions for having fallen short of the goal in late 1962 because our skipper, Commander Kelly, covered those not contributing the required amount out of his own pocket. Such was not the case this year, however. Because *Skipjack's* officers and men had once more not achieved the required 100 percent participation, we soon learned that instead of having Thanksgiving at home, we would be getting under way early in the Thanksgiving week to proceed over 1,500 nautical miles to Flemish Cap, to the east of Newfoundland. Once there, we would render target services to ASW aircraft based out of Argentia, Newfoundland, which would practice detecting and tracking us over the holiday.

This news was not well received on *Skipjack,* much less by our families, who were devastated. But orders were orders, and with a cheery "Aye, aye," off we went at top speed. We reached the assigned exercise area early morning on Thanksgiving, only to discover there would be no aircraft that day. We learned further that the local area commander had canceled the entire exercise and that we were released to return home. To the credit of the captain and our cooks, *Skipjack* threw a superb Thanksgiving dinner at sea, but we would have much preferred to enjoy it with our families and friends at home. General morale remained good in spite of the grousing about this bit of petty, time-wasting, and unnecessary family-separation idiocy. There was no fondness in our hearts for the United Way Drive or the strong-arm methods used by our seniors to raise money for this particular charity. We headed home at top speed and three days later were moored once again at State Pier, New London. We remained in port this time for a lengthy upkeep and a leave period that to our delight extended through the Christmas period and well into the new year.

# CHAPTER 18

# A Year to Remember

S*kipjack* began 1964 by taking part in a submarine ASW exercise, which added to the Submarine Development Group Two's much-needed barrier exercise data. This exercise involved submarines patrolling a stationary or fixed barrier against aggressor submarines attempting to transit or penetrate the barrier without being detected and attacked. As a transiting submarine, we demonstrated once again our capabilities as a high-speed, extremely maneuverable attack boat. It was during this time that Capt. Michael U. Moore relieved Capt. Frank A. Andrews as commander of Submarine Development Group Two, and the Big Daddy series of submarine-versus-submarine exercises intensified. We spent most of February and March at sea, simulating wartime transiting and patrol conditions, broken only by a pleasurable visit to San Juan, Puerto Rico, and several brief pit stops at our home port.

## Taking Their Picture

Our skipper, Shep Jenks, was promoted to full commander on 1 April 1964. *Skipjack*'s wardroom did a fine job of "wetting down"—pouring Scotch over the skipper's new full gold stripe at the officers club the following Saturday evening. As it happened, in the main dining room the Blue Crew wardroom of one of the New London–based fleet ballistic missile submarines (FBM) was celebrating, too. Possibly it was the anniversary of their launching or commissioning. The officers were in full dress, giving long serious speeches, all very formal and dull. Behind their table a blown-up photograph of their beloved FBM was mounted on the wall. The event was a fine candidate for a disruption of some sort, courtesy of our raucous gang.

Commanding officer Shepherd M. Jenks (far left) and officers, USS *Skipjack* (SSN 585), 1964. *U.S. Navy*

The bright idea was hatched of trying to find some way of stealing the photograph without their noticing it. It was not long before we hit on the solution: Captain Jenks and I would respectfully approach their table and ask the Blue Crew officers if they would all please assemble in our room so that we could "take their picture." Pleased as punch, they dutifully got up and followed us back, where we asked them to line up against the wall "by height and rank." It was all we could do to keep a straight face when they had more than a little trouble figuring out just how they would do this. In the meantime, one of *Skipjack*'s officers who had stayed back quickly took down the photo of their FBM, hustled it down the stairs to the club's storeroom, shoved it in, and locked the door. Another *Skipjack* officer stepped forward with a camera and asked the FBM officers to adjust their positions, pose, and smile as he pretended to photograph them. After the photos were taken, Captain Jenks and I waved, thanked them in a friendly fashion, and returned to our table. Our coconspirators who had hidden the photograph preceded us to the table, soon followed by our erstwhile cameraman. We carried on as if nothing had happened to disrupt the good time we'd been having.

We were in the midst of telling jokes, laughing loudly, and making a great deal of noise as the officers of the FBM Blue Crew solemnly filed back into the main dining room and took their seats. They resumed the speech-making associated with whatever their formal occasion was all about.

It was at least a half hour before one of them suddenly noticed that their photograph was no longer on the wall. The table broke up as some officers began looking under their own and adjacent tables, while others began frantically searching the room. We feigned indifference to the goings on until their exec approached and asked if we had seen their picture. Our exec, Lt. Cdr. William H. "Bill" Purdum, answered, "Yes, we had seen and admired it earlier. Why are you asking?" The FBM exec, in a high state of agitation, pointed to the wall and said, "It's gone." Some of us rose to our feet and, with concerned looks, expressed surprise that the picture was no longer there. Our exec offered to assist in whatever way we could, and with a gruff "thanks" the FBM exec turned on his heel and abruptly departed.

The FBM officers searched and searched and came up empty handed. We caught them looking at our group suspiciously from time to time, but they never quite got up the nerve to come over and make a direct accusation. They finally called it a night and left in a deflated mood. The club staff kicked us out well after midnight, and that was the last we heard about it until the following week when the club's cooks discovered the picture in the storeroom. We subsequently heard from our DivCom that the theft was brought up at a high-level staff meeting, mentioning that we were the prime suspects. He didn't ask us directly, and although we laughed loudly, we didn't admit to a thing, nor were we ever asked for the photographs that we supposedly took that night.

We spent the remainder of the month in dry dock at the submarine base in New London. There we accomplished minor repairs following the recent period at sea. The hull was thoroughly cleaned and repainted. The marine growth acquired on the underside of our hull during the brief time in San Juan had been enough to drop *Skipjack*'s top speed by several knots.

The month of May was devoted to advanced exercises with U.S. Navy ASW surface forces. *Skipjack*'s capabilities conclusively demonstrated several crucial combat needs among our surface forces. One was for more-advanced sonar detection and attack systems on all ASW ships. Another was for higher-speed ASW torpedoes capable of acoustically acquiring and destroying high-speed nuclear attack submarines.

## Dropping Off the Step

It was during this period of ASW exercises that USS *Skipjack* was visited by a near catastrophe, to be followed by a personnel tragedy of the worst sort.

*Skipjack* had been at sea in the North Atlantic for several weeks, participating in a major fleet exercise with surface ships of the U.S. Navy and Royal Navy. We had been tasked with playing the role of an enemy or "red" submarine—a simulated Soviet submarine whose mission was to oppose an allied powers' fast-carrier task force en route to forward strike positions off the coast of the "red" nation.

*Skipjack* had already executed a series of surprise attacks on the Royal Navy aircraft carrier HMS *Hermes* and evaded detection and counterattack by her ASW destroyer escorts. In May 1964 she broke off contact and headed for her next assigned patrol area at maximum speed. Once there, our plan was to proceed to the surface just after sunset and celestially fix our position. It would be good practice for our navigator, his quartermaster assistants, and various junior officers for their qualification in submarines.

At the edge of our new patrol area, *Skipjack* slowed and ascended to periscope depth. We were greeted by a beautifully clear evening twilight with an almost flat, calm sea, which were perfect conditions for the training planned. It was even better for the conduct of an airless surface, another important training evolution for a number of our boat's officers and crewmembers.

A normal submarine surfacing involves the simultaneous blowing of seawater from the six soft ballast tanks that surround the submarine's pressure hull. High-pressure air at three thousand pounds per square inch is stored in banks located within these tanks. A full blow of all tanks using this air is normally ordered in order to expel the water and achieve the requisite positive buoyancy to reach the surface as rapidly as possible. Once on the surface, seawater remaining in the ballast tanks is removed through the continued use of a low-pressure blower, until the boat is riding high and dry on the surface. In the case of *Skipjack* with its rounded hull, the higher the submarine, the less surface drag and thus the greater speed that she could obtain.

The high-pressure air used to accomplish the initial blow, however, must be fully replenished as soon as possible. With two high-pressure air compressors on line, it was a noisy operation that usually required several hours, making it more detectable to potential adversaries. It should be noted that the air used in any surfacing evolution was an important part of a submarine's store of emergency breathing air. This was air that would be needed when submerged should a casualty occur to both of the submarine's oxygen generators. For these reasons, an airless surface was the preferred method of surfacing *Skipjack*.

The airless surface procedure consisted of driving the submarine to the surface at full speed at a relatively steep up-angle with all vents atop the six ballast tanks open. This permitted seawater to drain by gravity from the ballast tanks as *Skipjack* was driven up to the surface and held, using speed and diving planes, at as shallow a depth as possible. All ballast tank vents were then shut, speed reduced, and the low-pressure blower used to remove all residual water, which usually took about ten minutes

Because of her football- or *Albacore*-shaped hull and the number of revolutions that her single five-bladed propeller could make, *Skipjack* could also be driven on to an essentially hydroplaning position once it was high and dry on the surface. We called this "getting on the step."

As mentioned earlier, the step was achieved, once the sub was fully surfaced, by placing the after-diving control surfaces or stern planes (already well submerged due to their location) on 3- to 5-degree rise, and then increasing speed to flank or the maximum allowable number of propeller revolutions. As *Skipjack*'s speed approached maximum, she would begin to squat slightly. The stern planes were then gradually eased to between a 1-degree and 2-degree rise. As she planed up to a more horizontal position on the surface, her speed through, or more properly over, the water surface would dramatically increase to well over twenty knots.

Extreme care had to be taken to maintain this position or *Skipjack* would suddenly drop off the step: her bow would nose down dramatically, and the boat would head for deeper depths at high speed. This was a known and ever-present hazard. It was also an inevitable outcome were the sea state or wave heights to rise. The consequences for an officer of the deck, watch section, and the crew as a whole could vary from a thorough drenching of the officer of the deck and bridge watch to catastrophic loss of the submarine if the upper and lower bridge trunk hatches were not immediately shut, speed reduced, and the boat leveled using both stern and sail planes on full rise.

On this particular evening *Skipjack* had conducted a flawless airless surfacing. All MBT vents were shut, and the low-pressure blower was hard at work removing the remaining seawater from the ballast tanks. The captain; the officer of the deck, Lt. Ron Eytchison; and a lookout had just ascended the bridge from the control room via the vertical ladder through an approximately twenty-foot steep access trunk and the now fully open lower- and upper-bridge trunk hatches.

I was senior watch officer as well as engineer officer of *Skipjack* at the time and had been on board for well over two years. It was, accordingly, my habit to ease into the control room during almost all surfacings and dives to keep an eye on things and to back up the captain while he was on the bridge. On this particular evening I had also just been the command watch officer while we were submerged. From appearances, all was well as both crew and boat operations appeared to have settled into a normal surface operations routine.

Not more than five minutes had passed when I was startled to hear the captain order, "Ahead flank!" This was soon followed by the order to the helmsman, in the control room, "Position the stern planes on 5 degrees rise!" The helmsman acknowledged both orders, and the remote speed indicator in front of the helmsman confirmed that the engineering officer of the watch in the maneuvering room was answering the flank speed order.

*Skipjack's* speed on the surface rapidly increased to ten knots, then twelve, and finally began to steady at between fifteen and sixteen knots. From the bridge then came the order, "Decrease the stern planes to 3 degrees rise!" The helmsman decreased the planes the ordered amount, and the boat's speed began to steadily increase to approximately eighteen knots. The bridge then ordered, "Decrease stern planes to 2 degrees rise!" Our speed began to increase again. Suddenly, *Skipjack's* bow abruptly dipped downward, and we found ourselves rapidly heading beneath the surface at high speed.

Without waiting for any order from the bridge or anyone else, I immediately ordered, "All back full! Blow the forward group!" I lunged forward at the same time, grabbed the lanyard to the lower bridge trunk hatch, yanked it shut, and held on tightly as a nearby watch stander dogged it. My orders were paralleled within seconds from the bridge. Nonetheless, during the next few minutes *Skipjack*, with a hefty down angle, plunged sufficiently beneath the sea surface to bring the captain, officer of the deck, and lookout within a few feet of the surface, ensuring that all were thoroughly drenched.

*Skipjack* quickly returned to the surface. I ordered "All stop!," and a high-pressure blow of the forward ballast tanks was secured.

Once we had all taken a deep breath, it became obvious to all that we had tried to get the boat on the step prematurely. The MBTs had not been blown sufficiently dry for *Skipjack* to ride high enough in the water to truly get on the step. We learned consequently that a requisite minimum draft had to be achieved and held before attempting any such maneuver in the future.

## A Tragic Accident

The near disaster of dropping off the step was followed a few days later by an incident that led to the death of one of *Skipjack's* best petty officers. To be electrocuted is the dread of all submariners, but it can only happen if all the required safeguards have been bypassed.

*Skipjack* was between exercises and proceeding at slow speed several hundred feet beneath the surface. An experienced internal communications and senior petty officer, James F. Twyford, decided on his own to crawl behind the fire-control display panels on the starboard side of the control room to repair something. Twyford was a fine young man with a nice family, and was much liked across the crew. He was working by himself. He had not informed anyone, including the chief of the watch, the conning officer, or his senior petty officer, where he would be working and what he would be doing. In addition, no electrical power of any sort had been secured and red tagged anywhere that might have been associated with Twyford's normal fire-control system responsibilities.

The first indication that something was seriously amiss was a very loud *pop* or explosion followed by a low agonized groan and then frantic thrashing from behind the forward fire-control display panel. The sounds abruptly ceased, and all became deathly quiet. A senior firecontrolman who happened to be sitting on a bench in front of the panel jumped up and went forward to check. As soon as he looked behind the forward panel, he yelled, "It's Twyford and he's badly hurt! Call the corpsman!" He proceeded, with assistance from an off watch stander, to untangle and drag an unconscious Twyford, heavily bleeding from the leg, from behind the panel and into the control room. The hospital corpsman who had been called over the 1MC arrived within minutes and checked him over. A large hole had burned through Twyford's right trouser leg and deep into his thigh.

We couldn't be sure, but it seemed that Twyford had somehow managed to electrocute himself by creating a massive electrical short with his leg. Across what and just how, we didn't know. The corpsman thumped Twyford's heart forcefully and began artificial resuscitation while continuing to apply pressure at regular intervals to the area just above his heart. I alternated with the corpsman, and we succeeded in getting Twyford to resume breathing on three occasions. Each time he would struggle very hard to sit up, but then collapse on the deck and cease to breathe.

The captain brought *Skipjack* to the surface and called for emergency medical assistance from one of the nearby surface ships that we had been operating with. The aircraft carrier helicoptered a doctor. In the meantime, Twyford revived yet one more time. He sat up, looked very intensely at something above him, and then with a loud gasp suddenly fell backward. He again ceased breathing, and it now appeared that his heart had stopped. The corpsman and I frantically resumed our efforts to revive him, but this time we knew that Twyford had departed this life for good and all.

The doctor arrived within ten minutes. He rushed below into the control room and had us stand aside so that he could examine Twyford. He put his ear to Twyford's chest and confirmed that he was no longer breathing and that his heart had stopped. The doctor removed a small flashlight from his pocket and peered deeply into Twyford's throat. After a few minutes, he removed the flashlight and slowly stood up. Shaking his head, he sadly told us that Twyford had drowned in his own vomit. He added that this must have begun almost immediately following his electrocution.

The hospital corpsman and I were at first thunderstruck, then overcome with grief. We both began weeping bitterly. How could we have missed seeing this? The hospital corpsman had in fact visually checked Twyford's airways before we commenced efforts to revive him and had not seen any obstruction and so reported. The doctor tried to explain that Twyford had probably vomited immediately after he had been electrocuted. He had then ingested most of the vomit into his lungs while he was still gasping behind the fire-control display panels. In this case it would have been very hard to detect. He repeatedly assured us that we had taken all the right steps in our efforts to revive Twyford. Even so, we could not be consoled, then or at any time in the future. We felt strongly that we had failed a shipmate in his time of greatest need. I am filled with remorse every time I think about this dark, ill-fated day.

*Skipjack* was detached from the exercise while petty officer Twyford's body was reverently wrapped with blankets and placed in the freeze box until we reached port. Returning home to New London, Twyford's mortal remains were off-loaded with full-military honors. All but the duty section left the boat several days later to attend our former shipmate's funeral service and interment at a large cemetery just north of New York City. He could not have received a more fitting tribute, but the occasion was terrible for us all. It was hard to believe that we would never again see Jim Twyford or enjoy his cheery disposition and comradeship during the long watch hours at sea.

A subsequent formal investigation confirmed that Twyford's death was accidental and not due to anyone's neglect or misconduct. He had apparently been working on something relatively minor and nonelectrical and had accidentally bumped or placed his leg across a hot, high-voltage circuit associated with the fire-control display panels.

In the wake of Twyford's death, *Skipjack*'s greatly shaken crew went through retraining in all aspects and requirements of onboard electrical safety. This included making sure that there was always a backup person standing by who fully understood what was being done by anyone working on an electrical circuit or any equipment connected to one. The backup had to be capable of both preventing an unsafe action by that person, or taking whatever emergency first aid action was necessary should something unexpected occur.

We subsequently remained in port several weeks for upkeep and for intensive preparations for a second Cold War mission to the Barents Sea under Cdr. Shep Jenks.

## CHAPTER 19

# One More Cold War Mission and a Change of Command

**S**kipjack's mission to the Barents Sea to collect intelligence during most of June and July 1964 was very much like the one we had conducted the previous summer. The Barents is a shallow continental shelf sea portion of the Arctic Ocean. It is 800 miles long and 650 miles wide. It covers some 542,000 square miles. The climate is subarctic, with summer air temperatures averaging 32° Fahrenheit in the north and 50° in the southwest. Branches of the Norway Current bring warm currents into the sea, but this heat is soon lost through mixing with colder waters from the north.[1]

As a result, many days during our mission were flat calm with heavy fog, making it difficult to see much of anything. We did sight several diesel electric-powered Soviet *Golf II*–class SSBs and tried to trail a nuclear-powered *Hotel II*–class SSBN.[2] Each had a long sail that housed three vertical missile tubes abaft the bridge. The SS-N-5 nuclear ballistic missiles they carried had a range of 750 nautical miles, according to a later analysis.[3] We hoped that the *Hotel II* might be deploying to a forward area off the continental United States, but we lost it shortly after it submerged and increased speed. We increased our own speed in order to remain within a comfortable trailing position, but that caused us to lose contact. For reasons mentioned earlier, *Skipjack* did not have good capability for detecting, much less tracking, a contact whenever it was necessary to increase her speed to more than five knots.

Among other duties during this mission, I was photographic officer, and one long-range photo of a Soviet submarine that I managed to take created some excitement on board and high interest back in port. The sub

I photographed was subsequently termed "the Monster" by the intelligence community. No one at the time had any idea what type it might be. In retrospect, it may well have been what was later to be termed the *Golf III*, a one-of-a-kind Soviet Northern Fleet SSBN, which had a much longer sail than usual, in order to accommodate six missile tubes. It was estimated that each could hold a Soviet SS-N-8 ballistic missile with a range of approximately 4,500 miles.[4]

During our transit home we were delighted to receive the news that *Skipjack* had been awarded the Battle Efficiency "E" for Submarine Division 102 for fiscal year 1964. The past twelve months had been tough. We all felt strongly that we richly deserved the accolades. We were also feeling quite pleased and proud that we had spent the better part of two successful, and undetected, months in what would surely have been our forward deployment area should the United States go into a hot war with the Soviets.

We were not in port at New London very long before our much-respected skipper, Cdr. Shep Jenks, was relieved on 7 August 1964 by Lt. Cdr. Paul D. Tomb. Commander Jenks went on to become commanding officer of a new-construction nuclear-powered ballistic missile submarine.

It was hard to see Shep Jenks leave. I had served with him as both navigator and engineer officer for over a year and a half. He was a quiet and reserved man, but a real professional. We all knew where we stood with him. I particularly admired the way he empowered each of us to take charge and fully do the job assigned. By not micromanaging us, he gave all of us maximum opportunity to grow professionally and helped us gain the necessary confidence to take on even greater responsibilities. At the same time, he was always available and approachable when we needed advice or instruction. As I reflect back, I appreciate even more fully his example. The two years I spent with him did much to prepare me for my own submarine command.

Our new skipper, Paul Tomb, came to us from the Blue Crew of the ballistic missile submarine, USS *Theodore Roosevelt* (SSBN 600), where he had been exec since September 1962. Prior to that, he had been *Roosevelt's* commissioning/new-construction engineer officer. Previous submarine duty included tours on both the nuclear attack submarine USS *Sargo* and the diesel attack boat USS *Tilefish* (SS 307).

## The Playmate of the Month's Short Reign

It was late August 1964 and we were preparing to head off to the North Atlantic in another month for a lengthy exercise with U.S. Navy and NATO forces. After that we were scheduled for visits to Le Havre, France; and Portland, England. Our crew was really looking forward to the months ahead. As part of our workup we would be going to sea on local operations with a new captain who had taken command just a few weeks earlier. It would be his first opportunity to show us what kind of skipper he would be. He was slated to remain with the boat through our remaining months at sea, until the spring of 1965. He would then take it through a lengthy overhaul and reactor refueling at the naval shipyard in Charleston, South Carolina.

Captain Tomb seemed a genial, confident sort—more informal with the officers and men than our previous two had been. He took part in the general kibitzing around the wardroom table during meals, and we soon became comfortable with him. Operationally, however, he was still an unknown. No one on board had previously served with him. We thus had no idea or feel for how he would handle stressful situations, which are certain to occur from time to time at sea and where a commanding officer's knowledge and experience really count. At least we were not heading off on a Cold War mission or special operation. The local operations followed by the voyage to the eastern Atlantic would be more of a lark. The mood that prevailed throughout the boat was thus more light-hearted and less tense than usual.

Within days of his reporting on board, it became obvious that Captain Tomb was fond of *Playboy* magazine. Rumors that he had a large cache of the magazines in his stateroom quickly spread throughout the boat. In the course of receiving routine reports, he was frequently seen to have his face deep in the centerfold of a playmate of the month. Our previous commanding officer, by contrast, had come across as somewhat austere and distant. None of us would dare to have been seen with any such magazine during his time. It's not that he ever said anything to discourage us—it just didn't seem like a good idea. Our wardroom bachelors were careful to tone down their descriptions of recent liberty escapades on shore whenever the captain was within listening distance. With this captain the wardroom atmosphere was just the opposite.

During the first days of a weeklong local operation, the new skipper became sufficiently comfortable with *Skipjack's* officers to share his playmate of the month centerfolds. The second morning under way he taped up one of his favorites on a wardroom bulkhead, or wall. He located it where he could best see and enjoy her from where he sat at the head of the dining table. She was certainly a lovely thing, with an exceptional smile in addition to all her other charms on display. One could readily see why the captain liked this particular playmate.

Well, after midnight some dirty dog—yours truly—altered the playmate of the month's appearance in a most dastardly fashion. She was now, inexplicably, missing two front teeth, leaving a disfiguring gap.

Probably no more than a half dozen of the officers and crew saw the altered playmate of the month before the captain did. After their initial laughter, they began to worry about his reaction. The senior steward's mate, SDC Peter William Ungacta Sococo, a commissioning crewmember on *Skipjack* and veteran of sixteen war patrols on USS *Stingray* (SS 186) during World War II, predicted fireworks.[5]

Captain Tomb, still half asleep, wandered into the wardroom and sat down in his usual seat at the head of the table. His mood was jovial, and he wished us all good morning as he took a first sip of coffee. The wardroom table was full. Those of us who had already begun our breakfast hunched over our plates or bowls as we waited for what was to come.

The captain looked up toward the bulkhead with a broad smile of pleasure to greet *la favorita*, as she was known. In a flash his expression changed to shocked disbelief, then to red-faced anger. "What the hell, what the GD hell!" he exclaimed.

He jumped up and ran out, dragging back the exec, Bill Purdum, from his bunk to view what he loudly swore was "an out-and-out atrocity." *Skipjack's* exec, whom we called the commissar for good reason, took one look and was not amused. Both captain and the exec scanned our faces hoping to detect the guilty party. They had no doubt it was an inside job. We officers greeted them with sorrowful expressions of sympathy and outrage, wanting to laugh but realizing this was definitely not the time.

The captain was angrier than any of us could possibly have expected. As we hurried to finish our breakfasts, he continued to rant and rave, promising it would go very hard on the culprit who had defaced *la favorita*, from restriction on board with only bread and water to a general court-martial. "Oh, boy," I thought to myself as I wolfed down my cereal. "I've done it now." Finishing up, I excused myself to "go take care of some urgent business in the control room" and made my exit.

Several officers riveted to the wardroom table later reported that the captain suddenly stormed out of his seat and ripped the centerfold off the bulkhead, tearing it into shreds and crumpling it. All agreed that, if discovered, the guilty party would find his naval career in jeopardy.

We tiptoed around the captain during the next several days. The exec tried his best to uncover the truth, but we held our tongues. Later in the day the captain announced that his "store of *Playboy* magazines would no longer be available to the wardroom."

I was glad not to have been standing the 8:00 p.m. to midnight watch, or I would have been part of the small group that fell under suspicion. Other than the occasional outburst by the captain that always seemed to occur when I was in the wardroom, the situation calmed down. By the time we reached our first liberty port of Le Havre, France, in mid-October, his good humor had returned, and the rest of our cruise proceeded without incident.

In the years that followed, Captain Tomb and I had occasion to serve in the same localities on both the East and West Coasts, and we often saw each other socially. Never, however, did I come close to confessing that I was the one who had despoiled his beloved playmate. Finally, at a party that he and his wife Beth were hosting, when he was in command of the submarine base in Pearl Harbor, just a few years short of my retirement, I confessed, after a few drinks. Paul Tomb roared with laughter.

"Hell, Fred, I knew it all along," he said. "Why do you think I carried on so whenever you were in the wardroom? I knew right away who had done it. Your reputation for general mischief was known to me long before I reported on board." We had a few more drinks, and I further confessed that he had certainly fooled me into uncharacteristically lying low for quite a while.

## The Mid-Atlantic Switch

*Skipjack* departed New London in mid-September 1964 for advanced operations with NATO forces in the mid- and eastern Atlantic. The crew looked forward to what constituted a minor deployment for the better part of two months. We would be operating fully submerged most of the time, both with and against British and French navy surface ASW forces in major exercises entitled Masterstroke and Teamwork. These exercises would be much as we had done in the past with both U.S. and Allied surface and air forces. The various higher commands claimed that sufficient advancement in their ASW tactics and capabilities against the nuclear attack submarine warranted putting these to the test. In between operations we would be enjoying a few days of liberty in Le Havre and, toward the end of our deployment, Portland. Le Havre would be our first pit stop. A great number of us had every intention, of course, of heading off to Paris. We just had to wait as patiently as we could until the lines went over and *Skipjack* was safely secured to the pier.

Mary and I were expecting our third child at the time. Captain Tomb most graciously arranged for me to remain behind in New London until after the baby was born. Also remaining on shore was our electrical officer, Lt. Thomas W. "Tom" Habermas, who would be getting married at roughly the same time. Arrangements were further made for Tom and me, and our DivCom Henry R. Hanssen, to be transferred to *Skipjack* in the mid-Atlantic. This would be courtesy of USS *Seawolf* (SSN 575), which was heading east for other, more-classified reasons. Hanssen in turn was excited about the trip and the prospects for going ashore in Le Havre—so much so that he sent his formal dinner dress plus some of his best civilian suits and golf clubs ahead on *Skipjack*. Commander Hanssen was a most genial and entertaining shipmate and much liked by us all, and we looked forward to having him with us.

My daughter Erin was born, and Tom got married, and he and the DivCom and I boarded *Seawolf* and got under way for a mid-ocean rendezvous with *Skipjack*. She came to the surface near the pre-agreed mid-Atlantic rendezvous point and established communications with *Skipjack*. We were within sight of each other within the hour.

It was a dark, overcast day in mid-September, although visibility was good with just a light wind. Of some concern was a heavy, rolling swell that dominated the sea surface. Conditions were determined to be safe enough, however, for an at-sea transfer via *Seawolf*'s two-man rubber life raft. The two submarines maneuvered to within twenty to thirty yards of each other. A heaving line was thrown from *Skipjack* to *Seawolf*. Attached to it was a somewhat larger-diameter line, which would be used to tow the life raft back and forth between our two boats. As soon as both boats were ready and the life raft lowered into the water, Tom and I quickly donned life jackets and boarded. Whatever we had carried with us on *Seawolf* was carefully lowered down to us. The DivCom was to follow on the second trip.

Once we were seated with our life vests tightened, *Skipjack*'s deck crew pulled us across the intervening water and secured us alongside with both bow and stern lines. Even so, the raft rode up and down *Skipjack*'s hull as much as eight to ten feet with every swell. We first had to throw the gear we were carrying with us to someone topside. That went fine. We then prepared to leap, on the upswing, from the narrow gunwale of the life raft to the out-stretched hand of one of the nearest men on deck. It was a somewhat hairy move, to put it mildly. I jumped first and got safely on board without diffi-culty, but Tom missed the outstretched hand. He fell back within the life raft sufficiently hard that one foot plunged straight through the bottom of the life raft. The raft immediately began flooding. Tom moved smartly and made it on his second try.

The raft was completely filled with water by this time and had to be towed back to *Seawolf*, hauled on board, and evaluated for its condition. Efforts to repair the leaking came to naught. A second life raft was not readily available. After much discussion, it was reluctantly agreed that it would not be safe to try to transfer the DivCom to *Skipjack*. I will never forget Commander Hanssen's disappointed expression as we waved goodbye to each other over the little stretch of water that separated us and headed off on our respective missions. Unfortunately for him, his clothing and golf clubs remained with us. If I had been in his shoes, I think I would have decided to swim for it.

Safe on board, Tom and I both looked forward to having a good steak.

### How to Save a Steak for Later

A typical crew of ninety men would eat almost four thousand pounds of steak during the course of a two-month operation or deployment such as the one we had recently completed. Steak, of course, meant T-bone, porterhouse, rib eye, sirloin, tenderloin, or New York strip cuts. It definitely did not mean Swiss steak or tough round steak. *Skipjack* had superb cooks, and steaks were served as often as four or five times a week for either lunch or dinner. Most crewmembers could put away a good pound of it at a sitting, and sometimes twice as much, preferably grilled. The cooks went to a lot of effort to ensure that those who liked them rare or well done got them that way. A few submarines, particularly in the Pacific, even carried their own homemade charcoal broilers—generally modified leftover, half-barrel drums—that could be placed on deck for barbeques during in-port or at-anchor periods.

My fellow officers were noted for their voracious appetites, so we had to be Johnny-on-the-spot to make sure we got all we wanted. The steward's mates always stored leftovers in the tiny wardroom pantry refrigerator following the meals when they were served. The pantry provided a last hope for those of us who hadn't had enough to eat to return to the trough one more time. As longtime steak lovers, a few of the sneakier crewmembers and I discovered that we had to get to those set-asides within an hour or so.

I had been assigned to stand the 8:00 p.m. to midnight watch as officer of the deck (conning officer) in the control room during *Skipjack*'s high-speed submerged transit across the eastern Atlantic, en route to the scheduled rendezvous for exercises with our NATO allies. I was to keep these same hours as a command watch officer during the course of the exercises. Back in New London before *Skipjack* departed, I noted that we had loaded a larger-than-normal supply of high-quality steaks. Following my debarkation from *Seawolf*, I was eagerly looking forward to eating my fair share. What I considered my fair share in those days should probably be explained: it generally consisted of at least two good-sized steaks during lunch or dinner, and then one more. The latter would be retrieved from the wardroom pantry ahead of the other "alligators" an hour or so after the meal. Not the most healthful diet, but very satisfying to a young man.

It had been some time since I had taken the 8:00 p.m. to midnight watch on a steady basis. It was generally assigned to the more junior officers, because it usually meant we had to leave our meal early in order to relieve the watch on time. It also meant we missed out on a leisurely dessert and the chance to visit and share a movie with our brother officers afterward. As I recall, I had been asked by the exec to take this particular watch to train up another prospective officer of the deck and submerged operations conning officer. In any case, it was not my favorite watch.

During the first few nights, as soon as I got off watch each evening, well after midnight, I immediately headed to the wardroom pantry to check what might be left over from dinner. Each time I found the pickings to be pretty slim, if not nonexistent. I quickly came up with a tactic to remedy the problem. After an hour or so on watch, I would call for a relief so I could use the head. I would then make a beeline for the wardroom pantry, open the refrigerator, spear a leftover steak, and take a few minutes to eat it. Soon the ruse caught the attention of the captain so that I considered it unwise to continue. Besides, it wasn't easy to get a brother officer to relieve me for longer than a few minutes.

Sooner or later, however, I came up with a better solution. Like my previous tactic, I would induce another qualified officer to relieve me for a minute or so, run down to the wardroom pantry, snap open the refrigerator door, seize the biggest and most desirable leftover steak, and take a big ragged bite out of it, then shove it beneath all the other steaks on the plate, close the door, and rush back to resume the watch.

This new tactic worked like a charm. "Ah, the devious submariner's mind," I thought, congratulating myself over and over as I enjoyed each steak in turn. But I should have expected that someone even more devious than I would come up with an effective check. One night, when I hungrily opened the refrigerator door to retrieve my prize, I discovered that all that was left on the plate was my "bite," surrounded by a very slim border of steak. One of my shipmates—officer or crewmember—had cut off the rest of the steak for himself and left me with a rim of meat showing my teeth marks. There was nothing more I could do, so I disgustedly gave up the game and worked to get off the 8:00 p.m. to midnight watch.

Reflecting back after all these years, it dawns on me that there was only one officer who had a sense of humor perverse enough to get to me in this way: our skipper, Paul Tomb who, given my own prank, had every reason to come up with a counter.

## Le Havre and Paree

In our first ASW exercise with NATO and U.S. forces, *Skipjack*'s capabilities vastly outmatched the "adversary's" ability to detect, much less to hold contact on us, sufficiently long to conduct a simulated attack. She was still invulnerable to detection and attack by any navy's ASW forces, or so we thought at the time. Such, however, was not the case with very quiet diesel attack boats on the battery. Incidentally, during the exercise *Skipjack* steamed past her 200,000th mile without having required refueling at any time.

Entering the outer harbor of the port of Le Havre at high tide—anywhere from twenty-two to twenty-seven feet—we passed through the series of locks en route to our assigned mooring. This was to be our first European liberty port since the Mediterranean back in 1962. We were somewhat disgruntled to find that reliable electrical shore power would not be available. Instead, we would be allowed to shut down the reactor and, once we had established an in-port condition that minimized electrical demands throughout the boat, use our diesel generator to supply all electrical power needs.

About half the crew and most of the officers took off for a few days' liberty in Paris. After twenty-four hours of duty, Lt. Howard D. "Joe" Mitchell and I managed to get away from the boat for one night to go revisit a few favorite places we had each, on our own, discovered in Paris during our U.S. Naval Academy midshipman summer cruises a decade earlier. We started by fortuitously discovering casino night at the NATO officers club, coming away with winnings of several hundred dollars' of francs. The devil in me led to my suggesting that Joe and I fill our pockets with the Monopoly money that was used for playing the various gambling games that night. Who knew what fun we could have with it later?

Off we went to the bars of Paris, one of them called Le Train Bleu that I had discovered back in 1952. We were sparing in what we ate and drank throughout the night and always paid with francs, leaving a generous tip but mischievously augmenting it with a large Monopoly money bill or two. This made us very popular wherever we went, especially with a few Scandinavian blondes of the Naples variety. Without going into self-incriminating detail, Joe and I were like pied pipers attracting new friends as we wound our way from bar to bar. It was a fun-filled night, culminating in the division of our remaining Monopoly money between two attractive waitresses who thought it was real and we were crazy. Although we had done nothing illegal, we said our goodbyes and wisely left the area, taking lodgings in the early morning hours in an entirely different area of Paris.

The next day, nursing colossal hangovers, we managed to combine pleasure with culture by visiting the Cathedral of Notre Dame, the Louvre, and the Tuileries Gardens before we caught a train back to Le Havre.

Back on the boat everyone had hilarious stories that they told over and over again. The most curious was that of Captain Tomb and the exec, Bill Purdum, who had accepted the invitation of a local noblewoman, a Madame Joubert, to attend an elegant cocktail party and formal dinner at her home. Neither man made it back to the boat. In the early morning hours in a chair and on a couch, they were awakened by the lapping tongues of two hugely affectionate dogs.

We started up the reactor and later stationed the sea and anchor detail, and crewmembers took their assigned watch stations in preparation for taking in our lines and getting under way. As Skipjack's engineer officer, I relieved the engineering officer of the watch shortly after the reactor was taken critical. We warmed up our two ships service turbine generators and secured the diesel generator once the former generator had assumed all electrical loads. This was followed by warming up the two main turbines in preparation and answering all bells.

The passage through the locks outbound, with the assistance of a French pilot, seemed slow and laborious. Unknown to me, the previous day's engineering duty officer had used an excessive amount of reserve feed water to flush another reserve feed tank that had somehow become infiltrated with salt water while we were at sea. Once I found out, the engineering watch and I closely monitored the usage of our remaining pure secondary system reserve feed water used to create the steam in each boiler that drove both ships service turbine generators and main turbines. There was always slight leakage through various valves in the supporting piping systems, so we watched the last remaining pure water level slowly drop with our hearts in our mouths.

We didn't want to operate either of our fresh-water-making stills because they would need to draw contaminated water from within the locks that we were passing through. The stills would produce water pure enough to use in our secondary water system, but not pure enough to drink safely. Thus, if we were required to operate a still, we would later have to shut the still down and go through an elaborate and lengthy decontamination process. This would be necessary to make absolutely certain that it produced water sufficiently safe to drink. What was our major worry? It was the risk of catching some form of water-borne disease injurious to the health of all on board. A submarine could not afford to have a single man taken seriously ill with a contagious or intestinal disease.

Once well clear of Le Havre, *Skipjack* rendezvoused with surface ASW units of the Royal Navy and commenced joint operations in the rough waters of the Bay of Biscay. The series of ASW exercises, termed Teamwork, that transpired during the week provided further proof that essentially no surface ASW forces of any navy at that time were a match for the modern high-speed, deep-diving nuclear attack submarine. By that time there was no doubt in anyone's mind that suitable sonar systems that could detect and track, and acoustic weapons that could acquire and hold, such an adversary had to be developed on an urgent basis by both U.S. and NATO navies. We, on the other hand, found we could detect, approach, and attack any surface warship from whatever quarter we chose and then dash away at speeds that neither our target's sensors nor weapons of that day could match.

# CHAPTER 20

# England and Then Home

O ur last port of call was Portland, England; it was not the easiest for us to reach because local area authorities required us to transit the English Channel in a surfaced condition. The Bay of Biscay had been bad enough with seemingly a major portion of the world's commercial traffic passing through its turbulent waters, but the narrow English Channel was downright hazardous. I had the officer of the deck watch up on the bridge atop the sail for much of the journey. *Skipjack* constantly pitched, rolled, and yawed as we ploughed through rough seas and into driving cold rain hour after hour. As we proceeded slowly toward Portland, it was necessary to maneuver constantly as we dodged hundreds of surface contacts, from small fishing boats to huge ocean liners. With a great sigh of relief we eventually found the harbor entrance and proceeded expeditiously to our assigned berth. Mercifully the weather there was much calmer than usual for the season.

A swarm of Royal Navy submariner hosts was there to receive us as we tied up. As soon as a gangway was lowered to connect us with the pier, more than a few of us, officer and enlisted, were escorted ashore to enjoy a fortifying drink on board the nearest submarine. Fellow officers Joe Mitchell and Howard Cornia, *Skipjack*'s main propulsion assistant and communications officer, respectively, and I were whisked away to the diesel-attack submarine HMS *Odin* (S10). Once below decks we were taken to the wardroom and squeezed into its innermost table seats where our hosts plied us with a great number of what they called horse's necks (cocktails). After much laughter and trading of sea stories, we all went off to a nearby favorite pub for dinner. I vaguely remember eating a kidney pie for the first time, but I don't remember much else. The long walk back to the boat in the miserable cold rain had a sobering effect on the three of us, however, and we arrived back on board in reasonably good shape.

It rained the entire four days we were in port, but that didn't dampen anyone's enthusiasm for this ancient port town, particularly for the fine drink. Most of us had the opportunity to make a quick trip to London via train to shop and/or down a number of "pints of the best" at some of the pubs around Piccadilly for a few hours. I was fortunate enough to be taken to see Stonehenge for the first time. At that time it was still possible to walk right up and closely examine every detail of this renowned megalithic monument.

The four days in port passed all too quickly, but there were no regrets as we were eager to head home in time for the Thanksgiving holidays. With no restrictions on *Skipjack*'s speed, once submerged we moved quickly across the Atlantic. We arrived back in New London in more than sufficient time to accomplish much-needed repairs and upkeep before we were allowed a generous liberty and leave period.

## Caught Napping

I was duty officer for several days after Thanksgiving. Since I was qualified both as an officer of the deck and as engineering officer of the watch, I was the only officer on board during that time. My usual habit while on duty was to inspect the boat topside and from stem to stern at rough intervals of every four hours or so. The reactor was shut down, and *Skipjack* was on shore power. Qualified crewmembers stood four-hour watches topside, in the control and torpedo rooms, and there were several constantly roving patrols in the engineering spaces. In addition, the reactor and electrical control panels were continuously manned in the maneuvering room where, when *Skipjack* was under way, the engineering officer of the watch, assisted by a maneuvering room supervisor, stood watch.

On one particular night I walked into the maneuvering room several hours after midnight. My purpose was to confirm that all was well with our shut-down reactor and the electrical distribution system throughout the boat. To my surprise, I found two of *Skipjack*'s senior petty officers, who were our most experienced engineering department watch standers, sound asleep. I stood there silently for a few more minutes watching them, then woke them up and ordered them to call their reliefs immediately. I also had the control room watch call the senior engineering department's chief petty officer and request that he come to the maneuvering room immediately. Upon his arrival I explained what I had found and ordered, asking him to ensure that a proper relief of both positions took place. Afterward I resumed my inspection of the boat.

The following morning I wrote both men up for sleeping on watch and deposited the slips in the exec's incoming box. The exec returned to the boat the Monday following Thanksgiving, found the report slips, and requested that I meet with him. I did so and explained what I had found and done. The exec was as surprised and disappointed in the senior petty officers as I was. After conferring with Captain Tomb several hours later, the exec scheduled a Captain's Mast the following day to deal with the two watch standers.

A green cloth was spread on the wardroom dining table shortly before 10:00 the next morning for Captain Tomb's first disciplinary Mast. The captain came in and took his seat at the end of the table, followed by the exec and me. I took a standing position at the opposite end of the table and across from where *Skipjack's* chief of the boat ushered in the two accused engineering department petty officers. Their division officers and leading petty officers also filed in.

The captain opened the Mast. He asked for the formal complaint, which the exec stood up and read, and then the captain asked me to elaborate on the circumstances. I repeated that I had discovered both petty officers sound asleep while on watch in the maneuvering room during a routine inspection on my duty day. The captain asked the accused petty officer's division officers and leading petty officers about their men and their performance of duty. All confirmed that the two men accused had always been responsible watch standers to the best of their knowledge. The captain then asked the two petty officers what they had to say for themselves. To my utter astonishment both vehemently denied they had been asleep at the time I entered *Skipjack's* maneuvering room. The captain asked no further questions of the accused or of me, and after considering for a moment, abruptly stated in a loud voice, "Case dismissed."

As *Skipjack's* chief engineer and senior watch officer, I was stunned. The accused were, of course, jubilant and smirked at me in triumph as we all departed the wardroom. I followed the exec into his stateroom, closed the door, and asked in utter outrage, "Exec, what the hell? The captain took their word over mine, his chief engineer and the most experienced officer on board. What was he thinking?"

The exec lowered his eyes and shrugged. He had nothing to say. I stormed out of his stateroom, through the wardroom and into the crews mess, where I heard the two accused holding forth and laughing loudly.

There were about twenty men in the crews mess, and there was sudden silence as I entered. I approached both men, ordered them to stand up and, looking them both straight in the eye, called them both liars. I then said, "OK, now let me give you both something more to laugh about. From this point on, you are both completely disqualified from all engineering department watches. You will remain so until you tell the captain the truth."

I returned to the wardroom and had the control room watch call the two men's division officers and leading petty officers, telling them to meet me in the control room immediately. As soon as all were assembled, I told them what I had mandated. I also added that this included all forward watches as well, such as topside watch and below deck security watches.

Several days later the exec called me into his stateroom and told me he and the captain had heard about and discussed what I had done. He said, "I am asking you to reconsider, because your decision is causing several of your men to go on port and starboard watches." I responded, "I am well aware of the situation and not particularly happy about that, either. However, the solution is very simple. As soon as the two men admit to you and the captain they were lying, they will go back on the watch bill."

I added that we were talking about safety of both the nuclear reactor power plant and the ship, not to mention principle, here. I said further, "I feel sure, as *Skipjack*'s engineer officer, that Admiral Rickover himself would back me up on this." The exec shook his head in response. I excused myself and returned to work.

The subject of returning the men to the watch bill came up from time to time. On one occasion both men came to plead with me to relent. My answer was always the same: "Admit you were lying and you go back on the watch bill." They would not do this, because they were afraid of the most likely punishment that they would receive: reduction in rate with accompanying loss of pay. The situation remained status quo until I was relieved as *Skipjack*'s engineer officer by Lt. Ralph W. West shortly before the boat entered Charleston Naval Shipyard for overhaul in April 1965. Interestingly, never a word was exchanged between the captain and me on the subject, although I later found, without explanation, that I had been marked down one notch on loyalty on my next fitness report.

I will never understand why Captain Tomb chose to take the word of the two senior petty officers over mine. By doing so he completely undermined his engineer officer with his entire engineering department, and with the rest of the crew, for that matter. Was it just an ill-thought-out impulsive gesture to gain popularity without considering the consequences? I will never know. His next step, logically, should have been to have me immediately relieved as engineer since my word could no longer be trusted. If I had not expected to receive orders to exec to another submarine, I would have demanded to be relieved as engineer officer. I did contact my first commanding officer on *Skipjack*, Les Kelly, told him the story, and asked his advice. He urged me to "keep calm and sit tight," since I would soon be receiving orders as prospective exec of a new-construction attack boat.

The lesson here is obvious. A commanding officer should either trust and back up his senior officers or immediately get rid of him if he believes that he cannot trust him.

## Final Months on Board

My remaining months on *Skipjack* were relatively quiet and uneventful. In early January of 1965 members of the crew had an opportunity to take their families out for a daylong Dependents' Cruise in Long Island Sound. The weather, although cold, was calm and pleasant. It was my first opportunity to take my eldest son, Fred Jr., age eight, to sea on a nuclear submarine. I was very interested in seeing how well he would adapt to the boat's extreme closeness and to its rolling and pitching motion on the surface, and what his reaction would be to submerging and operating beneath the sea. To my delight he took it completely in stride. He asked all sorts of questions of crewmembers and made me very proud with his obvious interest in what we were doing and why.[1]

The months of February and part of March were spent taking part in Submarine ASW Exercise 1–65, a part of Submarine Development Group Two's continuing and very important Big Daddy submarine-versus-submarine series. This exercise proved once again that our submarine force did not have a torpedo that could acquire and close a nuclear attack submarine transiting or evading at high speed. The exercise also demonstrated, conclusively in my opinion, that the next class of nuclear attack submarine had to be infinitely quieter throughout its entire speed range. Ideally, its radiated noise across all frequencies would be considerably lower than that of the surrounding sea state.

This next class was the *Sturgeon*, already under construction in several shipyards. There it would be equipped with several sonar systems capable of detecting and tracking adversaries, both surfaced or submerged, at long ranges no matter what speed she was making. Finally, it had already been determined that existing sonar arrays and torpedo tubes were in too-close proximity to each other on all U.S. nuclear submarines. The noise involved in preparing a torpedo or torpedoes for launching could cause the submarine's sonar to lose contact on the potential target at a critical time. This finding resulted in the relocation and reorientation of the four torpedo tubes to an amidships positions, where they were angled outward both port and starboard.

During the course of the exercise, *Skipjack* made one final visit to Bermuda. A number of us managed to find our way, in spite of almost non-existent transportation, to the famous old Elbow Beach Hotel for some final nights of good fun and drinking.

After concluding this final submarine-versus-submarine exercise for *Skipjack*, we pulled into Charleston for a port visit and to lay important pre-liminary groundwork for entering the shipyard for an extensive overhaul a month's hence. It was during this time that Lt. Ralph West, from USS *Tullibee*, relieved me as engineer. I assumed the duties of navigator and operations officer one last time.

After a pleasant week in Charleston, *Skipjack* departed for State Pier, New London, and a final pre-overhaul upkeep alongside the submarine tender *Fulton*. The exec's and officers' time was spent, in addition, accomplishing the myriad tasks associated with moving the families of all those crewmembers who would be with *Skipjack* during the course of the overhaul.

The upkeep completed in late March 1965, I had one last opportunity to plan and execute a maximum-speed submerged transit to a point to the east of the entrance buoys to the port of Charleston. We reached that point in early April and surfaced. With the assistance of a pilot, I was allowed to conn *Skipjack* for one final time up the Cooper River. We moored within the Charleston Naval Shipyard where *Skipjack*'s overhaul was to include the refueling of its S-5-W reactor, a process that would take almost a year and a half.

I remained on board with little to do as navigator and operations officer for the better part of the month. It was to prove a most enjoyable and relaxing time. I house-sat for some good friends on Sullivan's Island, took part in the Annual Submarine Ball with gusto, and played a lot of tennis with my commanding officer, Paul Tomb. I was then detached and returned north to the U.S. naval submarine base in Groton, where I began a series of intensive weapons and sonar schools and training courses, including the Prospective Commanding Officers Course, that would prepare me for my next duty, first as officer in charge, and then as precommissioning exec of the second in the *Sturgeon*-class nuclear attack submarine, the *Whale* (SSN 638).

*Skipjack*'s high speed and maneuverability enabled her to remain an effective attack submarine and she stayed in service for another twenty-four years. She received a new seven-bladed propeller in the mid-1970s, replacing a noisier five-bladed propeller with which she had earlier set so many speed records. She was deployed to the Mediterranean on several occasions and, in addition, was assigned Cold War missions until well into the mid-1980s.

In October 1989 this proud boat that had inaugurated a new era of submarine warfare entered the Newport News Shipyard and Dry Dock Company for decommissioning. On 19 April 1990 she was officially decommissioned and stricken from the Naval Vessel Register. The ex-*Skipjack* subsequently entered the Nuclear Powered Ship and Submarine Recycling Program in Bremerton, Washington, on 17 March 1996. On 1 September 1998, this beautiful entity ceased to exist.[2]

# Epilogue

I have written this memoir of seven years of rich and varied experience on board three Cold War attack submarines to interest students and aficionados of submarines and in hope that it will prove to be of value to submarine officers aspiring to submarine command.

I have not mentioned the unique opportunity I had to act as fire control coordinator throughout my service and training on *Seadragon*, under the command of George Steele, and on *Skipjack* under the commands of Leslie Kelly, Shepherd Jenks, and Paul Tomb. The position of fire control coordinator is key, second only to that of the captain during Cold War trailing operations and all submarine battle stations approaches and attacks. The opportunity to perform this function for considerable lengths of time on all three boats was an essential component of my preparation for command of a nuclear attack submarine.

It is the fire control coordinator who coordinates the collection of information from all sources—sonar, visual, electronic, and intelligence—on the threat target of interest; who analyzes all this information, using the boat's fire control equipment, and who comes up with a best estimate of target identity, range to the target, and the target's course, speed, depth, and mode of operation.

In wartime the fire control coordinator is further responsible for producing a hitting solution for best destroying the threat target, for recommending the most appropriate weapon to be used and how many to use for maximum weapons system effectiveness, and for advising the commanding officer when to launch, or fire, the weapon(s).

Lt. Cdr. Alfred S. McLaren receiving Commander Submarine Force Atlantic Letter of Commendation from Rear Adm. John A. Tyree Jr., USN, Deputy Commander Submarine Force Atlantic, 1965. *U.S. Navy*

The foregoing experience was to prove invaluable as I proceeded through my various training courses: AN/BQQ-2 Sonar School, the Submarine Prospective Commanding Officers courses at the submarine base in Groton; and the SSN Navigator Course at Dam Neck, Virginia, following my detachment from *Skipjack*. Most importantly, the experience gained enabled me to serve as a command watch officer for four months on board USS *Greenling* during a still-classified Cold War operation through the summer and early fall of 1968, and to carry out with great success the many Cold War special operations conducted during my four-year command of USS *Queenfish*.

I owe a deep debt of gratitude to three of my former commanding officers, Vice Adm. George Steele, Capt. Les Kelly, and Capt. Shep Jenks, who prepared me for submarine command by creating an onboard atmosphere of forceful backup. No officer or crewmember was ever afraid to speak up whenever an unsafe course of action was contemplated or undertaken, there was a better way of doing something, or a wrong order was inadvertently given. Such an atmosphere was, and is, absolutely essential on board an attack submarine if it is going to operate safely and to maximum effectiveness. I strove to create this same environment as skipper of USS *Queenfish*, particularly during our 1970 Arctic Ocean Expedition and numerous Cold War operations from 1969 to 1973.

In August 1965 I reported as officer in charge of the new nuclear attack submarine, *Whale* (SSN 638), at the Quincy Fore River Shipyard in Massachusetts, and four months later I reported as precommissioning exec of *Queenfish*, being constructed at the Newport News Shipbuilding and Drydock Company, Virginia. It was during this time that I was pleasantly surprised with the presentation of a ComSubLant Letter of Commendation by Rear Adm. John A. Tyree Jr., deputy ComSubLant, for my performance of duty during *Skipjack*'s last Cold War mission.

*Queenfish*, although ninth in the new *Sturgeon*-class nuclear attack submarine, with its keel laid a year and a half after the lead submarine *Sturgeon*, was the first to be completed and to go to sea, which it did during the fall of 1966.

From being precommissioning, and later commissioning, exec of *Queenfish*, I was to go on to the U.S. Naval War College, Newport, Rhode Island, for duty as a student in the Command and Staff course, 1967–68, and the first nuclear-trained officer to serve on the staff of the War Gaming Department from 1968 to 1969.

I was detached from the War College in April 1969 to proceed to the command of USS *Queenfish* at Pearl Harbor following my completion of Admiral Rickover's three-and-a-half-month Prospective Commanding Officers course at his Naval Reactors headquarters in Washington, DC.

The details of this later challenging period will be covered in a planned third book, as soon as declassification permits.

# Notes

## Introduction

1. Alfred S. McLaren, *Unknown Waters: A First-Hand Account of the Historic Under-Ice Survey of the Siberian Continental Shelf by USS* Queenfish (SSN-651) (Tuscaloosa: University of Alabama Press, 2008).

## Chapter 1. Early History and Post–World War II Modifications

1. David L. Johnston, *A Visual Guide to the U.S. Fleet Submarines Part Three: Balao and Tench Classes 1942–1950* (NavSource Naval History, 2012), http://navsource.org/archives/08/pdf/0829295.pdf.
2. Electric Boat Company is now General Dynamics Corporation, Electric Boat Division, Groton, Connecticut.
3. Joseph Mark Scalia, *Germany's Last Mission to Japan: The Failed Voyage of U-234* (Annapolis: Naval Institute Press, 2000), 185. Uranium oxide is used in producing nuclear weapons.
4. Gary Weir, "Silent Defense: One Hundred Years of the American Submarine Force," Chief of Naval Operations, Submarine Warfare Division, Submarine Force History, 27 April 1999, http://www.navy.mil/navydata/cno/n87/history/fullhist.html.
5. Conning the submarine means directing a submarine's movements through appropriate orders to the helmsman (course and speed) and diving officer of the watch (depth).
6. P. D. Hulme, "USN Guppy Submarine Conversions 1947–1954: The Quest for Higher Submerged Speed & Greater Underwater Propulsion Power," Barrow-in-Furness Submariners Association, http://www.rnsubs.co.uk/Dits/Articles/guppy.php.
7. A polynya hop is transit under ice from open-water area to open-water area, using each surfacing to recharge the boat's batteries.

## Chapter 2. On Board USS *Greenfish*

1. Norman Friedman, *U.S. Submarines through 1945: An Illustrated Design History* (Annapolis: Naval Institute Press, 1995), 242.

2. The 1MC is the primary system for electronically broadcasting communications throughout the submarine.
3. "Five Sailors Die in Explosions on Snorkel Submarine," *Chicago Tribune*, 22 February 1955.
4. Submarine school instructor during my class, September 1957.
5. "Project 611 Zulu class," GlobalSecurity.org, http://www.globalsecurity .org/military/world/russia/611.htm. Twenty-eight had been built and were in service in 1952.
6. Shannon Rankin and Jay Barlow, "Source of the North Pacific 'Boing' Sound Attributed to Minke Whales," *Journal of the Acoustical Society of America* 118, no. 5 (2005): 3346–51, doi:10.1121/1.2046747.
7. Terry Rodgers, "Mysterious Underwater Noise Is Likely a Whale Mating Call," http://legacy.utsandiego.com/news/science/20021227-9999_2m27whales .html.
8. "The Mysterious Music of Minke Whales," by Scott Simon, *Weekend Edition Saturday*, NPR, 9 April 2005, http://www.npr.org/templates/story/story.php ?storyId=4584101.
9. Commanders and lieutenant commanders, or any rank for that matter, who are in command of a submarine or ship are usually addressed as captain by their subordinates by centuries-old naval custom.
10. A ship or submarine captain has the power to award a Captain's Mast, or non-judicial punishment, for minor offenses committed by the enlisted personnel under his command.

## Chapter 3. Our First Deployment

1. The diving officer of the watch is responsible for keeping the submarine at ordered depth, in a condition of neutral buoyancy overall, and trimmed to a zero bubble (perfectly horizontal) fore and aft (similar to using a carpenter's level). He reports to the officer of the deck under way. The officer of the deck in port is responsible for the security and safety of the submarine in port. The officer of the deck under way is responsible for the safe navigation and maneuvering of the submarine both on the surface and when submerged. He has control of course, speed, and depth. He reports directly to the commanding officer or command watch officer.
2. Trim means flooded from or pumped to sea internal, hard variable ballast or "trim tanks" as necessary to achieve overall neutral buoyancy. No way on means no forward motion.
3. This layer is where the water temperature decreases such that active sonar emissions from either an ASW surface warship or aircraft sonobuoy are deflected away from the depth to which the boat is headed.
4. To dog a watertight door or hatch is to seal it securely with each of the sealing levers provided.
5. Commands to maneuvering are to the senior and assistant controllers (electrician's mates) who stand their watch in the maneuvering room.
6. The sonar supervisor and several additional sonar watch standers who man the various passive and active sonars are located in the sonar room. The attack

periscope presented a very small radar or visual cross-section and hence was very difficult to detect.

7. So the periscope does not create a wake or "feather" that can be visually detected. The creation of fluorescence trails in the water could also be a problem, particularly in warmer water.

8. During patrol-quiet all noise-making activities and equipment, such as high-pressure compressors, are secured to minimize radiated underwater noise.

9. A snapshot refers to launch of an acoustic homing warshot from an already flooded or ready torpedo tube (as soon as the torpedo tube outer door is open) directly at an immediate threat, ideally within thirty to forty-five seconds of initial detection.

10. Current to real dollars converter (using GDP deflator), http://stats.areppim .com/calc/calc_usdlrxdeflator.php, accessed 29 April 2014.

## Chapter 4. Coming into Yokosuka

1. Martin W. Lewis, "Subic Bay: From American Servicemen to Korean Business-men," GeoCurrents, 22 October 2010, http://www.geocurrents.info/geopolitics/ subic-bay-from-american-servicemen-to-korean-businessmen#ixzz30DLzs2yp

2. Shane Tuck, "Mess Management Specialists Transform into Culinary Specialist," Navy.mil, 3 March 2004, http://www.navy.mil/submit/display .asp?story_id=12134.

## Chapter 5. Off the Soviet Far East Coast

1. Emanuel M. Ballenzweig, "The Weather and Circulation of September 1958," *Monthly Weather Review* 86, no. 11 (1958): 359–82, http://docs.lib .noaa.gov/rescue/mwr/086/mwr-086-09-0359.pdf.

2. These were not absolute sound pressure recordings. *Greenfish* did not have this capability at the time. The captain was to play the most interesting of these recordings at subsequent debriefings in Yokosuka and Pearl Harbor and, on special occasions, for certain high-level visitors on board *Greenfish*.

## Chapter 6. Homeward to Pearl Harbor

1. Cumshaw is an international seagoing term for petty graft and secret commissions.

2. Clay Blair Jr., *The Atomic Submarine and Admiral Rickover* (New York: Henry Holt and Company, 1954).

3. Described in McLaren, *Unknown Waters*, 6–8.

4. There were not more than seven such submarines: *Nautilus, Seawolf, Triton, Skate, Sargo, Swordfish,* and *Skipjack,* plus another half dozen under construction.

5. This chapter is a difficult and complex portion of the Submarine Qualification notebook that consisted of hand-drawn reproduction of each and every shipboard electrical system as one personally hand-over-hand traced it. The production of each drawing that would meet engineering drawing standards took many hours.

6. McLaren, *Unknown Waters*, 9.
7. "USS *Greenfish* (SS 351) Deployments & History," HullNumber.com, http://www.hullnumber.com/SS-351.
8. "Museum Visit to the Scrapping of USS *Greenfish*," San Francisco Maritime National Park Association, http://www.maritime.org/rioweb/.

## Chapter 7. My First Nuclear Submarine

1. The chief operator is a top supervisory position, equivalent to engineering officer of the watch, on an operational nuclear-powered submarine.
2. USS *Skate* (SSN 578) was the lead nuclear attack submarine in the class, followed by USS *Swordfish* (SSN 579), USS *Sargo* (SSN 583), and USS *Seadragon* (SSN 584).
3. "Milestones: 1953–1960," U.S. Department of State, Office of the Historian, https://history.state.gov/milestones/1953-1960/u2-incident.
4. "584 Commissioning Tomorrow: RADM Grenfel Speaker," *Portsmouth Periscope*, 4 December 1959.
5. Dictionary of American Naval Fighting Ships, *Seadragon*, http://www.history.navy.mil/danfs/s8/seadragon-ii.htm.
6. John Lyman was later to fleet up to engineer officer of *Thresher* and was, sadly, one of the some 130 who were on board when she was lost during a dive to test depth in 1964.
7. I was to be the thirty-seventh president of the Explorers Club for four years, beginning in 1996.
8. William Edward Parry, *Journal of a voyage for the discovery of a north-west passage from the Atlantic to the Pacific: Performed in the years 1819-20, in His Majesty's ships* Hecla *and* Griper, *under the orders of William Edward Parry; with the appendix containing scientific and other observations* (London: John Murray, 1821); Robert John Le Mesurier McClure, *The Discovery of the North-West Passage by H.M.S.* "Investigator," *Capt. R. M'Clure, 1850, 1851, 1852, 1853, 1854* (London: Longman, Brown, Green, Longmans, & Roberts, 1856).

## Chapter 8. Into Davis Strait and Baffin Bay

1. Clive Holland, *Arctic Exploration and Development c. 500 B.C. to 1915: An Encyclopedia* (New York: Garland, 1994), 3–11.
2. Ibid., 22, 185–86, 222–23.
3. An 8kHZ active scanning sonar.
4. George P. Steele, *Seadragon: Northwest under the Ice* (New York: E. P. Dutton, 1962), 118.
5. Gerald E. Synhorst, "Soviet Strategic Interest in the Maritime Arctic," U.S. Naval Institute *Proceedings* 99, no. 5 (1973): 843.
6. A Williamson Turn, used to bring a vessel back to a point it has previously passed through, calls for running a short distance, then changing course to port or starboard 60 degrees using 15 degrees rudder then reversing course and heading back toward the center of the area where the vessel wants to return.

7. Steele, *Seadragon*, 128.
8. Crewmembers were known to relieve themselves in the bilges after a night of heavy drinking in port.
9. An 8kHZ active scanning sonar.
10. William M. Leary, *Under Ice: Waldo Lyon and the Development of the Arctic Submarine* (College Station: Texas A&M University Press, 1998), 193.
11. Steele, *Seadragon*, 134.
12. Ibid., 138–39.
13. Ibid., 140.
14. Ibid., 140–41.
15. Leary, *Under Ice*, 195; Steele, *Seadragon*, 20.
16. Leary, *Under Ice*, 195.
17. Steele, *Seadragon*, 148.

## Chapter 9. Through the Northwest Passage

1. The author was a watch officer throughout *Seadragon*'s survey of the Northwest Passage, and remembered much of what we accomplished, However, he found his commanding officer, Cdr. George P. Steele's book, *Seadragon*, invaluable for the reconstruction of dates, times, and some very important quotes.
2. Ibid., 153, 156, 158.
3. Ibid., 160.
4. Holland, *Arctic Exploration and Development*, 185.
5. Steele, *Seadragon*, 161.
6. This paragraph is based on, and quotes are taken from, ibid., 164.
7. Ibid.
8. Ibid., 165.
9. Ibid.
10. Ibid., 168–69.
11. One fathom equals six feet, so this was a depth of 420 feet.
12. Steele, *Seadragon*, 174.
13. Ibid., 179.
14. Ibid., 181.
15. Ibid., 182.
16. Ibid., 182–83.
17. Ibid., 184–85.
18. Ibid., 186.
19. Ibid., 187.
20. Ibid., 185. Interestingly, fifty-four years later the Northwest Passage has become navigable during the summer months due to the warming of the seas during the past several years. However, no Arctic communities to date are provided heat and power by nuclear power, nor do any nuclear submarine cargo vessels and tankers ply the waters. Finally, the Northwest Passage is still far from becoming a major thoroughfare.
21. Ibid., 187.
22. Ibid., 189–91; Leary, *Under Ice*, 197.
23. Steele, *Seadragon*, 189.

24. Ibid., 192; Holland, *Arctic Exploration and Development*, 203.
25. Steele, *Seadragon*, 193–94.
26. Ibid., 194.
27. Ibid., 199–200; McClure, *The Discovery of the North-West Passage*.
28. Steele, *Seadragon*, 200. Polynyas were circular or oval in shape, leads were long and thin, and skylights were either of these covered over with thin ice.
29. Ibid., 201.

## Chapter 10: Surfacing at the Pole

1. Ibid., 202–3.
2. Ibid., 203–5.
3. Ibid.
4. Ibid., 206.
5. Ibid.
6. Bob Doelling had an interesting background. It was said that his father had been a German U-boat commander during World War I and apparently remained in the German navy after the war, where he once served as a naval attaché in the United States. Bob was born in the States but grew up in Argentina, where his family finally settled following his father's retirement from the German navy. He later entered the U.S. Naval Academy and graduated with the class of 1953.
7. Steele, *Seadragon*, 206–7.
8. Ibid., 207.
9. Ibid., 209.
10. Ibid., 211.
11. Ibid., 214–15.
12. Ibid., 216–17.
13. This was the first U.S. South Pole station that was built during the International Geophysical Year in 1956–57. The original station was abandoned in 1975.

## Chapter 11. The Bering Strait and Nome

1. Howard Newmann, "The North-Pole Drifting Stations and the High-Latitude Air Expedition of 1954" (Air Intelligence Information Report IR-226-55, AF-656791, 1955), http://docs.lib.noaa.gov/rescue/IPY/IPY_020_pdf/ G630S65N481955.pdf.
2. *Encyclopaedia Britannica Online*, s.v. "Mikhail Vasilyevich Lomonosov," by Luce-Andrée Langevin, http://www.britannica.com/EBchecked/topic/346787/ Mikhail-Vasilyevich-Lomonosov; "World University Rankings 2013–2014," TimesHigherEducation.co.uk, http://www.timeshighereducation.co.uk/world -university-rankings/2013-14/world-ranking; "Further Education Programs at MSU," Lomonosov Moscow State University, http://www.msu.ru/en/science/ further.html.
3. Encyclopedia Britannica, http://britannica.com/EBchecked/topic/346795/Lo monosov-Ridge

4. A. P. Crary, R. D. Cotell, and T. F. Sexton, "Preliminary Report on Scientific Work on 'Fletcher's Ice Island,' T3," *ARCTIC* 5, no. 4 (1952): 211–23, doi:http://dx.doi.org/10.14430/arctic3913.

5. Throat singing begins deep in the abdomen and thorax and consists of rhythmic grunts emitted at various pitches; there are often two or more singing at the same time.

## Chapter 12. Pearl Harbor at Last

1. USS *Sargo* (SSN 583), USS *Halibut* (SSGN 587), and USS *Swordfish* (SSN 579) preceded us.

2. Cdr. George P. Steele, USN, Commanding Officer, USS *Seadragon* (SSN 584). Lieutenant Alfred S. McLaren, USN, Fitness Report, 27 May 1961.

## Chapter 13. A New Commanding Officer

1. I was to hit on the solution many years later as commanding officer of USS *Queenfish:* I had the navigator compute the number of miles to our first checkpoint of many across the Pacific, and then determine how many hours this would require if *Queenfish* were to proceed at flank speed immediately following our dive beneath the surface shortly after exiting the Pearl Harbor channel. For both six-month deployments to WestPac during my four-year command, we found that we could depart at 1:00 a.m. the following day. This gave everyone not on duty an extra thirteen hours with their family and an opportunity to be seen off with late evening toasts of champagne courtesy of *Queenfish's* captain and our squadron commander. It also meant that those not on duty could immediately hit the sack and sleep away what had been the most painful hours—the ones immediately following our departure. My crew and their families loved it, and we all parted company in much better spirits than we would have if we had left earlier and lost the best of one last beautiful day at home.

2. Roy A. Grossnick, *Dictionary of American Naval Aviation Squadrons*, vol. 1, *The History of VA, VAH, VAK, VAL, VAP and VFA Squadrons* (Washington, DC: Naval Historical Center, 1995), 295–96, http://www.history.navy.mil/download/dictnry//Chapter3.pdf.

3. *Seadragon* had conducted the SDGE test without difficulty under Captain Steele's command during the spring of 1961. I was officer of the deck at the time and hence was not overly concerned that we would have any difficulties.

4. At this early point in the Cold War, U.S. nuclear attack submarines, from the *Nautilus* to the newly launched *Skipjack* class, had not yet achieved the degree of sound quieting that would become standard for later *Thresher*- and *Sturgeon*-class submarines.

5. "*Seadragon* History SSN 584," Seadragon Alumni Association, http://ssn584.homestead.com/HISTORY1.html.

6. Ibid.

7. "USS *Seadragon* (SSN 584)," NavySite.de, last accessed April 30, 2014, http://navysite.de/ssn/ssn584.htm.

## Chapter 14. First Months on Board

1. Nimitz was later to become a fleet admiral and commander of American forces in the Pacific theater during World War II.

2. NavSource Online: Submarine Photo Archive, *Skipjack* SSN 585, http://www.navsource.org/archives/08/08585.htm.

3. USS *Albacore* (AGSS 569) was basically a full-sized undersea test vessel whose numerous undersea tests over a period of six years, beginning in 1954, proved that a round-nosed, tear drop–shaped hull was hydrodynamically superior to that of all previous U.S. submarines. The *Albacore* could go twice as fast as a GUPPY sub under water, with less than half of the GUPPY's shaft horsepower. The S-5-W nuclear power plant was eventually to be used in ninety-eight U.S. nuclear submarines and the first British nuclear submarine, HMS *Dreadnought* (S-101).

4. "Cuban Missile Crisis," GlobalSecurity.org, http://www.globalsecurity.org/military/ops/cuba-62.htm.

5. Senior Submarine Force authorities speculated that rupture of one or more sil-brazed joints in an engine room seawater system led to the loss of USS *Thresher* (SSN 593) on 10 April 1963.

6. Submarine Squadron Ten, based on the submarine tender USS *Fulton* (AS 11), comprised four nuclear and five diesel attack submarines at this time.

7. "NATO Code Names for Submarines and Ships," AIS.org, Association for Information Systems, http://www.ais.org/~schnars/aero/nato-shp.htm; NATO designation. Soviet Project "627." "November-class Submarine Project 627," Federation of American Scientists, https://www.fas.org/man/dod-101/sys/ship/row/rus/627.htm.

8. "NATO Code Names for Submarines and Ships," NATO designations, Soviet Projects, "613," "641," and "611," AIS.org, http://www.ais.org/~schnars/aero/nato-shp.htm. The diesel is used when surfaced and when snorkeling at periscope depth. The battery or electrical power is used when submerged or at periscope depth (except when snorkeling).

9. "Project 613," Russian-Ships.info, http://russian-ships.info/eng/submarines/project_613.htm; "Project 641," Russian-Ships.info, http://russian-ships.info/eng/submarines/project_641.htm; "Project 611," Russian-Ships.info, http://russian-ships.info/eng/submarines/project_611.htm.

## Chapter 15. In the Mediterranean

1. They were later determined to be *Foxtrot* diesel attack submarines armed with nuclear torpedoes.William Burr and Thomas Blanton, editors, National Security Archive Electronic Briefing Book No. 75, 31 October 2002, The Submarines of Ocrober, U.S. and Soviet Naval Encounters During the Cuban Missile Crisis, http://www2.gwu.edu/~nsarchiv/NSAEBB/NSAEBB75/.

2. "Inflation Calculator," DollarTimes, accessed 30 April 2014, http://www.dollartimes.com/calculators/inflation.htm.

## Chapter 16. Home Port in New London

1. Emergency drills were eventualities, such as fire, flooding, collision, both submerged and while on the surface.
2. Harry Aisncough, "USS *Thresher*: The Loss, the Inquiry and the Lessons Learned," *EB News*, March 2013, 6–7, http://www.gdeb.com/news/ebnews/PDF/ebnews_2013_03.pdf.
3. "History of USS *Thresher* (SSN-593)," Navy.mil, http://www.history.navy.mil/danfs/t/thresher.htm.
4. Loran is short for long range navigation, a low-frequency radio shipborne navigation system, that enabled a submarine to receive bearing or direction information from Loran transmitting stations.
5. Omega was a shipborne very low-frequency radio navigation system that enabled a submarine to receive bearing or direction information from Omega transmitting stations. A Radio Direction Finder was a shipborne navigation equipment that provided bearings to/from high and medium frequency radio transmissions received from both shipborne and shore based stations.
6. Burnout of the uranium fuel core was never really achieved, and as *Skipjack*'s engineer I can report that, at the time we entered Charleston Naval Shipyard in April of 1965, *Skipjack* could still make some twenty-two knots at only 17 percent power. She didn't dare slow down for too long, however, because a buildup of xenon 131 within the reactor core would increasingly absorb neutrons such that the reactor would go subcritical and shut down.
7. "Parhelion," *Encyclopedia Britannica*, http://www.britannica.com/EBchecked/topic/443546/parhelion.

## Chapter 17. Evaluation of the Nuclear Attack Submarine

1. Chief of Naval Operations to Commander in Chief, U.S. Atlantic Fleet and Commander in Chief, U.S. Pacific Fleet, 31 January 1949, *Submarine Warfare and Tactical Development 50th Anniversary Symposium: A Look: Past, Present and Future 1949–1999* (Groton, CT: Naval Submarine Base New London, 1999), 124–25.
2. Benson was later to be promoted to admiral and to become ComSubPac.
3. Chief of Naval Operations to Commander Submarine Force, U.S. Atlantic Fleet and Commander Submarine Force, U.S. Pacific Fleet, 11 March 1949, *Submarine Warfare and Tactical Development 50th Anniversary Symposium*, 128–31.
4. A conformal long-range passive array sonar.
5. Frank Andrews, "My View—Submarine Development Group Two," May 1999, Paper prepared for the 50th Anniversary of Submarine Development Group Two, http://www.pdfio.net/k-34642702.html.
6. Ibid.
7. J. R. Potts, "USS *Tullibee* (SSN 597) ASW Fast Attack Submarine (Nuclear)," MilitaryFactory.com, http://www.militaryfactory.com/ships/detail.asp?ship_id=USS-Tullibee-SSN597. The AN/BQQ Sonar System was subsequently installed on both the new SSN 594 *Permit* and SSN 637 *Sturgeon*-class

nuclear attack submarines. The AN/BQQ-2 is a low-frequency spherical bow passive array sonar.

8. D. W. Mitchell, *United States Navy, Submarine Development Group Two and Submarine Development Squadron Twelve, A Royal Navy Perspective, 1955 TO DATE* (unpublished monograph, Submarine Force Museum Archives, Groton, CT, March 2003, revised June 2007).

9. Potts, *"Tullibee."*

### Chapter 19. One More Cold War Mission and a Change of Command

1. *Encyclopaedia Britannica Online*, s.v. "Barents Sea," http://www.britannica .com/EBchecked/topic/53189/Barents-Sea.

2. "NATO Code Names for Submarines and Ships," AIS.org, http://www.ais .org/~schnars/aero/nato-shp.htm. Soviet "Project 629." Thirteen *Golf I*–class diesel electric SSBs were converted from an original twenty to accommodate the more advanced SS-N-5 ballistic missile. Ibid. Soviet "Project 658." Eight (possibly nine) were built originally as the nuclear-powered *Hotel I* and converted to *Hotel II* to accommodate the more advanced ballistic missile SS-N-5.

3. John Berg, *The Soviet Submarine Fleet: A Photographic Survey* (London: Jane's Publishing, 1985), 64.

4. Ibid., 62.

5. The late steward's mate, SDC Peter William Ungacta Sococo, was one of the finest men I had the pleasure of serving with in the U.S. Navy. He was a gentleman in the truest sense of the word and an exemplary role model for both officers and crew alike. He was born in Guam in 1921, enlisted in the U.S. Navy in 1939, and served thirty-one years in the submarine force.

### Chapter 20. England and Then Home

1. Fred Jr. later was awarded a full four-year NROTC scholarship to Villanova, where he majored in mathematics. Although he qualified as a diving officer of the watch on board the USS *William H. Bates* (SSN 680) during his final summer as a Midshipman, USNR, he decided to take a commission as a second lieutenant in the United States Marine Corps upon graduation. He served as an infantry officer for thirteen years, achieving both platoon and company commander, at which time he resigned to join the civil service.

2. "Skipjack (SSN-585)," NavSource.org, http://www.navsource.org/archives/ 08/08585.htm.

# Index

231

# About the Author

Capt. **Alfred Scott McLaren**, USN (Ret.), PhD, former nuclear attack submarine officer and commander, served on USS *Greenfish* (SS 351), *Seadragon* (SSN 584), *Skipjack* (SSN 585), *Greenling* (SSN 614), and *Queenfish* (SSN 651). He is a veteran of more than twenty Cold War missions and three Arctic expeditions. He took part in the first submerged transit of the Northwest Passage, a Baffin Bay expedition, and, as commander of USS *Queenfish* (SSN 651), a North Pole expedition that completed the first survey of the entire Siberian Continental Shelf. His awards include the Distinguished Service Medal, two Legions of Merit, Meritorious Service Medal, Navy Commendation Medal, and four Navy Unit Commendations. He graduated from the U.S. Naval Academy and Naval War College and holds graduate degrees from George Washington, Cambridge, and Colorado Universities.

Captain McLaren is president of the American Polar Society, former president of The Explorers Club, and senior pilot of Sub Aviator System LLC's Super Aviator submersible. A deep-sea explorer, he completed dives to the RMS *Titanic*, Mid-Atlantic Ridge hydrothermal vents, and the first manned dives to the German battleship *Bismarck*. Honors include The Explorers Club's Lowell Thomas Medal for Ocean Exploration and its highest honor, "The Explorers Club Medal" for "extraordinary contributions to Arctic exploration and deep sea research." He also received medals from The Societe de Geographic Paris and La Ville De Paris for Polar exploration. His first book, *Unknown Waters* (University of Alabama Press, 2008), was judged a Notable Naval Book of 2008 by the U.S. Naval Institute.

The **Naval Institute Press** is the book-publishing arm of the U.S. Naval Institute, a private, nonprofit, membership society for sea service professionals and others who share an interest in naval and maritime affairs. Established in 1873 at the U.S. Naval Academy in Annapolis, Maryland, where its offices remain today, the Naval Institute has members worldwide.

Members of the Naval Institute support the education programs of the society and receive the influential monthly magazine *Proceedings* or the colorful bimonthly magazine *Naval History* and discounts on fine nautical prints and on ship and aircraft photos. They also have access to the transcripts of the Institute's Oral History Program and get discounted admission to any of the Institute-sponsored seminars offered around the country.

The Naval Institute's book-publishing program, begun in 1898 with basic guides to naval practices, has broadened its scope to include books of more general interest. Now the Naval Institute Press publishes about seventy titles each year, ranging from how-to books on boating and navigation to battle histories, biographies, ship and aircraft guides, and novels. Institute members receive significant discounts on the Press's more than eight hundred books in print.

Full-time students are eligible for special half-price membership rates. Life memberships are also available.

For a free catalog describing Naval Institute Press books currently available, and for further information about joining the U.S. Naval Institute, please write to:

Member Services
**U.S. Naval Institute**
291 Wood Road
Annapolis, MD 21402-5034
Telephone: (800) 233-8764
Fax: (410) 571-1703
Web address: www.usni.org